RCC Pilotage Foundation
North Brittany
St-Malo to Ouessant

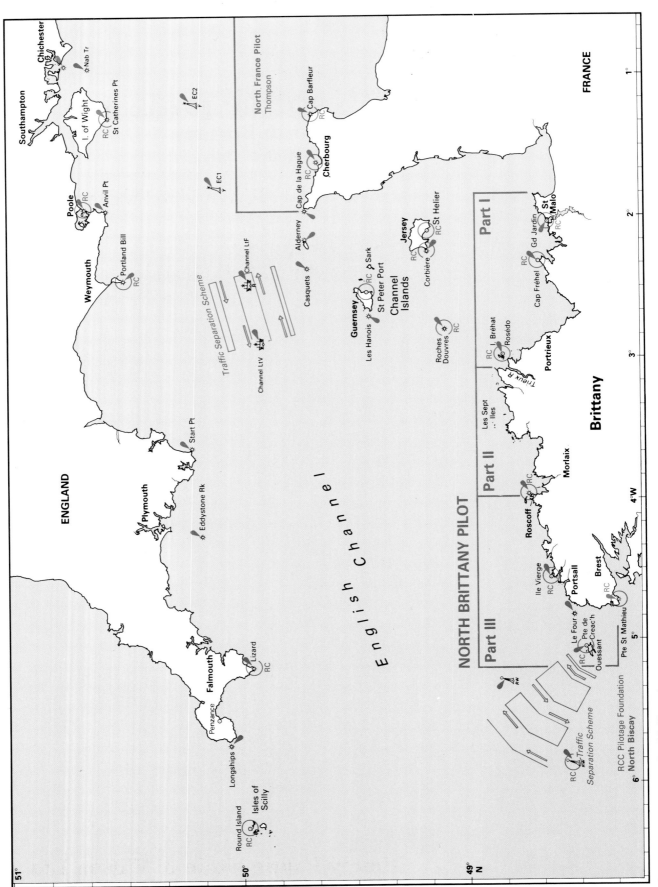

Frontispiece. The Western English Channel

North Brittany

St-Malo to Ouessant

RCC PILOTAGE FOUNDATION

K. Adlard Coles
Revised by Nick Heath

Imray Laurie Norie & Wilson Ltd
St Ives Cambridgeshire England

Published by
Imray, Laurie, Norie & Wilson Ltd
Wych House, St Ives, Huntingdon,
Cambridgeshire, PE17 4BT, England
☎ 0480 62114 *Fax* 0480 496109
1992

Partly based on *Harbours and Anchorages of the North Coast of Brittany* by H.G. Hasler, first published by Robert Ross and Co. Ltd, 1952
Second Edition 1965, published by Adlard Coles Ltd
Third Edition 1972
Reprinted 1973, 1976 (twice), 1977 (with amendments)
Fourth Edition 1980
Fifth Edition 1984
Revised reprint 1987
Revised reprint 1989
Sixth Edition 1992

ISBN 0 85288 162 2

British Library Cataloguing in Publication Data
A catalogue record for this title is available from the British Library.

CAUTION
Every effort has been made to ensure the accuracy of this book. It contains selected information and thus is not definitive and does not include all known information on the subject in hand; this is particularly relevant to the plans which should not be used for navigation. The Pilotage Foundation believes that its selection is a useful aid to prudent navigation but the safety of a vessel depends ultimately on the judgement of the navigator who should assess all information, published or unpublished.

PLANS
The plans in this guide are not to be used for navigation. They are designed to support the text and should always be used with navigational charts. They are based on charts published by Service Hydrographique et Océanographique de la Marine.

The last input of technical information was April 1992.

Printed in England by Tabro Litho Ltd, Ramsey Forty-Foot, Huntingdon, Cambridgeshire.

Contents

Preface

The first edition of this pilot, written by the late H. G. (Blondie) Hasler, was published in 1952 under the title *Harbours and Anchorages of the North Coast of Brittany*. This made use of sketches and coloured plans and has been regarded by many as a model for pilot books.

Unfortunately, production costs dictated that later editions were to be illustrated in black and white only. In 1965 a second edition was published, edited by the late K. Adlard Coles, in which, for the first time, he added many photographs of approaches and leading marks, as well as details of many small harbours and anchorages. A third edition was published in 1972 and the title changed to *North Brittany Pilot*. In 1977 Adlard Coles transferred his interests in the book to the RCC Pilotage Foundation, and Donald Beswick was asked to edit a fourth edition, to incorporate the changes in buoyage and lights, which were to be made to conform with the IALA system. The entire area was visited in 1978 and 1979. Apart from the IALA system, the situation had changed in many other ways. Notably there had been an explosion in boat ownership by the French, and formal yacht harbours were being built in the popular harbours.

When editing the 4th edition, followed by a 5th edition in 1982, revised in 1987, Donald Beswick, besides bringing the text up to date and introducing new plans, took the opportunity, where appropriate, to link the various harbours and anchorages by the tortuous, but well marked, inshore channels which must have afforded coastal sailing vessels, with local knowledge, relative safety from enemy fleets patrolling offshore.

For this 6th edition, during the spring or summer of 1989, '90 and '91, the present editor visited every harbour and anchorage in the area in *Capelan*, a twin-keel ketch drawing 1·1 metres. The area was photographed in colour from sea level and from the air and new plans in colour were prepared.

The anchorages which were deserted and free of charge when Blondie Hasler visited them are now largely served, regulated and charged for by formal marinas, which, in some cases, are almost completely occupied by residents' boats. At the same time however, there are now many more boats capable of taking the ground, enabling their owners to visit drying harbours in which they may anchor, with due care, and so avoid paying the ever increasing marina charges.

Nick Heath
Kingsbridge, Devon 1992

Acknowledgements

The plans in this book are based on the official French charts, with the kind permission of the Directeur du Service Hydrographique and Océanographique de la Marine. They have been painstakingly drawn by the staff of Imray, Laurie, Norie and Wilson, and to them full thanks are due.

Details of tidal movement, buoys, beacons and lights have been checked against the French almanac *Votre Livre de Bord*; the British Admiralty (BA) *Tide Tables, European Waters; Channel Pilot;* and *List of Lights Volume A;* together with supplementary information contained in the RCC portfolios on foreign ports.

Help has also come, as usual, from sources too many and varied to mention. Suffice it to say that it has all been useful and much appreciated. Finally, the finished book would have been a poor shadow of itself but for the original work on which to build.

THE RCC PILOTAGE FOUNDATION

The RCC Pilotage Foundation was created to enable members of the Royal Cruising Club and others to bring their experience of sailing and cruising to a wider public and encourage the aspiring sailor to extend his range with confidence.

The Foundation, a registered charity, is based on a very generous benefaction by an American member of the RCC, Dr Fred Ellis. It fulfills its objectives in a number of ways, among them re-editing and updating existing pilot books or initiating its own where a need is recognised. The first works undertaken were new editions of *North Brittany* by Adlard Coles, a member of the Club who gave the copyright of the Pilot to the Foundation, and of *North Biscay* which he wrote in collaboration with Professor Black. With these and its other works, the Foundation now covers a substantial part of the eastern North Atlantic seaboard as well as the Mediterranean coast of North Africa as far as Libya.

The work of the Foundation is carried out through the voluntary effort of members of the RCC who in turn rely on the support of yachtsmen and shore sources. This edition of *North Brittany* is the result of meticulous work by Nick Heath (RCC) who both maintains close contact with local sources and continually takes his own boat to the area. It has also been made possible through a bequest from the late Waldo Dowson, RCC, which enabled the Foundation to provide aerial photographs of the region, in which he was particularly interested.

O. H. Robinson
Director
RCC Pilotage Foundation

Also by the RCC Pilotage Foundation
North Biscay Pilot (A. & C. Black Ltd)
Atlantic Spain and Portugal
Atlantic Islands
North Africa
Atlantic Crossing Guide (A. & C. Black Ltd)
Lesser Antilles (with SHOM)

In preparation
The Baltic Sea

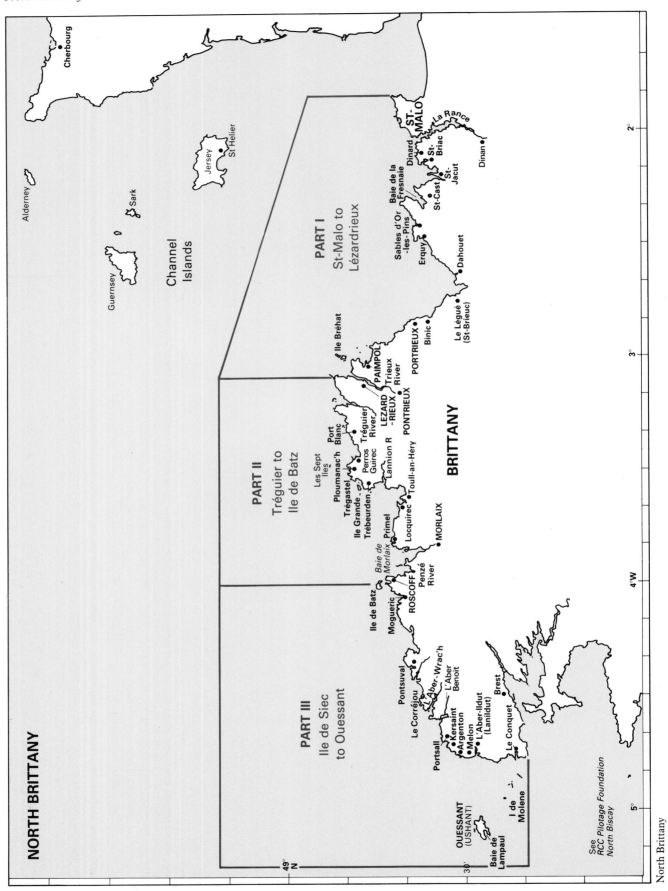

NORTH BRITTANY

Cherbourg

Alderney

Jersey
St Helier

Sark

Guernsey

Channel Islands

PART I
St-Malo to Lézardrieux

ST-MALO
La Rance
Dinard
St-Briac
Dinan
St-Jacut
Baie de la Fresnaie
St-Cast
Sables d'Or -les-Pins
Erquy
Dahouet
Le Légué (St-Brieuc)
Binic
PORTRIEUX
Ile Bréhat
PAIMPOL
Trieux River
LEZARD -RIEUX
PONTRIEUX

PART II
Tréguier to Ile de Batz

Les Sept Iles
Port Blanc
Tréguier River
Ploumanac'h
Perros Guirec
Lannion R
Toull-an-Héry
Trégastel
Ile Grande
Trébeurden
Primel
Locquirec
MORLAIX

BRITTANY

Baie de Morlaix
Ile de Batz
Mogueric
ROSCOFF
Penzé River

PART III
Ile de Siec to Ouessant

Pontsuval
Le Corréjou
L'Aber-Wrac'h
L'Aber Benoît
Kersaint
Argenton
Portsall
Melon
L'Aber-Ildut (Lanildut)
Brest
Le Conquet

OUESSANT (USHANT)
I de Molene
Baie de Lampaul

See *RCC Pilotage Foundation North Biscay*

49° N
30'

2°

3°

4° W

5°

North Brittany Pilot

6th Edition 1992
RCC Pilotage Foundation

Supplement No. 7 cumulative to January 1998

Imray Laurie Norie and Wilson Ltd
Wych House The Broadway St Ives Cambridgeshire PE17 4BT England
☎ +44(0)1480 462114 Fax +44(0)1480 496109 *E-mail* ilnw@imray.com

North Brittany

RCC Pilotage Foundation
6th Edition, 1992
Supplement No. 7 cumulative to January 1998

This document contains information and corrections for the RCC Pilotage Foundation pilot book *North Brittany*, 6th Edition. Material in it is derived from RCC members and other private sailors as well as from official Notices to Mariners.

The Editor is most grateful for the information that he has received from yachtsmen who visited the area in the past year and will be grateful for further reports from those sailors visiting the area in 1998. He is particularly grateful for the contributions of Ted Hawkins, Cyril Harber, Ben Pester, Nick Heath, Peter Adam, Chris Dawson, Archie Young, Tony Daniels, Tony Bolingbroke, Maurice Treboal, Wil Oliver, Sarah Watson, Elizabeth Bourne, Jeremy Burnett, Peter Eddis, Pierre Maillet and Ted Osborn, who collated several contributions from members of the Cruising Association.

CAUTION

These amendments contain selected information. They are thus not definitive and do not include all known information on the subject in hand; this is particularly relevant to plans, which should not be used for navigation. The Pilotage Foundation and Imray Laurie Norie and Wilson believe that their selection is a useful aid to prudent navigation but the safety of a vessel depends ultimately on the judgement of the navigator who should assess all information, published and unpublished, available to him or her.

Copies of these Supplements can be obtained from Imray Laurie Norie and Wilson Ltd, Wych House, The Broadway, St Ives, Huntingdon, Cambridgeshire. PE17 4BT.

Michael Grubb
Falmouth
January, 1998

* Denotes new or updated correction

Page 2 and 6 **Introduction**
Delete all reference to *Reed's*.

Page 2 **Customs**
The situation continued in 1997 whereby yachts travelling within the EU are not required to report arrival or departure unless dutiable goods are carried. Evidence that VAT has been paid may still be required. The Channel Islands are not, of course, within the EU and the 'old' rules continue.

Page 3 **Introduction**
French Telephone Numbers
To telephone France from the UK a number must be added:
To Brittany and Normandy – (00 33) 2 + old 8 figure number.
To South of the Loire – (00 33) 5 + old 8 figure number.

Fuel
Lead-free petrol is also available (*Sans Plomb*).
Currency (1997)
Some banks will no longer accept Eurocheques – but credit cards are generally accepted.

Page 5 **Inland Waterways**
It is now necessary for the person helming a yacht in the inland waterways of France to hold the ICC (International Certificate of Competence). The old document can be exchanged by the RYA for the new certificate, but the first issue of the ICC now requires a short practical test, conducted at many clubs and sailing schools. It has recently been reported, though, that the certificate is not required for passage through the Canal d'Ille-et-Rance.

Page 5 **Traffic Separation Schemes**
There is now no requirement to report by VHF to Ushant Traffic when rounding Ushant (inside or outside) for vessels under 300 GRT. However, Ushant Traffic will, if requested, give position and navigational assistance (Ch 13). (The original requirement was largely ignored by small craft.)

*Page 6 **SatNav and GPS**
Delete paragraph and substitute:
At present the British Admiralty charts for the area covered by this pilot are prepared using the European Datum (1950) while GPS operates on WGS 84. Before fixing a position with GPS, the chart datum should first be read and the necessary correction made. The corrections to be applied are noted on each BA Chart.
The 'selective availability' errors introduced by the US Defense Department make it inadvisable to rely solely on GPS for pilotage among rocks.

Page 7 **Tides**
Under 'Tidal Data' in all sections of this Pilot delete all references to 'Index'.

*Page 8 **Weather Forecasts**
Add new section:
CROSS (Centres Régionaux Opérationnels de Surveillance et de Sauvetage)

Station	Ch	Local time
Zone Cap de la Hague to Penmarch – CROSS CORSEN		
Jobourg	80	0715, 1545, 1915
Granville	80	0703, 1533, 1903
Raz	79	0445, 0703, 1103*, 1533, 1903
Stiff	79	0503, 0715, 1115*, 1545, 1915
Batz	79	0515, 0733, 1133*, 1603, 1933
Bodic	79	0533, 0745, 1145*, 1615, 1945
Fréhel	79	0545, 0803, 1203*, 1633, 2003

(* from 1 May to 30 September)
Offshore forecasts are broadcast:

Jobourg	80	Gale warnings on receipt and
(Jobourg Traffic)		every half hour at H+20, H+50
Corsen	79	Gale warnings on receipt and
(Ouessant Traffic)		every half hour at H+20, H+50

Forecasts every 3 hours at H+50 commencing at 0850 (winter), 0950 (summer).

Yachtsmen's Forecast
France-Inter 162kHz,1852m. Forecasts are broadcast at the following times: 0654 Sat and Sun. 2003 Daily (all local times).

NAVTEX

If a dedicated receiver is carried on board, meteorological, navigational and other safety information may be received by automatic print-out or on a screen. Broadcasts, in English, are on 518kHz.

Note Full details of all French Méteo broadcasts can be found in: *Le Guide Marine de Météo-France* – published annually and which can be obtained from: Météo-France, 1 Quai Branly, 75340 Paris Cedex 07 *Fax* No 00 33 1 45 56 71 11 and on Internet http//www.meteo.fr.

*Page 10 and 12 **St Malo to Lezardrieux Approaches**
Delete RC (Radiobeacon) at Cap Fréhel Lighthouse.

Page 13 **St-Malo ,Approaches (Plan 2)**
a. Insert rock awash at LW, from La Crolant (white) Bn Tower 050° 0·38M. This position is on the 2m line, E of the figure 236° on line W just E of the dashed part of Chenal de la Bigne line. (Chart 2700 shows this rock.)
*b. La Grande Hupée – substitute depth 0·7m for depth 1·3m. (48°40'·9 N 2°05'·8W)

*Page 20 **Plan 3**
The cardinal N buoy, Plateau de la Rance has been moved 160m to the SE. The lat stbd buoy SSW of the end of the Môle des Noires and W of the ferry terminal is now lit: Fl(4)G.15s.
Caution A recent report (1997) indicates that currents caused by the tidal power station on the Rance may attain six knots in the vicinity of Bizeux (0·8'N of lock) and that the area to the east of Bizeux is most unsuitable for anchoring. The scouring has also caused depths to be greater than indicated.

Page 22 **St Malo, St Servan, Port des Bas-Sablons**
The marina entrance is only 40 metres wide and is approached immediately south of the new extended ferry pier (running W from N corner of Bas-Sablons). There are two white waiting buoys outside – S of the new ferry pier. Depth of water over the sill is clearly shown on a depth gauge on northern end of the marina breakwater and on another gauge in the marina situated above the slipway on the NE side.

It has been reported that only French credit cards can be used to obtain fuel in this marina.

Page 23 – **Dinard**
First paragraph line 3: 'plan 4' should read 'plan 3 '.
Line 9: 'plans 3 and 4' should read 'plans 2 and 3'.

Page 27 – **Plan 4, Inset**
The metres scale should read 0 – 1000 (Not 100).

Page 30 – **Canal de l'Ille-et-Rance**
In normal conditions there is a minimum depth of about 2m as far as the lock at Le Châtelier – but it is recommended to seek local advice as unusual electricity requirements can cause a lower level.

*Page 42 – **Dahouet, Approaches**
Below the two white stakes on the end of the wall 3m above the harbour bottom and covering at HW is a tide gauge.

Page 43 and 46 – **Le Légué landfall buoy.**
Amend light to read 12s.

*Page 44 – **Dahouet, Facilities**
Yacht club and harbour office in old camp site buildings by the marina, with showers, toilets and telephone. Only a baker and café/bar on quay otherwise Val André (3km) or Pléneuf (3½km) must be visited for all facilities. Depth in the marina 2m, with a sill gauge on the stbd entrance beacon, covering at 2·6m.

Page 51 – **St-Quay, Portrieux**
Southern entrance: the 0.3m patch referred to is not shown on Plan 12 but lies virtually on line R, 0·2M (400m) East of the E cardinal buoy marking a wreck. The patch is shown on BA 3674 and 3672 and is about 75m NE of the leading line.

*Page 53 – **Facilities**
The fifth night is no longer free, (not the second, as stated).

Plan 13
Insert the *sémaphore* on the Point de St-Quay as in photo on page 52. Insert rock 1·2m in position 48°38'·84N 2°48'·79W.

Pages 57 and 64 – **Plans 15 and 16**
The clearing height of the suspension bridge S of Lézardrieux is 17m (not 18m).

Page 60 – **Chenal de la Trinité**
La Madeleine W cardinal beacon should be left to port. (as shown in Plan 15)

Page 62 – **Paimpol, Approach**
Line K should be amended to read 262°, the directional light (DirF.R – rear leading light in Paimpol) shows from 260° to 264°.

Paimpol, Harbour
The lock gates open from HW −2½ to HW +2½.

Page 65 – **Lézardrieux, Plan 16**
Delete the lights on the pontoons.

*Page 69 – **Lézardrieux, Anchorages**
The marina referred to on Page 69 (south of existing pontoons) is now fully operational and is complete with showers, 'continental' toilets and a chandlery. Entry over the sill at half-tide (a depth gauge shows depth of water over the sill) and is controlled by 'traffic lights'

Three red lights facing	*No passage*
Three green lights facing	*Pass*
Two green and a white	*Passage either way*

Rivière de Trieux, Approaches
The 'unmarked wreck' referred to in the second paragraph has been removed.

Anchorages (and Plan 16)
There are now no mooring buoys below the Château de la Roche-Jagu. Care is needed when

anchoring, clear of sand-barges, as the stream may swing you onto the mud.

Page 75 – La Chambre, Anchorages

There are several visitors' mooring buoys just S of La Chambre and E of the Men Alan beacon. Caution – the depth of water is not known and should be checked. (The beacon is clearly shown on Chart 3673 – but not on Plan 17).

*Page 77 – Tréguier to Ile de Batz, Lights

Delete RC (Radiobeacon) on Port de Bloscon jetty head light.

*Page 80 – Plan 19

Insert a rock – depth unknown – which may be dangerous to navigation, close S of Line B and S of the stbd bn which is W of the Line B symbol. There are three green Buoys marking the channel between No 12 red and the marina.

Page 84 – Passe de la Gaine

Vertical bars of reflective material have been placed on either side of the outer mark (Men Noblance) making it conspicuous in afternoon sunlight.

*Page 86 – Tréguier, Facilities

Dinghy landing 'b' can no longer be used – but dinghies may be left at the marina. Due to the strong tidal conditions it is recommended to arrive or leave the marina at slack water – which, in any case, is to be preferred in order to catch the E or W going stream, as required.

The end pontoons are reported to be fragile in relation to the fast flowing current and larger boats may be turned away at spring tides.

The fuelling pontoon only sells diesel.

Page 91 – Perros Guirec, Anchorages

There are reported to be several white waiting buoys in the roads, in the vicinity of Pointe du Chateau – although somewhat uncomfortable at high tide. There are 70 berths for visitors in the marina.

*Page 96 – Ploumanac'h, Plan 23

The channel now has several more port and stbd beacons (unlit) but the danger still exists of a drying rock some 150 metres to the NE of the first stbd beacon. The sill now dries at 2·55m – maintaining at least 1·5m in the pool. An extension to the eastern slip allows easier 'dry' dinghy landing at LW. Due to electric cables, anchoring is prohibited anywhere is the entrance from a line drawn west from Méan Ruz Light and south to the sill. (See BA Chart 3670.)

*Page 99 – Les Sept Isles

No navigation among the islands is permitted (see BA Chart 3669 for prohibited area). The anchorage off Ile aux Moines may be used and landing on this island is permitted, via the pier.

*Page 102 – Trégastel Sainte Anne

Le Taureau beacon was in position (1997) and entry was found to be not difficult. The eastern bay is full of white moorings for local boats; outside these is a row of red mooring buoys for visitors.

Page 103 – Trébeurden, Facilities

The new marina is now fully operational. Access is controlled by red and green traffic lights – the green light shows when there is a minimum of 1·5 metres over the sill. There is also an illuminated tide gauge at the entrance. Reports of good local facilities. When the gate over the sill is dropped there can be a strong surge in the marina – and boats should not attempt to move for at least 10 minutes. The marina also guards VHF Ch 9.

Page 116 – Plan 30

Top of plan – 'See Plan 31' should read 'See Plan 32'.

Bottom of plan – 'See Plan 30' should read 'see Plan 31'.

Page 116, 117, 118 and 120 Plans 30, 31 and Text

Right-hand column, line 6 and page 120 line 3, Stolvezen lat port buoy, 48°42'·6N, 3°53'·2W converted to can buoy.

*Page 118 Plan 31

Delete all of line T to the E of line J. Le Menk beacon tower (0.7M east of Bloscon breakwater) is a W cardinal (not N). Line J should read 176°/356° (not 256°). The fish farm tanker and buoys marking a prohibited area have been removed. (1997).

Page 119 Plan 31

Longitude is 3°W not 4°W.

Page 121 Baie de Morlaix

There is a useful anchorage, waiting for the tide, clear of the moorings to the E of Penn Lann (and one buoy for visitors).

*Page 122 Morlaix, Approaches

A recent report (1997) indicates that silting has taken place in the approaches to Morlaix and that particular care should be taken during periods of neap tides (when the Coefficient is below 55). In the vicinity of the bridge, just to the north of the lock into Morlaix, it is essential to keep towards the starboard (west) side of the River. (The Coefficients can be found in the *Macmillan Almanac* for 1998 on page 710 or in the latest *Votre Livre du Bord*.)

Page 127 Chenal de l'Ile de Batz

Tidal stream, line 4 – the W going stream begins at +0110 Brest (not -0110 Brest).

Page 128 Plan 32

The rocky patch 0·2M SE of Basse Platte N cardinal Bn Tr dries 9·5m and a second patch 0·13M to the ENE of the first, dries 6·8m. (See Chart 2745.)

Page 129 Plan 32

Bottom right: red square marking Roscoff plan should be titled 'Plan 33', not 'Plan 31'.

Page 131 Chenal de l'Ile de Batz

Left column, line 10 – delete S cardinal light beacon. Insert white beacon tower.

*Page 133 – Roscoff – Bloscon, Plan 33

Amend the sectors of the light Fl.WG.4s9m10/7M as follows: G-200°-shore-W-210°-G-shore. Delete the radiobeacon at the light.

Page 135 **Roscoff, Facilities**
Recent report (1997) indicates fuel is tax-free and not available to private pleasure craft.

Page 136 **Bloscon, Anchorage**
Visitors' mooring buoys have been laid SW of pier end, with a convenient slipway. (Clear of the ferry turning circle).

Page 139 **Lights and Fog Signals**
Ile Vierge – amend 'Siren' to read 'Horn'
Le Four – amend 'Siren (3+2) 75s' to read 'Horn (3+2) 60s'
La Grande Vinotière – amend 'Oc.R.6s15m5M' to read 'LFl.R10s15m5M'. Amend Plans accordingly.

Page 145 **Mouguériec, Anchorage**
There are still two visitors' moorings (drying) on the sandbank in the middle of the harbour. The village *alimentation* mentioned on p.145 is no longer there but there is a shop on the camping site at the W end of the village, open all the year round. There is now no actual causeway to the mainland from Ile de Sieck (new spelling) – but the sand is hard and a walk to Dossen is possible (tide permitting) where you can find the usual shops and restaurants.

Page 149 **Le Correjou, Approaches**
First paragraph – plan 5 should read plan 37.

Page 150 **Plan 37**
Lat stbd buoy established just E of Men Yan, in position 48°39'·00N 4°29'·7W.

Page 152 **L'Aber-wrac'h, Plan 38**
The cardinal buoy to the W of Petite Fourche should be a west cardinal (not east).

Page 154 **L'Aber-wrac'h**
Lower photo caption line 2 – for 'town' read 'tower'.

Page 156 **L'Aber-wrac'h, Anchorage**
2. Delete last sentence – there is now adequate room between moorings (1997).
3. Maximum length on pontoon is now 12m. Only restriction is depth of water towards root of pontoons. Current practice is to find vacant berth and then report to *Capitainerie*. Private berths when vacated for a short time may have lines strung across to prevent access. Electricity and water available on pontoons (included in the price). Charges are the same as for moorings but a free water taxi service is included. A brightly illuminated square sign at the end of the access pontoon (hammerhead) is clearly visible at night from the channel to locate pontoons. Showers available at the club (and washing machines etc). The harbour launch should be called on Ch 9 and not by using a fog horn. There is now a supermarket nearby.

Page 164 **Chenal du Raous**
Right-hand column, line 17 – amend 'Barrou Néves' to read 'Barrou Nèvez'.

Page 165 **Chenal Meridional de Portsall**
Top photo caption, line 2 – change 'starboard' to 'port'.

Page 166 **Chenal Meridional de Portsall**
Left-hand column – first two paragraphs should read:
When Bosven Kreiz and Bosven Aval white pyramids come into line, bearing 035°, follow this line exactly until Men ar Pic bears 090°, then alter to starboard and, when the east side of Men Gouzain rock touches the tip of Landunvez bearing 210°, steer 030° to maintain this stern transit. Follow this line leaving Sélédran rock (dries 0·8m) close to starboard and Bosven Aval 120m to port. When Bosven Aval is abaft the beam, alter slightly to starboard to avoid Karreg Luth (drying 5·2m) and bring Bosven Kreiz in line with Barrou Névez (almost covered at HWS) bearing 025°. Follow this line until Le Four lighthouse is just open to the left of Bosven Aval astern bearing 228°, when alter to hold this stern transit making good 048°.

Page 167 **Portsall – Plan 41**
Several positional inaccuracies have come to light in this Plan; in particular, the latitude scale is incorrectly marked. Readers are reminded that Plans should not be used for navigation; the appropriate largest scale chart for the area should be used.

Page 169 **Calerec Passage**
Left-hand column: Losquet pyramid is white with a red top as described, but is incorrectly shown as white in Plan 40 and BA 1432 and white and yellow in Plan 41.

Page 172 **Plan 42**
Delete the word 'dest' from Le Belier R beacon tower.

Page 176 **Plan 43, Plan 45 and text.**
Grande Vinotière Bn Tr. Amend to read LFl.R.10s15m5M.

Page 179 **L'Aber-Ildut, Approaches**
Caution – many small fishing floats have been observed in the entrance.

Page 180 **L'Aber-Ildut, Facilities.** Free showers at the *Capitainerie* in the commercial port. The caption to the photo should read 'tower' not 'town'.

Page 184 **Ile de Molène, Plan 4**
The southern mill, west of the lifeboat station, may have been made more conspicuous and SHOM has reinstated an old leading line for an approach from the north, only as far as a point midway between Bazou Real E card bn Tr and Roche Goulin W card buoy: Transit 190° South Mill x white marks on old môle. Further reports would be appreciated.

Page 187 **Ouessant**
Tidal Streams – 1. Amend to read 'page 188'.

Page 189 **Plan 48**
By Creac'h lighthouse, delete the easternmost of the pair of RC pylon symbols.

List of plans

Cruising in Brittany

Brittany is rich in deep-water and small secluded anchorages, and has held a particular fascination for British yachtsmen ever since Frank Cowper demonstrated that foreign cruising does not necessarily require a large yacht. It is a wonderful coastline in its indentations and in its contrasts between rugged rocks and sands. North Brittany is the nearest foreign shore to the western part of the south coast of England and, with a fair wind, it is only a 24-hour sail from our overcrowded but rather lovable Solent to the peaceful river of Tréguier where a different world is entered – a completely contrasting coastline and a foreign country with different customs and outlook. From Falmouth to l'Aber-Wrac'h the distance across the Channel is even less.

The features of the Brittany coast are the rocks, the inlets, the large tidal range and the strong tidal streams. So the navigator, unfamiliar with local conditions, has several factors to contend with:

a. The numerous rocks which are difficult to identify except in clear visibility.

b. The strong tidal streams especially between St-Malo and Les Sept Iles, which at spring tides will quickly raise severe overfalls on many parts of the coast, if the wind rises contrary to them. The streams also set towards rocks in certain positions.

c. The Atlantic swell, particularly between Ile de Batz and Ouessant which becomes very steep against a westerly running stream. A big swell may also restrict visibility so that landmarks and buoys can only be seen when one is perched at the top of each sea.

d. In summer there is often a haze which makes it difficult to identify leading marks at a distance, and fog is by no means uncommon. If when approaching the coast of Brittany visibility becomes poor, whether from fog or rain squalls, it is best to return to the open water of the English Channel, even if one has to ride out a gale there. The coast can only be approached safely if one is certain of position and of picking up the leading marks or outer beacons.

It would be irresponsible not to mention the possibility of these dangers as, although North Brittany is near to us, the navigation is more difficult than farther afield on the coast of the Bay of Biscay, and there is often no margin for mistakes. A stranger to the coast should at first be content with the straight-forward deep anchorages and only attempt the comparatively out of the way ones after he has gained experience, and even then only in the right conditions. The relieving factors are that the coast is extremely well marked by beacon towers, beacons and buoys, and that at neap tides the streams are moderate. Even at spring tides there are many days when the seas are smooth, the weather is sunny, the visibility is clear and there are no exceptional hazards if proper care is taken in navigation.

From the yachtsman's point of view there are three pictures of North Brittany. The first is at low water spring tides, when a maze of rocks and glorious stretches of yellow sands are uncovered. The second is at high water spring tides, when most of the rocks have plenty of water over them and, with the aid of large-scale charts, it is often possible to depart from the recognised channels. The third is at low water neap tides. Here the picture in the approach is more moderate, but there is about 3m or more water above chart datum, which is then deep enough to provide anchorage in many of the most interesting and picturesque harbours such as at Bréhat, and Ile Grande, which may be termed neap-tide anchorages.

Many of the best harbours in North Brittany, e.g. Roscoff, dry out at low water. It is a great advantage to have a yacht equipped with legs or constructed with suitable bilge keels, so that she can take the bottom; but there is rarely any difficulty in lying alongside the quay. Booms, dinghy, anchors and chains can be placed on the side of the yacht which is against the quay and, as a precaution, but not in fact at Roscoff as the wall is too high, a halyard can be secured to a ring ashore to ensure that the yacht will not fall outwards as she takes the bottom. Some modern yachts have very short keels and fall by the bows as the tide recedes. This is uncomfortable but not dangerous, providing that she still heels towards the quay and is secured by a halyard. Such yachts should be berthed heading inwards towards the shore end of a jetty, as the slope of the bottom usually rises from the outer end of the quay towards the inner end which dries out further. Good fenders are required and the modern type of long plastic ones with a line at each end are excellent, as they act as elastic rollers between the yacht and the quay. In drying harbours yachtsmen should if possible avoid mooring against the seamost ladder, as this position is often needed by fishermen.

Where a sea lock gives access to a freshwater dock or river, e.g. Morlaix, there is heavy turbulence and a strong current when the gates are opened and the fresh and salt water mix. Yachts should remain secured until this dies down. Where the dock remains salt, being periodically filled from the sea, e.g. St-Malo, this does not happen to the same extent. The coastline of North Brittany, composed of rocks and sand, alters little but there are frequent changes in lights, fog signals, beacons and buoys, and sometimes in their names and positions. The navigator must be prepared for alterations, as they continue even while a book is being compiled and printed. See also page 6.

Lights

Particulars of lights are given each year in *Reed's* and *Macmillan's Nautical Almanac*, and in the Admiralty *List of Lights, Volume A (NP 74)*, published every year or two.

Alterations are published weekly in Admiralty *Notices to Mariners* and are also shown on new charts corrected up to the date of sale. Particulars of light buoys are given in the *Channel Pilot (NP 27)* and also on large-scale charts, but see the warning on page 5.

Particulars of radiobeacons are given in *Reed's* and *Macmillan's Nautical Almanac*, and in the Admiralty *List of Radio Signals Volume 2 (NP 282a)*.

Charts

English

Recent editions of Admiralty (BA) charts have been prepared with the yachtsman very much in mind and, besides indicating yacht harbours, slipways and fuel berths, inset plans of small havens are being introduced. As well as reports of corrections, the Hydrographic Department, Ministry of Defence, Taunton, Somerset, TA1 2DN, are pleased to receive suggestions from yachtsmen for improvements in the design of their charts.

Imray charts *C33B*, *C34*, *C35* and *C36* cover the area at medium scales with plan insets. Stanford charts *17* and *18* offer small-scale coverage.

French

Since 1988 the French hydrographers (SHOM) have been producing a new style of chart, using symbols to conform with the international system. The British Hydrographic Department is now adopting the latest French charts as part of the international standardisation of charts, but using its own colour scheme. To some users, the present advantage of the French charts is that they can be purchased folded and printed on a waterproof, tearproof material, and so can safely be used in the cockpit. They may be obtained by post from Service Hydrographique et Océanographique de la Marine at 29283 Brest Cedex, France; payment can be made through any bank. They can also be bought at the Librairies Maritimes at various ports, although sometimes the selection may be limited. Imray, Laurie, Norie & Wilson Ltd will also obtain copies if required (Wych House, St Ives, Cambs, PE17 4BT, England, ☎ 0480 62114 *Fax* 0480 496109).

It has been the custom of SHOM, when publishing a new edition of a chart, to give it a new number so that an up-to-date catalogue is necessary when ordering a chart by post.

Note that the spelling of Breton place names is phonetic and is subject to alteration from time to time. In this edition an attempt has been made to match the spelling with that on the most recent French charts.

A series of charts, ECM Navicarte, is also obtainable published by Grafocarte, 64 rue des Meuniers, 92220 Bagneux. These have been designed especially for yachtsmen and many may find the style attractive.

Appendix II lists all these charts in detail.

Customs

Passports

These are essential, except for members of a professional crew. They are required for production to the *douane*, when cashing traveller's cheques, Euro-cheques, or collecting post and, not least, should it be necessary to re-enter the UK by public transport.

British customs

Customs declaration *C1328* must be completed and the instructions thereon complied with before departure and parts *II* and *III* retained for delivery to customs on return.

French customs and requirements

Regulations, which can be expected to be strictly enforced and which carry penalties, impose restrictions on:

1. Pursuing any paid activity on land.
2. The arranging of skippered or bare-boat charters, without first paying import charges and taxes.
3. Cruising in French waters without carrying a Certificate of Registry or an international certificate of ownership.
4. The carrying of drugs, whatever the quantity.
5. The carrying of goods other than (a) personal effects, (b) authorised goods intended for personal use within the limits of duty-free allowances and (c) foreign currency in excess of the authorised amount (the equivalent of 50,000F in 1991). If the restrictions imposed by these regulations are complied with, no 'Q' flag or other formalities are required on arrival in Brittany. There is no need to enter at a port with a *douane*, no need to report departure, freedom to berth anywhere, subject to local restrictions, and freedom to stay in French waters and canals for an aggregate of six months in any period of twelve consecutive months. If the restrictions are not being complied with, then entry must be made at a port with a *douane* and a 'Q' flag must be flown until cleared.

The *douane* have the right to make random inspections anywhere and, as well as calling for the Certificate of Registry or other approved document, they will require proof that the boat and the goods on board conform to the regulations. When visited by the *douane* for the first time during a cruise, ask for *une Fiche*, a clearance certificate, which can be shown in the event of a further visit. There will be alterations to the requirements in 1993.

Harbours and facilities

Harbour dues

These are now the rule in Brittany.

Ensign

French courtesy ensign should always be worn, and a Breton ensign is appreciated as an addition.

Echo soundings

The modern echo sounder is a great advance on the older method of measuring depth by lead and line. It is particularly useful on the Brittany coast, as it enables a navigator to feel his way into secluded anchorages where the bottom is sand or gradually shelving rocks. Echo sounders must not, however, be relied upon to give warning of steep-to rocks, where at one moment a yacht may be in deep water and the next on top of them.

Fresh water

Most marina pontoons and commercial jetties can supply water by hose. The smaller towns and villages often have public water taps near the landing place but one should enquire before using it whether the water is *potable* (for drinking). Restaurants or cafés will usually oblige by filling jerrycans. A yacht intending to stay some time in French waters would find it useful to carry a length of hose with a universal tap adaptor, since hoses are not always available.

Fuel

With some exceptions, it is normal for a fuel pontoon to be found in a yacht harbour. Note the following translations:

Petrol (two star), *essence (f)*
Diesel oil, *gasoil (m)* (pronounced 'gaswahl')
Paraffin, *pétrole (m)*

There are no arrangements for the supply of petrol or diesel oil to yachts at reduced prices. The pumps on the quays at most fishing harbours can only supply petrol and diesel oil to fishermen and commercial users through the customs officer. Paraffin, *pétrole*, can be bought at *drogueries* or sometimes at *épiceries*. Ask for refined *(raffiné)* paraffin for a *Primus* stove, as the inferior grade quickly chokes the jets. It is not so easily obtained as *Camping gaz* which is available anywhere, and an accessory can be bought to connect the cylinder to a *Calor Gas* regulator. There are no facilities for refilling *Calor Gas* cylinders, but the screw connections on French Butagas cylinders are interchangeable with those on 10lb *Calor Gas*. These can be obtained in most ports subject to the payment of a deposit, similar to that on a *Calor Gas* cylinder. Methylated spirits (*alcool*) may easily be obtained at a *pharmacien* or at a *droguerie*. It is colourless in France.

Yacht clubs

The large yacht clubs of France are hospitable to foreign yachtsmen belonging to recognised clubs, and put all facilities at their disposal. The smaller clubs, of which there are now a great number, are equally helpful within the limits of their smaller premises, and a visitor need not hesitate to call and ask for local advice. There are centres and sailing schools in almost every harbour and sheltered bay, and many plans for the further improvement of facilities.

Currency

Eurocheques can be cashed on production of a Eurocheque card. Traveller's cheques are still negotiable. New cheque guarantee cards are available from UK banks and one is recommended to approach one's own bank for details. Traveller's cheques can sometimes be cashed at hotels and shops where money is spent. Many French banks are closed on Saturdays, all on Sundays and holidays, and most on Mondays. Non-French currency may be carried on board but if more than the permitted amount (the equivalent of 50,000F in 1991) is carried it must be declared to the *douane*.

Post offices

These are normally open from Monday to Friday (0900–1700). Postboxes are painted blue and yellow, and are often recessed into the wall of a house.

Telephones are well provided in kiosks (*cabines*), also in post offices where one's call is metered and paid for at the counter and the charge appears to be less. To ring a UK number dial 19, then pause until a low pitched continuous note is heard, then dial 44, followed by the UK STD code and number, but omitting the first 0 of the code. Thus for London dial 71 or 81.

It is essential to carry a phone card (*telecarte*) on board as the kiosks in various ports may be either coin or card operated. A *telecarte* may be purchased in a bar or at a post office.

History

For those who are not well acquainted with the French coast the following notes may be useful:

France, like Great Britain, is subdivided into ancient kingdoms, each of which contains a number of *départements* corresponding roughly to British counties. The coast of Brittany stretches from Mont Saint Michel round Ouessant and down as far as the Loire, and its *départements*, taken in order, are Ille et Vilaine, Côtes du Nord, Finistère, Morbihan, and Loire Atlantique. Only the first three concern us here.

Historically, the connection between Great Britain and Brittany is very close. Brittany, whose ancient name was Armorica, was originally peopled by the race of Dolmen-builders, whose stone monuments (*dolmens*, *allées couvertes*, *menhirs*, *cromlechs* and *lechs*) are still to be seen everywhere. Next came the Gauls, later to be subjugated by Caesar and incorporated in the Roman Empire.

The links between the Celtic tribes of Armorica and those of Britain had always been close, and from about 460 AD Britons began to seek refuge there, first from raids by Picts and Scots and much more so after the Anglo-Saxon invasions began. This resulted in the region being known as Lesser Britain, with the inhabitants speaking the British tongue, closely akin to present-day Welsh and to the old Cornish language (which some enthusiasts are attempting to revive).

At first these settlers retained links with Celtic chieftains in SW Britain but gradually accepted allegiance to the Frankish kings who had conquered most of Gaul by the end of the 5th century and, after much turbulence, the emerging Breton ruler became a duke, nominally under the French crown.

The early British settlers, joined by others from Ireland, helped to spread Christianity beyond the few Christian centres founded under the Roman Empire, and many Breton legends are no more than distorted accounts of the work of these 'saints' in teaching the gospel.

The early colonisers formed settlements of two kinds: civil communities called 'Plous', and religious settlements called 'Lanns'. A glance at the map will show the extent to which these two words still occur in the names of towns and villages. Many other towns are named after the missionaries themselves, such as St-Malo, St-Servan, St-Brieuc, St-Pol de Leon and St-Lunaire. Brittany suffered from raids by the Norsemen and the Danes and, especially after the Norman conquest of England, by civil war between the great feudal families, usually supported by either France or England, each trying to gain control of the dukedom. In 1491 it was finally united with the French crown by marriage, but was soon involved in the French wars of religion, with the result that by the end of the 16th century it is described as having been almost depopulated by war and plague.

During the Revolution the Breton peasantry made a stand against the Terror, and Brittany is still the stronghold of Catholicism in France. Fifty years ago the western half of Brittany still spoke the Breton tongue almost exclusively, but this is now slowly on the way to extinction. The rest of France has discovered the charm of Brittany, and many of its coastal villages now rely more on holidaymakers than on fishing. Nevertheless, it is still common for the people to speak Breton amongst themselves, particularly in the extreme northwest, and the correct pronunciation of Breton place names is often nearer to English than French practice. Recently in Brittany (as in the West Highlands of Scotland and Wales) local spelling of place names is being adopted, e.g. l'Aber-Wrac'h instead of l'Abervrach.

A surviving Breton custom is the *pardon*, a religious gathering centred around a particular locality. *Pardons* take place on the same date each year, and some of the better known ones are mentioned later in this book.

Sailing directions

The book is divided into three parts, as indicated on the frontispiece. Each part starts with general information, then goes on to a description of the individual ports and anchorages; these are arranged as far as possible in the order in which they would be encountered when sailing down-Channel.

Chausey, Cancale and the coast east of St-Malo have been omitted as they are covered elsewhere, but St-Malo is described as it is a principal port of entry whether one is cruising east or west. At the other end of the book the scope has been extended westward to fill the gap between Ouessant and Brest, where *North Biscay Pilot* begins.

Plans

The plans reproduced here are of three general kinds:

a. Small-scale plans showing the scope of the book and Brittany which form part of the introduction and general plans at the start of each section.
b. Medium-scale plans covering the north coast of Brittany in sections, and showing the positions of the harbours and anchorages mentioned.
c. Large-scale plans showing details of the main anchorages and their approaches.

Of these, only the large-scale plans are intended to aid navigation. In addition adequate charts of the coastline and seaward approaches, together with the latest light list and tide tables, are essential.

Depth of water and unmarked dangers

The plans in this book have been kept as simple as possible, but are designed for the navigator who likes to use secondary entrances as well as the main channels of approach. Most of these channels are well marked by leading lines, buoys and beacons. In addition to the normal leading lines shown on the official charts, H. G. Hasler put in many leading lines and lines of bearing of his own, and this convention has been followed since. Most of these have been labelled with a letter, for ease of reference.

Even when under power, however, it may be necessary to depart from a chosen line on occasions, such as when passing another vessel; while for a sailing vessel beating to windward the question of following a leading line does not arise. The aim throughout has been to simplify the plans to such an extent that the owner of a small boat can sit at the helm with the book beside him and beat to windward through the approach channels single handed, if necessary.

In effect, the plans suggest how far, and in which direction, a small craft may depart from the given lines in suitable weather and state of tide. The method used has been to apply a blue tint to areas which have a depth of less than 2m or which contain unmarked dangers with less than 2m over them. In some cases the chosen contour has been 3m. Drying areas are tinted grey/blue and soundings are shown only where they are considered to be essential.

Areas tinted blue should only be entered with caution at all states of tide as they may contain rocks which cover, but which are too small to be shown on the scale of the plan.

Areas which are left plain white carry 2m of water or more except where lesser soundings are shown. If such lesser soundings mark a small isolated danger, they are surrounded by a line and tinted. In seaward areas and approach channels, few soundings over 2m are normally shown. This is in order to make the plans as easy as possible to read.

In the anchorages, a few soundings are usually shown, whether over 2m or not, so that scope of chain and swinging room can be estimated, but in all cases soundings should be taken and the depth at low water calculated. See page 7.

All soundings are in metres relative to chart datum.

Chart datum is LAT which is explained on page 7, so that it is only necessary to point out here that at MLWS there is usually at least 1m more water than at datum (so that 2m will then be 3m or more) and at least 3m more water at MLWN (so that 2m will then be 5m or more).

Leading lines

These often do not follow the centre of the navigable channel. Except where otherwise stated, it is considered safe to follow such lines exactly, but where they can be seen from the chart to pass very close to a danger on one side, it is advisable to borrow slightly towards the other.

Leading marks often cover only part of the approach, after which course has to be altered to a new transit. Care should be taken not to overstand on a transit which eventually leads over dangers. It is frequently easier for a stranger approaching a harbour to navigate by the nearer buoys and marks, as the recognised leading marks are often difficult to pick out even in clear weather. They may be far away and indistinct in haze.

The sailing directions in this book provide for either method, including a description of each mark and how far to port or starboard it is left when following the line.

As a general rule, it is much easier to pick up the leading marks when leaving harbour than when entering. It is therefore a good plan to get to know some of the more difficult secondary channels as exits, before trying them as entrances.

Caution

A word of caution may not be out of place to those who are visiting these anchorages for the first time. It is not safe to follow the tracks of other craft instead of relying on one's own navigation. They may themselves be strangers and on a wrong course, or local boats which know every rock in the district and are dodging between unmarked dangers. Fishing boats, in particular, are the most dangerous of guides, as they frequently draw less water than yachts of the same size, and seldom follow the safest channel, unless it happens to be the shortest.

System of buoyage

The International Association of Lighthouse Authorities (IALA) has drawn up the 'Combined Cardinal and Lateral System' (IALA Maritime Buoyage System, Region A) which now applies to the waters covered by this book. Full details of the scheme are published in the Admiralty *Channel Pilot (NP 27)*, *Symbols and Abbreviations (NP 5011)*, and elsewhere. The French have adapted their traditional system to conform where possible and their navigational marks are summarised on page 7.

Magnetic variation, courses and bearings

All bearings, courses and light sectors, expressed in 360° notation, are true and are from ship or seaward as the case may be. Cardinal points are used to give general directions. To convert to magnetic, variation must of course be added. It is essential to consult the relevant charts and publications for accurate conversion to magnetic bearings.

Clock times

All times, time differences and time corrections are expressed in four-figure notation and 24-hour clock; e.g. 5 minutes past ten in the forenoon is 1005, and 25 minutes past two in the afternoon is 1425.

Traffic separation schemes

A separation zone exists NW of Ouessant at the extreme western end of the area covered by this book, and another exists outside its scope, NW of the Casquets light. These have been shown on plan 1, since yachts sailing from Poole or ports east of Poole direct to NE Brittany will pass through or close to the zone off the Casquets. These zones are monitored by their respective traffic controls on VHF channel 11, in English.

Lights and fog signals

These are subject to frequent alteration. Many are being automated. Whilst the light characteristics may remain unaltered, and even be increased in intensity, the fog signals can be of low strength or even inaudible. See:
a. The *Admiralty List of Lights Volume A (NP 74)*, for shore lights and light vessels.
b. The *Channel Pilot (NP 27)*, or charts, for light buoys.
c. *Votre Livre de Bord* or *Almanach du marin breton*, the French almanacs, for all shore lights and light buoys.

Electronic navigational aids

For reasons indicated below, all navigational information received electronically needs interpreting and checking against other inputs and none should be taken at face value. On this coast it is sensible, especially in poor visibility, to make a position well off an identifiable landfall feature, clear of dangers, and then close in with careful pilotage.

Radiobeacons

Details of marine radiobeacons and air radiobeacons of use to shipping are given in the text where appropriate and on the plans. Beacons may be withdrawn and their characteristics altered; major changes to European beacons will be made from April 1992 onwards. The authoritative list is to be found in the *Admiralty List of Radio Signals Volume 2 (NP 282a)* as modified by notices to mariners, which is repeated in *Reed's* and *Macmillan's* nautical almanacs.

Radar

Particular caution should be excercised when using radar for navigation on the North Brittany coast. When approaching the coast from seaward, offshore dangers may be encountered before the main shore features show up on the screen, or before they can be relied on to give an accurate indication of one's position.

Whilst many of the offshore dangers are marked by buoys, those without radar reflectors cannot be relied on to produce a strong echo. Certain inshore buoys are fitted with radar reflectors, particularly when they mark dangers close to harbour approaches.

Decca

The coast of North Brittany is served by the SW British chain 1B and coverage should be regular. There are however anomalies which have not been fully documented and Decca cannot be relied upon to give an accurate fix everywhere.

A separate issue is that the positional datum of the chart may not be identical to the datum for Decca which must also be taken into account when entering waypoints.

SatNav and GPS

The positional datum for SatNav and GPS systems frequently differs from the datum of any particular chart. The error is noted on recently issued charts and must be applied. It must also be applied in reverse when entering waypoints into such systems.

Lobster/crab pots and buoyed fishing lines

These are to be found throughout the waters covered by this book, even in deep water and approach channels, especially in secondary channels. They usually have two floats on the surface, the end one with or without a flag. The lines are often of buoyant rope and present a considerable hazard, especially when laid in narrow channels on the line of leading marks. A good lookout is essential. Occasionally one sees a coil of surplus rope close to the inner float, which would badly foul a propeller. Particular care needs to be taken when motoring, and night passage-making under engine must be hazardous.

Abbreviations used in this book

B	black
bg	bearing
cheq	chequered
Dir	directional
E	east
ev	every
F	fixed
Fl	flashing
Fl( )	flashing (group)
G	green
Gy	grey
HW	high water
Iso	isophase
LAT	lowest astronomical tide
LFl	long flashing
LtHo	lighthouse
LW	low water
m	metre(s)
M	mile(s)
N	north
MHWN	mean high water neaps
MHWS	mean high water springs
MLWN	mean low water neaps
MLWS	mean low water springs
MTL	mean tide level
Mo( )	Morse code (letter)
Oc	occulting
Pyr	pyramid
pt/pte	*petit/petite*
Pte	*pointe*
Q	continuous quick flashing
R	red, or rock (*Roc'h, Roche, Rocher*)
RC	radiobeacon
s	second(s)
S	south
Vi	violet
VQ	continuous very quick flashing
VQ( )	continuous very quick flashing (group)
Whis	whistle
W	west, or white in multicoloured lights; no colour in a light characteristic infers white
Y	yellow

Tides

Tidal heights and tidal streams

The plans in this book are drawn to the same datum as the appropriate French charts. This datum is also used in Admiralty and other British reproduction charts for this coast. It is taken as the lowest astronomical tide (LAT) which can occur at any particular place. This prediction, therefore, applies only to equinoctial tides, but meteorological conditions can cause these levels to occur at other times and even produce tides lower than LAT.

Tidal heights and tidal streams are given in the preamble for each principal port. Time differences for high and low water are actual differences from the standard port, and correction should be made for any difference in zone or local time.

To predict tidal levels, reference should be made to the data and instructions contained in the *Admiralty Tide Tables Volume 1* or to the French or British almanacs. In using English tide tables, particular care must be taken with French secondary ports based on St Helier. The time correction for the French port, applied to UT St Helier, corrects also for the difference between UT and the standard zone time for the secondary port. For example, find the time of low water at Ile Bréhat on Saturday 10 August 1991:

Low water St Helier 1307 UT
Correction for Ile Bréhat +0011 (add 11 minutes)
Low water Ile Bréhat 1318 zone −0100
Low water Ile Bréhat 1218 UT
Low water Ile Bréhat 1418 French summer time, UT+2 or *Heures Locales*.

In 1992 the Admiralty introduced the *Admiralty Tide Tables for Yachtsmen, NP 192*. These cover the Channel Islands and the French coast from Cherbourg to Port Navalo. They contain tidal curves and predictions using French time of UT+1 (zone −0100) for St-Malo, Paimpol, Roscoff and Brest among their reference ports, thus reducing the difficulty of calculating tide levels for secondary ports in the area.

A rough and rapid method of estimating the height of tide for any place at any given time is by the well known 'twelfths' method. Having arrived at the range of the tide for the day, divide by twelve then adjust as follows: first hour's rise or fall 1/12th of range, second hour 2/12ths, third hour 3/12ths, fourth hour 3/12ths, fifth hour 2/12ths, and sixth hour 1/12th of range.

It must be appreciated that tidal heights are influenced by atmospheric pressure and wind so that no method of calculation can be relied on absolutely.

To predict tidal streams, reference should be made to the tidal data given on the largest scale Admiralty chart available for the area. For rough use, and particularly for planning passages, reference can be made to the tidal charts published by the Admiralty and by Imray, Laurie, Norie & Wilson Ltd.

French navigational marks and plan symbols

The IALA Buoyage System A is very largely based on the lateral and cardinal systems which the French themselves developed, except that the lights for cardinal marks have all had to be changed; otherwise the old lateral and cardinal marks have been adapted to conform with IALA. Former marks which remain, but which have not been given IALA designations, have been painted white. Some light towers have been painted as IALA marks; but some still retain coloured sectors, so that they serve as beacon towers by day and lighthouses by night.

Near low water, care needs to be taken not to mistake the portion of a tower between HW and LW as a black band, especially when viewed from a distance. The following are examples of descriptions and symbols used in this book:

Lighthouses (*phares*)
a. All lights: ☀
b. Where a radiobeacon is operated: RC ⊛

Sectors are indicated by pecked lines radiating outwards.

Beacons

Beacon towers (*tourelles*) Masonry towers, painted in appropriate IALA colours, otherwise white, e.g. ⌂

Beacons (*balises*) Iron, masonry or wooden pole-like structures painted in IALA colours and usually with the appropriate topmark, e.g. ↓

Pyramids (*pyramides*) Conical beacon towers, usually white and quite narrow for their height, like obelisks with flat tops. Mainly used for leading and clearing marks e.g. △

Buoys (*bouées*)

Pillar Usually lattice structures. The colours on the latticework are not always easy to distinguish and from a distance the shape is considerably distorted when solar panels are fitted. Where a radar reflector is mounted, it is often larger than the topmark shown e.g. ⌇ ⌇ ⌇ ⌇
BY BYB YB YBY

Spindle Basically can-shaped cylindrical, but much higher in relation to its diameter. Invariably a lateral port mark, e.g. ↗

Spar A narrow steel cylinder mounted on a float. Usually painted in IALA colours, with appropriate topmark. Not always conspicuous, e.g. ↗

Can Generally used only as lateral and safe water marks e.g. ⊠

Conical Generally used as lateral starboard marks but occasionally as lateral port marks. ◁

In relation to all buoys:
Those fitted with lights are shown: ⚑
Those fitted with bells are noted 'Bell'
Those fitted with whistles are noted 'Whis'

Daymarks (*amers*)
Stone walls or other structures built on dry land as navigational marks, and usually painted white, or black and white.

Withies (*perches*)
Small saplings stuck into the mud to mark the edge of oyster beds and the like, being light and flexible, they are not themselves a danger to navigation.

Leading marks (*alignements*)
These fall into the following categories:

a. Natural objects, such as a headland or one edge of a prominent rock.
b. Lighthouses, church spires, old mill towers and the like.
c. Beacon towers or pyramids, usually painted white or black and white.
d. Daymarks, usually painted white, or black and white.

Painted rocks A few above-water rocks near certain entrances are painted white, red, green, red and white, or green and white, to serve as leading marks or simply to help in identification.

Other symbols used on the plans

Fuel,	
Customs,	
Water,	
Harbourmaster,	
Lifeboat,	
Slip,	
Yacht harbour,	

I. St-Malo to Lézardrieux

Between St-Malo and Lézardrieux the coast consists mainly of cliffs of steep rock with small sandy bays, and is encumbered with off-lying rocks and shoals, extending in places over 7M offshore. Beyond these coastal dangers lie the Iles Chausey, Plateau des Minquiers, Grand Léjon, Roches Douvres, and Plateau de Barnouic, all of which contain sunken rocks and should not be approached close-to without consulting a large-scale chart. The range of tide is very great, and the tidal streams reach 5·5 knots on the NE side of the Ile Bréhat.

Lights and fog signals

Details of the main coastal lights and fog signals are given below. All bearings are given in degrees true. To convert to magnetic, one must of course add variation, which is approximately 5°W during the 1990s on this part of the coast. The height of the light structures is measured from the lantern to the base of the structure; elevation is measured between the centre of the lantern and MHWS. *See Warning on page 5.*

La Corbière (Jersey) 49°10'·8N 2°14'·9W Iso.WR.10s36m 18/16M From shore-W-294°-R-328°-W-148°-R-shore. Horn Mo(C)60s. Circular stone tower 19m high. Signal Station. RC *CB* 295·5kHz 20M; wind strength and direction coded in signal.

Le Sénéquet 49°05'·5N 01°39'·7W Fl(3)WR.12s18m 13/10M 083·5°-R-116·5°-W-083·5° White circular tower with B base, 26m high.

Regnéville 49°00'·2N 1°34'·6W Oc(2)WR.6s12m10/7M 063°-R-110°-W-063° White tower 12m high, upper part R, white dwellings.

Pointe du Roc (Granville) 48°50'·1N 1°36'·8W Fl(4)15s 49m23M Grey circular tower, R top, 16m high.

Tourelle Fourchie 310m NW of Pointe du Roc, Horn(4) 60s.

Grande Ile (Chausey) 48°52'·2N 1°49'·3W Fl.5s39m23M Horn30s Grey square tower, 19m high.

Pierre de Herpin 48°43'·8N 1°48'·9W Oc(2)6s20m17M Siren Mo(N)60s, in daylight hours. BW circular tower, 28m high.

Les Courtis (St-Malo) 48°40'·5N 2°05'·8W Fl(3)G.12s14m 9M G tower, 21m high.

Le Grand Jardin (St-Malo) 48°40'·2N 2°05'·0W Fl(2)R.10s 24m15M Tall concrete tower R top, 38m high. RC *GJ* 306·5kHz 10M

Cap Fréhel 48°41'·1N 2°19'·1W Fl(2)10s85m29M Horn(2) 60s Brown square tower G lantern, 33m high. RC *FÉ* (··—·/·—··) 286·5kHz 20M.

Le Rohein 48°38'·9N 2°37'·8W VQ(9)WRG.10s13m10-8M 072°-R-105°-W-180°-G-193°-W-237°-G-282°-W-301°-G-330°-W-072° W cardinal tower, 15m high.

Le Grand Léjon 48°44'·9N 2°39'·9W Fl(5)WR.20s17m18/14M 058°-W-283°-R-350°-W-015°-R-058° R circular tower with white bands, 24m high.

Ile Harbour (Portrieux-St-Quay) 48°40'·0N 2°48'·5W Oc(2)WRG.6s16m11-8M 011°-R-133°-G-270°-R-306°-G-358°-W-011° White square house with small white tower with R top on its roof, 13m high.

L'Ost Pic (Paimpol) 48°46'·8N 2°56'·5W Oc.WR.4s20m 11/8M 116°-R-221°-W-253°-R-291°-W-329° Two white towers, R tops, 15m high.

La Horaine (Lézardrieux approaches) 48°53'·5N 2°55'·3W Fl(3)12s13m11M Grey octagonal tower, black top, 20m high.

Barnouic 49°01'·7N 2°48'·4W VQ(3)5s15m9M E cardinal octagonal tower, 19m high, (unreliable).

Roches Douvres 49°06'·5N 2°48'·8W Fl.5s60m28M Siren 60s Pink tower on dwelling with dark green roof, 65m high. RC *RD* 308kHz 70M.

Les Héaux (Tréguier approaches) 48°54'·5N 3°05'·2W Oc(3)WRG.12s48m17/12M 227°-R-247°-W-270°-G-302°-W-227° Grey granite tower, 57m high.

Le Paon (Bréhat) F.WRG.22m12/9M 033°-W-078°-G-181°-W-196°-R-307°-W-316°-R-348°-obscd-033° Yellowish tower, 12m high.

Rosédo (Bréhat) Fl.5s29m20M White tower green gallery, 13m high RC *DO* 287·5kHz 10M.

Off-lying buoys and marks

In addition to the lighthouses listed above, the following off-lying buoys and marks may be useful when making passages along this coast. They are unlit unless otherwise stated.

Plateau des Minquiers. Not all the buoys marking the perimeter are shown on plan 1; it will be seen that some of them are lit.

La Fille (½M NE of Pierre de Herpin LtHo). N cardinal whistle buoy.

Rochefort (6M W of Pierre de Herpin LtHo). W cardinal beacon tower and Basse aux Chiens E cardinal buoy.

Le Vieux Banc (6M ENE of Cap Fréhel). N cardinal bell light buoy, and a W cardinal pillar light buoy.

Banchenou (5M E of Cap Fréhel). Starboard pillar light buoy.

On the N side of Chenal d'Erquy

Les Justières Q(6)+LFl.15s, S cardinal spar light buoy.
Basses du Courant Q(6)+LFl.10s, S cardinal spar light buoy.

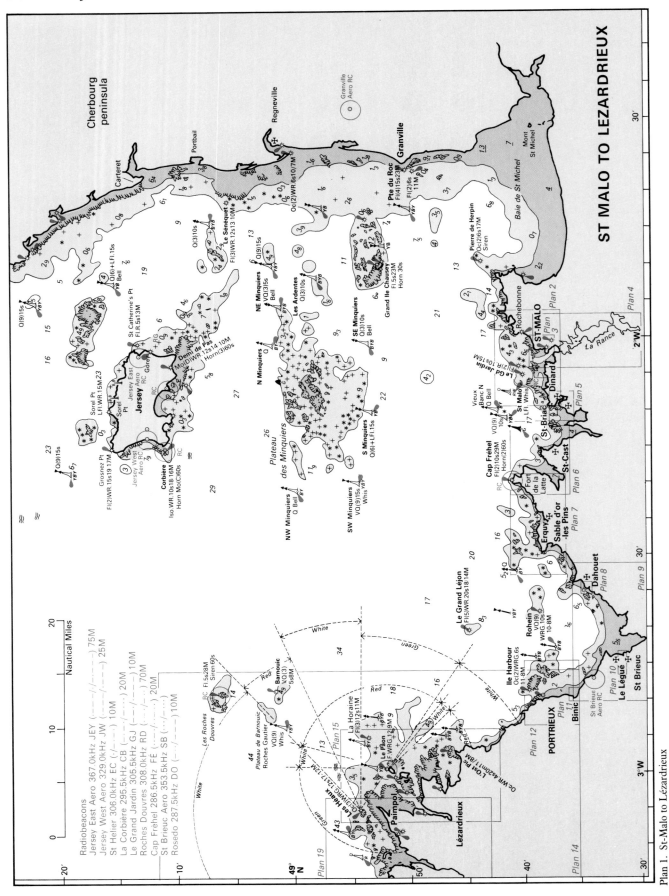

Plan 1. St-Malo to Lézardrieux

Les Landas (6·5M SE of Le Grand Léjon). N cardinal spar light buoy.

Le Petit Léjon (3·5M SSE of Le Grand Léjon). W cardinal spar bell buoy.

For buoys and beacons in the close approaches to harbours, see the appropriate chapters.

Air radiobeacon

Saint Brieuc 48°34′·1N 2°46′·9W SB 353kHz 25M

1. St-Malo and Dinard

Charts

BA *3659, 2700*
Imray *C33B*
SHOM *844, 7130*
ECM Navicarte *535*

Tidal data

Tidal heights (approx)

HW −0020 St Helier, −0515 Dover, +0205 Brest
MTL 6·75m. Index 13A
Heights of tide above chart datum
MHWS 12·1m, MLWS 1·4m, MHWN 9·1m, MLWN 4·4m

Tidal streams

1. In the offing between the Minquiers and Ile Cézembre the ESE-going stream begins about −0445 St Helier (+0245 Dover), reaching 3 knots at springs; and the WSW about +0040 St Helier (−0415 Dover), reaching 2·5 knots.
2. In the eastern approach north of Tourelle Rochefort and in the Chenal de la Petite Porte the ENE-going stream (NE in Chenal de la Petite Porte), reaching 3 knots at springs, begins at −0510 St Helier (+0220 Dover); and the WSW at +0030 St Helier (−0425 Dover), reaching 3 knots.
3. In the Chenal de la Grande Porte the stream turns at the same times as in 2 above, but the directions are E and W and both streams reach 3·8 knots at springs.
4. In Chenal de la Bigne the ENE-going stream, reaching 3·8 knots at springs, begins at −0540 St Helier (+0150 Dover); and the SW-going stream at 0000 St Helier (−0455 Dover), reaching 3·3 knots.
5. In the Chenal de la Grande Conchée and Chenal des Petits Pointus the times are the same, but the directions and rates differ, ENE reaching 2·8 knots and SW 1·5 knots.
6. Between St-Malo and Dinard, the SSE-going stream begins −0525 St Helier (+0205 Dover); and the NNW-going stream begins HW St Helier (−0455 Dover), maximum rate 2·5 knots.

General

St-Malo is by far the most important commercial harbour on the north coast of Brittany, but remains an attractive and convenient port of call for yachts. It is possible to anchor in the river abreast the town, but there is little shelter here and yachts usually lock through into the basin, where they can lie alongside floating pontoons or alongside the wall, with all the amenities of a marina close to the town and the *plage*.

Alternatively, yachts can, when depths over the sill permit, secure to a visitors' pontoon in the yacht marina at Port des Sablons. This is more expensive, less convenient and in a NW blow less comfortable than a berth in the basin. However, chandlers, engineers, a travel-lift and fuel pontoon are available in this expanding marina.

Opposite St-Malo, across the entrance to La Rance river, is the town of Dinard, mainly a large holiday resort with several adjacent bathing beaches. There is an anchorage in the Rade de Dinard abreast the town, but unless a yacht is prepared to take the ground, this is rather inconvenient at springs. La Rance is a charming river and above the barrage (see page 24) is navigable at low water level almost to St-Suliac, 5M from the entrance. There are several good anchorages on the way. Above St-Suliac the river dries at chart datum, but when the water level is high enough it is navigable for a further 2M to Port St-Hubert, where there is a pool in which a yacht can lie afloat, even at low water.

When the water level has risen sufficiently it is possible to continue over the drying river bed to L'Ecluse du Châtelier. The bridge here swings to pass masted vessels, so yachts can lock through into the Canal de l'Ile-et-Rance and proceed up to Dinan. From Dinan, except in a dry summer, small craft drawing less than 1·4m and needing less than 2·3m headroom, may pass by canal and river to Redon, and thence down the Vilaine to the Bay of Biscay. Before planning this passage, it is necessary to find out whether the canal system will be open at that time; it usually closes for maintenance for about a fortnight in late August and early September. A timetable for *chômages* (maintenance work) on the French canals can be obtained from the French Government Tourist Office (FGTO), 178 Piccadilly, London W1V 0AL, ☎ 071-491 7622.

The seaward approaches to St-Malo are complicated, but splendidly marked. There are two channels which can be taken by day or night at any state of the tide, and three more which can be used in daylight except near LWS.

Approaches

By day

The following can be used for fixing position during the approach:

Cap Fréhel (10M west of the Ile de Cézembre) a high headland with steep cliffs, with a lighthouse (tower 30m high, elevation 85m), a disused light tower, and a disused signal station. This has a radiobeacon: *FÉ* (··—·/··—··) 286·5kHz 20M.

Le Grand Jardin lighthouse, a tall concrete tower with red lantern (29m high, elevation 24m) standing about 0·4M WSW of the Ile de Cézembre. This also has a radiobeacon: *GJ* 306·5kHz 10M.

Ile de Cézembre a prominent island 32m high with several rounded summits.

St-Malo, looking east. Port des Bas Sablons far right. Lock into Bassin Vauban centre. Photo *Brian J. Green*

ST-MALO APPROACHES

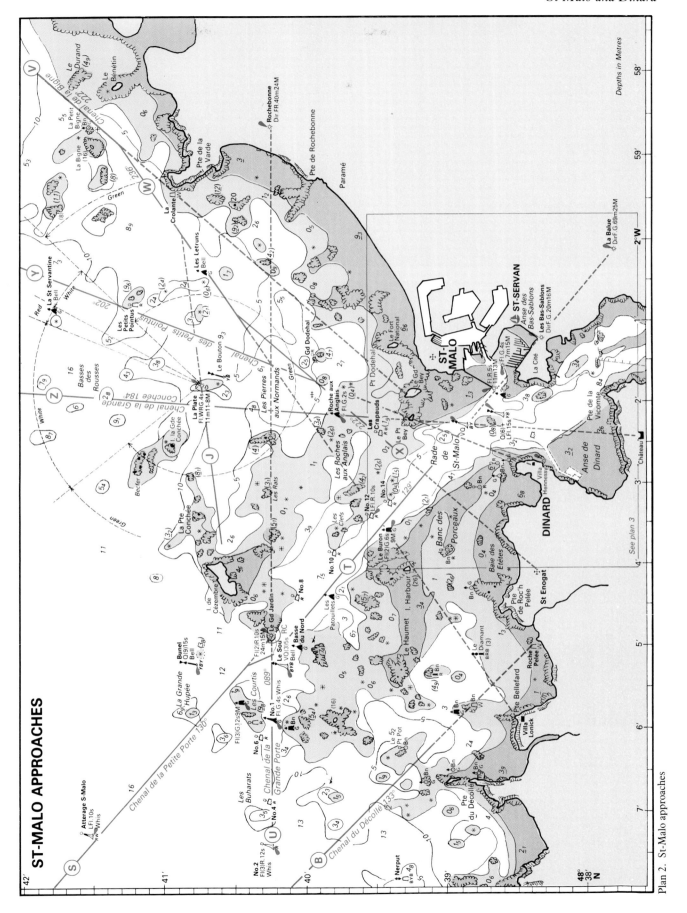

Depths in Metres

Plan 2. St-Malo approaches

Le Grand Jardin lighthouse with St-Malo spire, right centre,
bearing 118°.

Leading marks for Rade de St-Malo (129°), Les Bas Sablons white
tower (centre) with La Balue tower on skyline, slightly left of Les
Bas Sablons tower.

La Grande Conchée rock with fort on it situated east of Ile de Cézembre.

Rochefort W cardinal beacon tower standing on a group of drying rocks 2·5M N of Rochebonne lighthouse, the E end being marked by Basse aux Chiens E cardinal pillar buoy. Many of the leading lines described below are rather difficult for a stranger to pick up, but the channels can equally well be used by locating the outer marks and then steering compass courses with allowance for tide, checking off the numerous buoys and beacons as they appear.

By night

Both the Chenal de la Grande Porte and the Chenal de la Petite Porte are excellently lit, and should not be difficult in reasonable visibility.

By day and by night

Approach can be made to either channel by homing on safe courses, on Le Grand Jardin radiobeacon (see plan 2 on page 13). Those wishing to use secondary approaches, navigable by day only, or to sail outside the two main channels should buy the large-scale BA chart *2700*, or the SHOM chart *7130*; these show detail which cannot be reproduced on small scale.

CHENAL DE LA PETITE PORTE

This is the principal approach. A yacht needs plenty of speed to cope with the strong cross tide in this channel, except at slack water. The least depth is 7·4m as far as the Rade de Dinard. If approaching from the NW, note Le Vieux Banc (dries). It is marked by two buoys, both of them lit.

By day

Approaching from any direction, first make a position about 150m to the NE of the fairway light-and-whistle (safe-water mark) buoy, moored about 2M NW of Le Grand Jardin lighthouse.

From here, the leading marks will be in line: Le Grand Jardin lighthouse in line with La Balue lighthouse (square tower with black lantern, 37m high, elevation 69m, standing on the skyline behind the town, bearing 130° (line S). This line leaves the unmarked Grande Hupée rock (least depth 1·3m) 0·1M to port; Bunel W cardinal bell buoy 0·3M to port; and Les Courtis lighthouse (lateral starboard 21m high, elevation 14m) 0·16M to starboard.

When this lighthouse tower bears 280°, quit line S and steer 160° for 0·2M then alter course to follow line T, which is marked by Les Bas Sablons lighthouse (white square tower 20m high, upper part black, elevation 20m) in line with La Balue lighthouse (elevation 69m) bearing 129°.

This line leaves the following marks on the sides shown:

Le Grand Jardin lighthouse 180m to port. A port beacon stands about 100m SW of the lighthouse and must also be left to port.
Le Sou E cardinal spar buoy 0·15M to starboard.
Basse du Nord starboard buoy 0·14M to starboard.
No. 8 port buoy 0·125M to port.
Les Patouillets starboard buoy 190m to starboard.
No. 10 port buoy 0·15M to port.
Le Buron starboard light tower 110m to starboard.
No. 12 port buoy 100m to port.
No. 14 port buoy 120m to port.

The channel now approaches the Plateau de la Rance, a shoal containing drying rocks, which may be left on either hand depending on destination:

For St-Malo or Sablons pass to the east of it, continuing along line T, leaving the N cardinal buoy marking the NE side of the shoal 60m to starboard.

When this buoy is abeam, hold on for 0·15M, sufficiently to leave Plateau de la Rance to starboard before altering course to 170° for 0·2M.

Then steer for the lock gates when they bear 070° leaving the end of the Môle des Noires about 100m to port.

If bound for Port des Sablons bear to starboard when the marina breakwater light is abaft the beam and check the depth of water shown on the tide gauge before crossing the sill. (See page 22.)

For Dinard or La Rance pass to the west of the Plateau de la Rance. When St-Malo Cathedral tower bears 085°, quit line T and steer 170°, leaving the S cardinal light buoy which marks the southern end of the Plateau de la Rance about 0·1M to port, and so into the Rade de Dinard.

By night

Approaching from any direction, it should be easy to fix position by the main coastal lights: Cap Fréhel, Les Courtis, Grand Jardin, Pierre de Herpin and Grande Ile, Chausey.

Then make a position close NE of the fairway light-and-whistle (safe-water mark) buoy, which is moored about 2M NW of Le Grand Jardin.

From here, follow line S by keeping Le Grand Jardin (Fl(2)R.10s) in line with La Balue (the upper of two fixed green lights south of St-Malo), bearing 130° and leaving Les Courtis (Fl(3)G.12s) 0·175M to starboard. Line S can often be picked up while still a long way to seaward. It leaves the Vieux Banc N cardinal lit bell buoy (plans 1 and 2) only about 150m to starboard, and the fairway light-and-whistle buoy about 180m to starboard.

From the deck of a small yacht, La Balue dips behind Le Grand Jardin tower at some point along this line. When this happens, borrow a few metres to the west and keep La Balue touching the west side of the tower. This line also clears all dangers. There are fixed red lights on pylons 0·7 and 1·2M SW of La Balue.

When Les Courtis bears 280°, at which position Le Grand Jardin should be 0·3M ahead, quit line S and steer 170° for 0·15M then pick up line T; the fixed green lights of Les Bas Sablons and La Balue in line bearing 129° (intensified 127·5° to 130·5° and 128·2° to 129·7° respectively). Follow this line closely leaving:

Le Grand Jardin lighthouse 150m to port.
Le Sou E cardinal light buoy 0·15m to starboard.
Le Buron light tower (Fl(2)G.6s) 120m to starboard.
No. 12 port buoy 100m to port.

If passing to the east of the Plateau de la Rance, continue along line T until the unlit buoy which marks the north side of the shoal is abeam to starboard, distant 60m.

Hold on for 0·15M then steer 170° until the light on the end of the Môle des Noires (Fl.R.5s Horn(2) 20s), bears 060°. Then alter course to approach the lock on the transit of the three F.R lights over and behind the lock, bearing 071°.

If passing to the west of the Plateau de la Rance, when the tower of St-Malo cathedral bears 085° quit line T and steer 160° leaving the S cardinal light buoy, marking the south end of the shoal, 0·1M to port, and so into the Rade de Dinard.

Alternatively, if the cathedral cannot be seen, quit line T when the light buoy bears 150°.

CHENAL DE LA GRANDE PORTE

This channel has a least depth of 6·5m as far as the Rade de Dinard. If approaching from the NW, note Le Vieux Banc (dries), which is beyond the limits of plan 3. It is marked by two buoys, one of them lit.

By day

First make a position 70m south of No. 2 port light and whistle buoy. From here, Le Grand Jardin lighthouse will be in line with (and obscuring) Rochebonne lighthouse (white-faced square tower, red top 20m high, elevation 40m) bearing 089°; line U. Follow this line which leaves the following marks on the sides shown:

No. 2 (Buharats Ouest) port pillar buoy 60m to port.
No. 4 Buharats port buoy 60m, to port.
Boujaron starboard Bn tower, 250m to starboard.
No. 6 port buoy, 140m to port.
No. 1 starboard pillar buoy, 40m to starboard.
Pierre des Portes port beacon tower, 0·15M to port.
Les Courtis starboard LtHo 0·225M to port.
Le Sou E cardinal pillar buoy 200m to starboard.

When Le Grand Jardin lighthouse is 240m distant, alter course to follow line T with Les Bas Sablons lighthouse (white square tower 14m high, upper part black, elevation 20m) in line with La Balue lighthouse (square grey tower 31m high, elevation 69m, the top only appearing on the skyline) bearing 129°. Thence proceed as described under *Chenal de la Petite Porte, by day*, above.

By night

While still west of No. 2 port light and whistle buoy (Fl(3)R.12s) bring Le Grand Jardin (Fl(2)R.10s) into line with Rochebonne (DirF.R) bearing 089° (line U). (When exactly on the line, Rochebonne will be obscured by the tower of Le Grand Jardin. It is best to keep it touching one side.) This line leaves:

No. 2 port light-and-whistle buoy 70m to port.
No. 4 unlit port buoy 40m to port.
No. 1 starboard light-and-whistle buoy 30m to starboard.
Les Courtis (Fl(3)12s) 0·225M to port.
Le Sou E cardinal pillar buoy 0·125M to starboard.

When just more than 0·1M from Le Grand Jardin lighthouse, the leading lights for line T will come into line: the fixed green lights of Les Bas Sablons and La Balue in line bearing 129°. Alter course to follow this line and proceed as described *under Chenal de la Petite Port, by night, above.*

CHENAL DE LA GRANDE CONCHEE
By day

This channel carries a least depth of 0m (i.e. 6·7m at half tide). It is the principal route used by the hydrofoils and other shallow-draught fast ferries which ply between St Helier and St-Malo via the east side of the Minquiers and also major ferries near HW.

Approaching from the north, first identify the Ile Cézembre, then Les Haies de la Conchée rocks about

Leading marks for Chenal de la Grande Conchée. For line Z, 183°, the half-completed *château*-like building (see photo page 23) should be just open to the right of Le Petit Bey fort.

4m high which lie about 1M ENE of the island. They are situated over 0·25M NNW of La Grande Conchée, which is easily identified as it has an old fortress on it, and form the NE corner of the group of rocks and dangers on this side.

Make a position from which these rocks bear 270° distant 0·4M then steer to make good 184° along line Z which is marked by a modern grey *château*-like building with a turret at either end, open to the right of the conspicuous fort on Le Petit Bey, behind and to the left of which will be seen a group of four electricity pylons (see photo).

This line passes over Basses des Rousses, a 2·8m rocky patch, which can be left to port should the water over it appear disturbed.

The old mark, a white reservoir, is no longer visible but the channel is wide and the dangers on either side are all marked.

This line leaves the following marks on the sides shown:

La Grande Conchée (4m high) with a fort on it, 0·3M to starboard.
La Plate N cardinal beacon tower, 0·2M to port
Le Bouton S cardinal buoy, 0·24M to port.
Les Pierres aux Normands starboard beacon, 0·2M to starboard.
Grand Dodehal port beacon, 0·5M to port.
Les Roches aux Anglais starboard buoy, close to starboard.

After proceeding a further 0·15M past this buoy alter course to make good 222° to follow line X heading for the eastern side of the Baie des Etetés and leaving Les Crapauds port buoy to port.

Then, when Les Bas Sablons lighthouse comes in line with La Balue lighthouse bearing 129° (line T) alter course to follow this line and proceed as *Chenal de la Petite Porte, by day*, above.

By night

From the north identify La Plate N cardinal tower, (Fl.WRG.4s11·8M 140°-W-203°-R-210°-W-225°-G-140°). Bring this on to a bearing of 180° (in a white

View to the west at half tide on entering Chenal de la Grande Conchée. From left to right: La Grande Conchée Fort with Le Grand Jardin lighthouse (centre) and Ile de Cézembre (right centre) behind the line of rocks, Les Haies de la Conchée.

sector) and steer to make good a course of 180° towards the light, leaving La St-Servantine unlit bell buoy 0·75M to port, then steer so as to leave the light 0·2M to port on a course of 186°. This course should then be heading for Les Roches aux Anglais starboard buoy, Fl.G.2s. Leave this close to starboard.

After proceeding a further 0·15M past this buoy, alter course to make good 222° to follow line X and leaving Les Crapauds unlit port buoy 60m to port.

When the F.G lights of Les Bas Sablons and La Balue come in line bearing 129° (line T) alter course to follow this line and proceed as described *under Chenal de la Petite Porte, by night, above.*

CHENAL DE LA BIGNE

By day only

This narrow channel has a least depth of 0m (i.e. 6·7m at half tide), and is the most direct entrance from the east. When employing the channel for the first time it might be considered prudent to use it for departure rather than for entry.

First make a position from which Rochefort shoal marked by W cardinal beacon tower bears 280°, distant 0·7M. From here pick up the leading marks for line V: La Crolante white beacon tower in line with the northwestern edge of Le Grand Bey (the larger of two islets close NW of St-Malo) bearing 222°. This line leaves:

Basse aux Chiens, E cardinal pillar buoy 75m to starboard.

Basse du Durand shoal, with a least depth of 0·7m, 0·1M to starboard.

Le Durand rocks, an unmarked group 0·2M wide, the nearest drying 4m, the farthest 10m, 100m to port.

La Petite Bigne starboard beacon, 80m to starboard.

After 0·4M further, alter course to 236° and follow line W keeping Le Buron green beacon tower in line with Lonick Villa, a house standing on the right edge of a wood near Pointe Bellefard, a point with a white stripe painted on it.

The house is not easy to identify from this position and in 1991 the white stripe needed repainting. An alternative is to keep the ruined fort on Ile Harbour open its width to the right of Le Buron.

Leading marks for Chenal de la Bigne 222°, La Crolante white beacon tower on the NW edge of Le Grand Bey island. Le Petit Bey fort is to the right.

This line leaves La Crolante beacon tower 0·14M to port (there may still be a range off La Varde point where red flags are flown when firing is in progress) and leads straight to Les Létruns starboard bell buoy, which should be left close to starboard.

Continuing along line W, when La Plate N cardinal beacon tower bears 300°, alter course to 222° and follow line X heading for the eastern side of the Baie des Etetés. This line leaves:

Le Bouton S cardinal buoy, 0·5M to starboard.
Grand Dodehal port beacon, 0·2M to port.
Petit Dodehal rock, unmarked and drying 0·9m, 0·1M to port.
Les Roches aux Anglais starboard buoy, 0·1M to starboard.
Les Crapauds port buoy, to port.

Then, when Les Bas Sablons lighthouse comes in line with La Balue lighthouse bearing 129° (line T) alter course to follow this line and proceed as described *under Chenal de la Petite Porte, by day, above.*

Second transit for Chenal de la Bigne, line W, 236°. Le Buron green tower in line with Lonick Villa. The white stripe is midway between Le Buron and Ile Harbour Fort.

CHENAL DES PETITS POINTUS
By day only
This channel has a least depth of 0m (i.e. 6·7m at half tide). First make a position from which Rochefort W cardinal beacon tower bears E, distant 1·25M.

From here, steer so as to make good 202° along line Y keeping the conspicuous fort on Le Petit Bey just open to the east of Villa Hennessy, a prominent house in the NE part of Dinard. This line leaves the following marks on the sides shown:

St-Servantine starboard buoy, 0·2M to starboard.
Les Petits Pointus port beacon, 170m to port.
Les Létruns starboard bell buoy, 0·5M to port.
La Plate N cardinal beacon tower, 0·35M to starboard.
Le Bouton S cardinal buoy, 0·2M to starboard.
Les Pierres aux Normands starboard beacon 0·5M to starboard.
Grand Dodehal port beacon 0·2M to port.

As soon as this latter beacon is abaft the beam alter course to 222° to follow line X and proceed as described *under Chenal de la Bigne, above*.

CHENAL DU DECOLLE
This channel, the entrance to which is shown as line B on plan 2, had until recently fallen out of use, being described as dangerous due to the continuing encroachment of the Banc des Porceaux into the channel at the east end, and the rear leading mark for the western entrance, Amer Pival, having become obscured by trees. However, Roche Pelée beacon has replaced Amer Pival as a rear leading mark, making entry from the west possible once more. At the east end, the shape of the encroaching sandspit is changing so rapidly that directions are not included in this edition. In 1990, on a calm sunny day, near low water, the editor made the passage east–west,

Looking SSE to the Pointe de Dinard on the left, with Dinard behind the bay in the centre. The large house on the left of the point is the rear mark for the Chenal des Petit Pointus, the front mark being the right-hand edge of the fort on Le Petit Bey, 202°.

equipped with a large-scale chart, corrected to date, but not showing the spit. He recommends it as an interesting exercise in pilotage, but as an entrance channel it affords no advantage in distance over the *Chenal de la Grande Porte*, above.

ILE DE CEZEMBRE

Two old forts stand on this rather desolate island, dominating the approaches to St-Malo. There is a landing slip which dries 3·3m in the middle of the south side of the island, and a temporary anchorage in 2·7m sheltered from the west, in a position from which the eastern corner of the island bears about 285° distant 0·1M. The easiest approach to this anchorage is made by sailing along line Z (*see under Chenal de la Grande Conchée*) until La Plate N cardinal beacon tower is in line with La Crolante beacon tower bearing E (line J). Follow this line west towards the anchorage.

St-Malo. From left to right: Môle des Noires below town, lock entrance between two cranes and ferry, entrance to Sablons marina behind three white waiting buoys.

St-Malo

Anchorages

1. In calm weather there is a reasonable temporary anchorage with the buoy marking the N corner of the Plateau de la Rance bearing about 280°. This is out of the main strength of the tidal stream, but it is well to keep as far inshore as possible, as a certain amount of commercial traffic uses this channel.
2. There is a temporary anchorage with the centre of the Fort de la Cité bearing about 100°, and La Mercière isolated danger beacon bearing about 180°. The least depth is 3m sand.

Prohibited anchorage

Vessels may not anchor in or near the channel leading from the light buoy, which marks the southern end of the Plateau de la Rance, to St-Malo lock. *See below under La Rance for prohibited zone near barrage.*

Docks

The docks consist of three main basins, in which a least depth of about 5·4m is maintained, and Bassin Jacques Cartier, which serves mainly as a reservoir. All four are at the same level, and are reached by way of locks which lie ENE of the end of the Môle des Noires. The names of the basins are shown on plan 3. Entry is made at the lock (Ecluse du Naye).

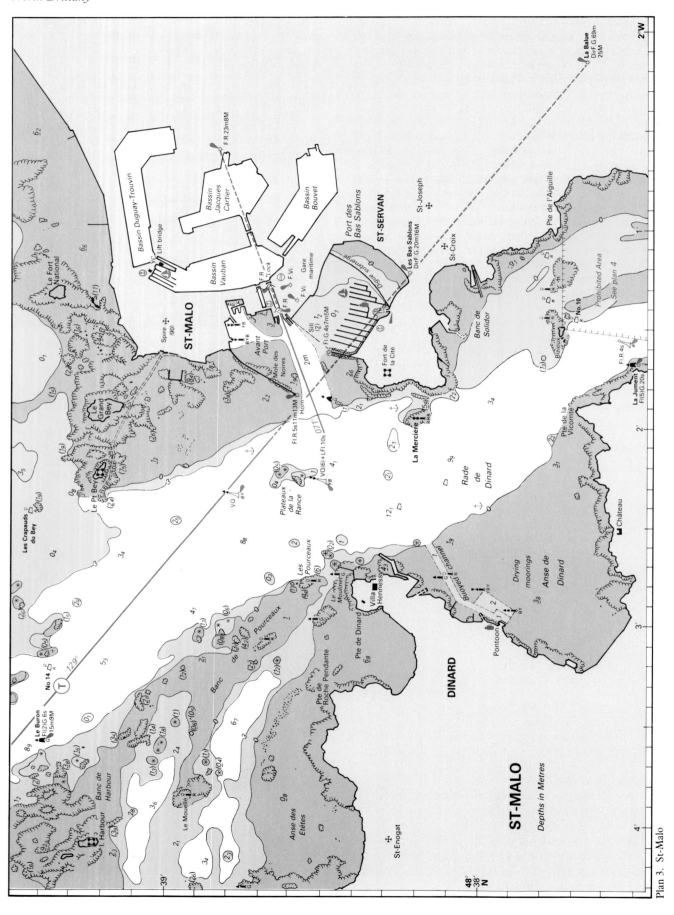

ST-MALO

Depths in Metres

Plan 3. St-Malo

Entry procedure

The port is open for entry 2½ hours before and for exit 2 hours before HW at St-Malo, both by day and by night, and thereafter as serves the traffic until about HW+1½ hours. Passage through the locks, or past the traversing bridges which separate the main basins, can be made only during these periods. When the tides are making, both gates of the lock are usually opened for a period of about 1½ hours just before HW. This is the best time for a yacht to pass through, but it is wise to keep plenty of way on, and to be ready for a strong set just outside the lock. The cross currents may attain 4 knots just before HW, on an 11m tide, when passage through can be dangerous and it is best to wait for slack water.

Unless the lock is very crowded, a yacht should secure against the side on which the lock-keeper is standing. The lock attendants will pass down heaving lines for the shore ends of the warps.

Signals

Light signals for regulating the passage of vessels through the lock, both by day and night, are exhibited on a mast by the side of the lock.

Normal working

G	A vessel may not enter the
W	lock unless authorisation
G	instructions have been received.
G	
G	Vessels may enter
G	
R	Vessels may not enter,
R	and must keep more than
R	200m clear of the gates.

Both gates open

G Y	Vessels may not pass through unless
W	authorisation instructions have been
G	received. (Attention to the current.)
G Y	Vessels may pass through.
G	(Attention to the current.)
G	
R Y	Vessels may not pass through,
R	and must keep more than 200m
R	from the lock.

Navigation control signal

Shown from the mast over the *capitainerie* on the north side of the lock. Yachts entering or leaving the Port des Sablons must also conform to this signal.

Y G	A vessel may not navigate in the Avant-Port
W	without special instructions from the
G	*capitainerie*.

Vessels navigating outside the channels can ignore this signal.

When signals prohibit entry it is necessary to lie off clear of the fairway, or temporarily on a mooring, but be ready to respond when the correct signal is made. When both gates are open and the signal is exhibited for entry, the current may at first be so fierce that entry is dangerous and the lock-master warns yachts away by loudspeaker.

Berthing

Yachts proceed to the northern end of the Bassin Vauban. Speed limit 5 knots. Berthing is allocated as follows:

Boats less than 7m on W side of No. 1 pontoon.

Boats between 7m and 10m on E side of No. 1, on both sides of No. 2, and on W side of No. 3 pontoon.

Boats between 9 and 12m on E side of No. 3 pontoon.

Boats above 11m, Quai St-Vincent (near town walls), Quai de Bajoyer (by yacht club) or Quai de L'Esplanade in the Bassin Dougay Trouin. Access to the latter is through a lifting bridge carrying a busy thoroughfare. Signal is one long blast.

Facilities

Water and electricity on the pontoons and quays. Showers, toilets, washing facilities and laundrette by harbour office. Fuel can now be obtained, by *Visa* and other cards, in the Bas-Sablons marina. Bins are provided for rubbish and there is a drum for waste oil opposite the harbourmaster's office.

The St-Malo Yacht Club is an active centre for yachtsmen. It has a bar and *poste restante*. The harbourmaster's office is at the N end of the Bassin Vauban. He does not now give information personally, but has a notice board on which is posted the day's heights for the Rance basin and the times of operation of the barrage. There is a stock of give-away literature, on signals and opening times for the lock and a programme of the times, during the summer season, when the water in the Rance basin will be maintained (a) at the higher level and (b) at the lower level, on local tides and services, and *pro forma* order forms for duty-free purchases.

There are banks, excellent shops, several shipwrights and engineers. French charts and publications can be obtained at the Librairie Maritime 5, Rue Broussais.

There is a casino and also many hotels among which the Hotel de l'Univers appears popular among yachtsmen. The restaurants are innumerable: the Duchesse Anne is nearest the quay and the cooking is good at an appropriate price.

St-Malo is a compact, closely built town, but a short walk from the club takes the visitor to the northern *plage* which is totally different in character, being a seaside resort with a front facing the sands extending for nearly 2M from St-Malo to Paramé with hotels, *pensions* and restaurants.

Vedettes leave the slip just east of the root of the Môle des Noires at frequent intervals for Dinard and, with sufficient rise of tide, for Dinan.

Hydrofoil and fast ferry services, weather permitting, run daily to the Channel Islands from a berth in the Avant-Port. Regular drive-on-off vehicle and passenger ferry services operate from the ferry terminal on the south side of L'Ecluse du Naye.

Regular rail service from station a mile from harbour office. Airport near Dinard with flights to the Channel Islands, Paris and Exeter.

Historical

The foundation of St-Malo is a single rock, which originally stood in the middle of a salt marsh but became an island in 1709 through an incursion of the sea. Later the causeway (Le Sillon) was built to connect it to Paramé, and the docks have slowly developed in the sheltered area to the south of it. The town itself started with a monastery founded in the 6th century by a monk named Aaron, who was succeeded by St-Malo (or St-Maclou) himself. St-Malo was actually Bishop of Aleth, the Gallo-Roman town which became St-Servan. As the centuries passed, a powerful walled town grew up on the isolated rock, and Aleth declined. The inhabitants, known as *Malouins*, were famous seamen, corsairs and explorers. They successfully resisted four English sieges, and even maintained themselves between 1390 and 1594, as an independent republic owing no allegiance to France or Brittany. *Ni Français, ni Bretons, Malouins seulement.*

Among the famous Malouins of history are Jacques Cartier, the discoverer of Canada, and Châteaubriand, who was born in the house which is now the Hotel de France and who is buried on Le Grand Bey. During the sixteenth and seventeenth centuries the walled town took on its present form, with immensely heavy fortifications, and streets of fine granite mansions for the rich sea captains and merchants. Towards the end of the Second World War most of the centre of the old town was demolished, but it is now restored as far as possible to its former condition.

St-Servan – Port des Sablons

Approaches

As for St-Malo

Anchorages

Off Fort de la Cité. (*See page 20*). Three mooring buoys have been laid in the dredged area close east of the new mole at Les Bas Sablons, for temporary mooring whilst waiting sufficient tide to cross the sill

and enter the yacht harbour. A rocky mole 250m long to the north of La Cité has been constructed and a sill from the end of this to the root of the ferry berth has been built making the Anse des Bas Sablons into a harbour for 1216 yachts. This sill dries 2m above chart datum leaving depths inside of 2·5m at the outer berths and less elsewhere. The dredged area to the northwest of the mole is being enlarged but drying sands still extend from near the root of this to the northwest. A yacht intending to enter the harbour should keep to the north of the end of the mole until it has been calculated that there will be adequate water over the sill or, when it is functioning, the illuminated panel, giving depth over the sill, can be seen. The depth is given in decimetres (065 = 6·5m and 000 = No entry).

The westernmost pontoon, with 35 berths for craft up to 12m LOA, is allocated to visitors. The outer berths on this pontoon can be uncomfortable in a northwesterly blow. It is proposed to extend the ferry terminal which should provide extra protection from NNW.

A light is exhibited at the end of the mole, 2Fl.G.4s(vert). When movement of ships is expected, a white light between the two green indicates that departure of yachts is prohibited.

Facilities

There is a hauling-out slip with a 9-ton travel-lift and a fuel pontoon (pumps operated by *Visa* and other cards) in the southern corner of the harbour. Masting crane for yachts intending to use the canal.

Water and electricity is laid on to the pontoons. The water may not be used for washing down. The harbour office is near the root of pontoon 9 where there is a bar-brasserie, WCs, showers, public telephones, chandlers and engineers. An indoor swimming pool has been built on the eastern side of the harbour. There are extensive car parks.

St-Servan town centre is about half a mile from the marina where there are shops, banks, hotels, restaurants, a laundrette and all the facilities of a large town. The village of Solidor is only a short walk from the marina and has small shops and restaurants. It overlooks its small harbour and anchorage which are dominated by the massive Tour de Solidor, built at the end of the 14th century and now a museum.

Dinard

Approach

See under St-Malo, Chenal de la Petite Porte

Anchorage

The best time to visit Dinard is at neap tides, as at springs the bottom drops steeply from the edge of the drying bank into depths of 7m (i.e. 18m at HWS). The holding ground, however, is good.

Drying moorings at Dinard, which is out of picture to the right. On skyline, water tower conspicuous from seaward and to the left the modern *château*-like building, completed in 1991, which can be used as a rear mark for the Chenal de la Grande Conchée. (See photo on page 16.)

A yacht should anchor as far in towards the Anse de Dinard as her draught will allow. Suitable anchoring positions can be chosen using plan 4, and at neap tides small craft will be able to stay afloat much farther in, in a position from which the small fixed green light on the *Cale des vedettes* bears about N, distant 0·1M or, with the aid of soundings, even nearer to the landings. There are two transits, refer to plans 3 and 4, which may help in selecting an anchorage by day or night:

Le Grand Jardin lighthouse (Fl(2)R.10s), touching the eastern side of the Point de Dinard.

Le Buron light tower (Fl(2)G.6s), touching the eastern side of Pointe de Dinard.

There is a row of yacht moorings in the northern part of the *anse*, near the edge of the bank. An area close to the club, with a narrow entrance channel, has been dredged and forms a small wet basin. Many small local yachts lie in this basin or on drying moorings near the town. Of recent years the number of moorings has greatly increased, and there are also many NW of Pointe de la Vicomté.

Facilities

The harbour facilities consist of the Quai de la Perle with a landing pontoon and fuel berth in the wet basin, and several small slips at the north end of the bay which are used by the *vedettes*. The most northerly of these does not dry.

The town is chiefly a residential and holiday resort, with excellent shopping facilities. There is a large yacht club, well known for its hospitality to British yachts, and a casino. Dinghies may conveniently be left on the endless mooring lines near the yacht club or at a slip. Cans can be filled with fresh water at the yacht club, but for large quantities it is necessary to go alongside the quay near high water. There are many hotels and restaurants. Dinard has an airport with a flight from Exeter via the Channel Islands. There is no bus service from the airport making it necessary to take a taxi.

2. La Rance

Before entering the river Rance it is necessary to consider the effects on its navigation caused by the construction of the hydroelectric barrage near the entrance. Silting is affecting the depths above the barrage. The water level above the dam changes by amounts comparable with the changes in tide level outside, but not at the same time.

Normally the rate of the streams is also comparable with what they were before; very strong at springs and in emergency substantially faster rates are permitted for short periods. Starting at or after high water there is a stand for an hour or two, at a level at or rather above the level of HW outside. Then the ebb begins suddenly. At neaps the level ceases to fall before it reaches LW outside, but at mean tides and springs the level may fall to LW outside. After a stand the level rises and continues to do so rapidly until about or after the time of HW outside.

It is thus possible to pass through the lock and sail in the river without special directions, providing the deep water (see plan 4) is adhered to. However, it is preferable to visit St-Malo first to obtain a copy of the programme from the port master's office (see above, page 21). This shows the periods when the level will be 4m and 8·5m above chart datum in the river during daytime from 15 June to 15 September, together with other relevant information.

The programmes are also available at the Barrage and at Le Châtelier or the information will be given by telephone (☎ 99 46 21 87) from any post office. If it is desired to ascertain accurately how far the level will fall for anchorage purposes, the information is available on the harbourmaster's notice board or by telephone as above. It is not possible, accurately, to interpolate for intermediate heights. It is recommended that, before anchoring, soundings are taken whilst the water is at the higher level. The difference between the day's height for this and the succeeding low water level is then subtracted from the sounding to find the minimum depth.

Alternatively, anchor whilst the water is at the lower level, allowing a suitable margin, as would normally be done at LW. The variation in height is not more than 4m per hour, or 1m in 15 minutes, except when necessitated in exceptional circumstances, when the maximum can be 1·4m in 10 minutes. Rapid changes such as these cause fierce currents. Reference should be made to Carte-guide Navicarte *No. 12 Bretagne: de Saint-Malo à Arzal, de Lorient à Nantes* (1:50,000), or Guide Vagnon *No. 10 Canaux Bretons et Loire* (1:100,000).

Yacht leaving the Rance by the barrage lock.

Bizeux to St-Suliac

There is a prohibited zone to the north and south of the barrage which is shown on plan 4. Yachts should keep to the west side of the river between Pointe de la Vicomté and the lock, leaving the port buoys marking the prohibited zone and the floating barrier to port.

The lock is worked from 0700 to 2100 (French civil time) during the season, when the tide or basin levels are 4m above datum or more. For entry from seaward yachts should arrive 20 minutes before, and from the basin between 40 and 20 minutes before the exact hour. Be ready to give draught and masthead height in metres should they be requested.

Vessels awaiting the lock may secure to one of the moorings nearby. There is a least depth of 1·5m at the seaward side and possibly less due to silting on the river side of the lock when the level is only 4m above datum, the minimum level for the lock to operate. In busy periods vessels without masts should enter after those with masts if proceeding upstream and first if proceeding downstream; this is because the lifting road bridge spans the north end of the lock and can be lowered without waiting for the lock to clear.

Within the lock ropes hang down to hold. There is very little swirl, and it is not necessary to make fast securely.

Traffic signals are shown at the lock:

Cone, hoisted point down, or green light – Entry permitted from seaward.

Ball, hoisted, or green light – Entry permitted from La Rance.

Cone and ball hoisted, or red light – No entry.

Signals on the centre of the dam indicate the flow through the turbines:

White cone over black cone, points up (green over white by night) indicate flood stream.

Black cone over white cone, points down (white over green by night) indicate ebb stream.

No signal, no stream.

Similar signals over the eastern end of the dam indicate the flow through the sluices there.

A boat which takes the first locking out of St-Malo, from 2 to 1½ hours before HW, should find no difficulty in reaching Le Châtelier lock before the water level falls. After passing through the barrage lock there are three port buoys and a floating barrier to be left to port. These mark the south side of the prohibited zone, which may be dangerous owing to the currents associated with the barrage and sluices. Anchorage is prohibited for a mile south of the dam on account of submarine telephone cables. The river above the barrage is unlit, except for the port buoy at the SW corner of the prohibited zone, and it would not be easy for strangers to navigate at night. If the channel is correctly followed it carries a least depth of 2m nearly to St-Suliac, plus the level at which the basin is maintained above datum. There is a certain amount of traffic in the river, mostly *vedettes* running between St-Malo and Dinan, and the number of yachts is increasing.

After clearing the SW prohibited zone a yacht can sail anywhere the depth of water permits at the level maintained above chart datum plus or minus the depths shown on your chart. After passing the prohibited zone, take care not to miss the inconspicuous Cancaval starboard beacon, but also leaving to port the Bancs des Rozais (drying 2·2m).

When approaching Cancaval beacon, leave it 100m and Pointe de Cancaval 150m to starboard, altering course to starboard, leaving Les Zèbres port beacon tower 200m to port and steering for the old ferry slip and hotel/restaurant on the west bank, thus avoiding a shallow patch south of the Pointe du Grouin ferry slip on the east bank.

On approaching the slip, steer to pass about 200m from it, 150m from the Pointe de la Landrais, and 100m from the Pointe du Thon.

From here steer so as to make good a course to leave La Morue (dries 3m) to port and Les Pierres du Fil (dry 1·2m) to starboard. (Note the latter are roughly in mid-stream, and on a line formed by Le Minihic spire and the southern side of Pointe Garel.) Note the seaplane landing areas on plan 4.

Then steer so as to leave Le Chaudron port beacon (and the concrete tower containing a tide gauge) 100m to port.

If bound for St-Suliac, cut in about 100m to the south of this beacon, leave Les Echaudières port beacon 50m to port, turn to starboard and bring up in the anchorage described below.

Anchorages

Anchorage is prohibited for a mile south of the barrage. At La Richardais there is a landing slip, a yacht yard, a small restaurant and shop. A yacht able to take the ground may be able to follow the winding drying channel, marked by beacons, and find room to dry out without breaking the regulations. Elsewhere it is possible to anchor almost anywhere in the river on the edges of the deep channel after taking soundings as mentioned on page 24. It is advisable to ease as close to the land as draught and low water level permit, in order to avoid the strength of the stream, particularly off headlands. Many of the bays are crowded with local moorings, many of which dry, but a number of visitors' moorings, white buoys without a yacht's name on them, are available for a one night stay.

1. Anse de Montmarin. At the southern end of the bay in 4m or closer in when programme permits. Good landing slip 0·15M south, near the conspicuous hotel.
2. In the pool north or east of Ile Chevret.
3. Anse de Gauthier. In 3·6m near the edge of the channel in the centre of the bay.
4. Off the bay between Pointe de Langrognais and Pointe du Thon. Moorings have been laid in this area, including some with heavy chains, but if anchoring it is best to take soundings and lie as far into the bay as possible as the current is astonishingly fast when the water level is being altered. The bay itself dries out. Slip and yacht yard. Restaurant at Le Minihic, ½M uphill walk.
5. St-Suliac. Between Les Ecrepières and local moorings to SE of Les Echaudières port beacon. It is a small, sleepy country town with post office, Restaurant de la Grève, *crêperie* and a few shops. There is good dinghy landing at the slip but beware the mud at low water!

Pardon, St-Suliac, Saturday mid-August, with a rather lovely candlelight procession up to the pagoda-shrine of Our Lady of the Rance on the point north of the village.

St-Suliac to l'Ecluse du Châtelier

Most of the estuary from St-Suliac to Port St-Hubert's two high road bridges dries out as shown on plan 4 on pages 26–7. This shows, in dotted line, the approximate track carrying the best water which, in summer months, is marked by a continuous line of port buoys. These and those between Port St-Hubert and Mordreuc should be given a berth of about 50m, as some sandbanks are developing.

Alternatively, with a rise in level above datum of about 7m, a yacht can sail straight up the middle of the river over the shoals as far as Port St-Hubert.

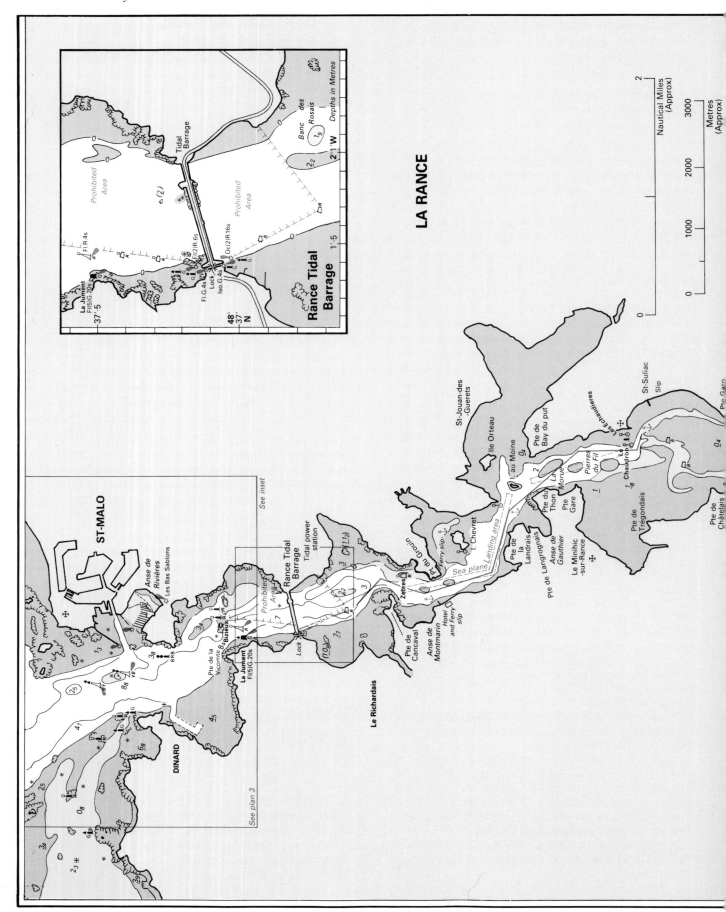

Rance Tidal Barrage 1'·5

La Jument
Fl(5)G.20s
37'·5
0
Prohibited
Area
Tidal
Barrage
Banc des
Rosais
1.9
2.2
2·1'W
48°
37'
N
FI.G.4s
Lock
Iso.G.4s
Fl(2)R.6s
Oc(2)R.16s
R
Fl.R.4s
Prohibited
Area
R
Depths in Metres

LA RANCE

St-Jouan-des
-Guerets
Ile Orteau
l'au Moine
Pte de Bay du put
Pte du
Thon
Pierres
du Fil
Le
Chaudron
St-Suliac
Slip
Les Echandrières
Pte de
Tregondais
Pte de
Châtelais
0.4
Pte de
la
Landrais
Anse de
Gauthier
Le Minihic
-sur-Rance
Pte de
Gare
1
8
2
I. Chevret
Ferry slip
Sea plane
Landing area
du Groun
Zebres
R
Hotel
and Ferry
slip
Anse de
Montmarin
Pte de Cancaval
Pte de Langrognais

Le Richardais

Rance Tidal
Barrage
Tidal power
station
Prohibited
Area
(1.2)
3
3
2
3
1.7
1.7
(10.8)
Lock
See inset

ST-MALO

Anse de
Rivières
Les Bas Sablons
3.8
BR B
Pte de la
Vicomte
Bizeux
R
La Jument
Fl(5)G.20s

DINARD

4.5
1.3
8.9
2.5
R
4.1
6.8
2.5
0.8
3.4
2.3

See plan 3

Nautical Miles
(Approx)
Metres
(Approx)
0   1000   2000   3000
0   1   2

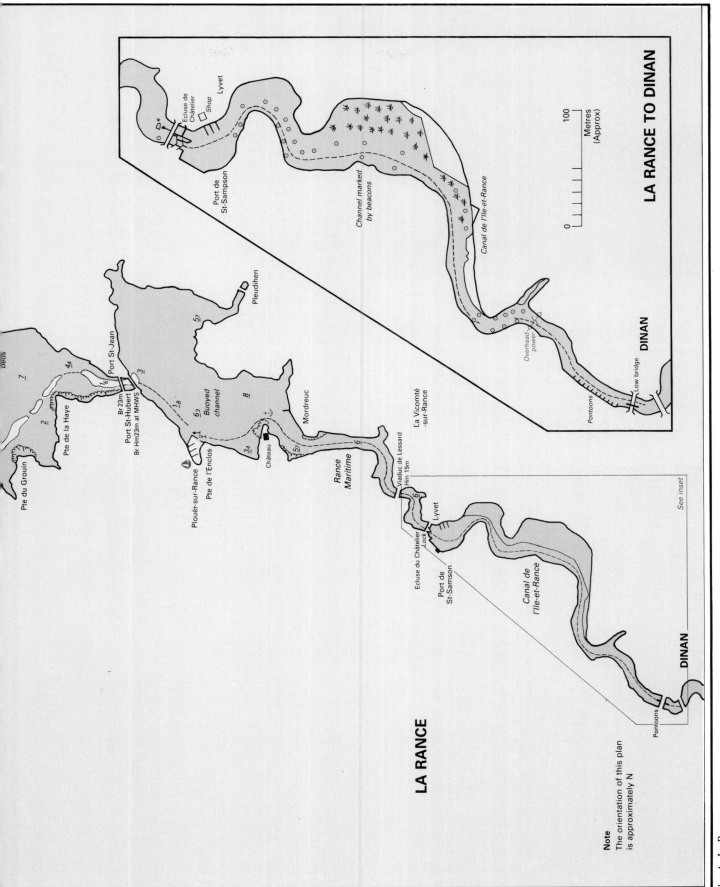

La Rance

LA RANCE TO DINAN

Metres
(Approx)

0   100

Écluse de
Châtelier

Shop

Lyvet

Port de
St-Sampson

Channel marked
by beacons

Canal de l'Ile-et-Rance

DINAN

Overhead
power

Low bridge

Pontoons

Pte du Grouin

beds

1

2

Pte de la Haye

4

1 6

Port St-Jean

3

Br 23m
Port St-Hubert
Br Hm23m at MHWS

1 8

Plouër-sur-Rance

Pte de l'Enclos

3 4

Château

6 3

Buoyed
channel

8

5 7

Mordreuc

Pleudihen

5 7

*Rance
Maritime*

6

Viaduc de Lessard
Hm 19m

La Vicomté
-sur-Rance

6

Écluse du Châtelier
Lock

Lyvet

Port de
St-Sampson

Canal de
l'Ile-et-Rance

See inset

LA RANCE

DINAN

Pontoons

Note
The orientation of this plan
is approximately N

Plan 4. La Rance

27

Looking upriver to the two road bridges across Port St-Hubert narrows.

Here the river is spanned by overhead cables and the two bridges. The clearance under the old suspension bridge is 22·8m at MHWS and even more under the new bridge and the cables. There is a pool over ¼M long in the narrows off Port St-Hubert which provides the only deep-water anchorage in this part of the river. Anchor near the sides of the fairway (which are very steep).

Beyond the pool the river dries out at low level and the channel may be taken as drying 7m above datum up to Le Châtelier lock. The time during which the depth above datum is more than 8·5m is the period during which the channel is taken to be open. The lock is worked when there is a minimum of about 1·5m in the channel, which is narrow and winding so that it is necessary to keep close to the line. Do not overlook the buoy at the corner 0·7M SSW of Mordreuc and then keep close to the buoys.

0·5M before Le Châtelier is reached the river is spanned by a viaduct with adequate clearance and the channel, now dredged, is marked by port and starboard beacons.

On the banks of the river there are one or two villages, of which the largest is Mordreuc. There are landing slips at Port St-Hubert, Port St-Jean, Mordreuc and L'Ecluse du Châtelier, amongst other places.

Anchorage
Drying anchorage at Mordreuc.

Plouër marina

In 1991 a marina was established in the tide-mill pool at Plouër. A depth of 2m is maintained by means of a *bascule* sill hydraulically operated by wooden counterweights. The depth over the sill is 1·5m when the level at St-Suliac is 8m, and 4m at high water.

Plouër marina entrance on 284°.

Château opposite Mordreuc looking downstream to the two bridges.

Early morning at Dinan.

Entrance

After passing under the twin road bridges at Port St-Hubert, carry on up the channel which is marked by three port buoys.

On reaching the third buoy the lights at the sill will be seen by day or by night if entry is possible. They are fixed red and green lights, both backed by a fixed white light. Enter by day with Plouër church midway between the entrance lights on 284°.

Facilities

Water and electricity on the pontoons, toilets and showers at the *capitainerie*. Two restaurants nearby and three in the village ¾M to the south where there are shops, a supermarket, two banks and a post office.

Canal de l'Ile-et-Rance

The bridge at Le Châtelier swings to allow passage of masted vessels. The sill is 6·34m above datum, but in 1991 there was silting in the basin and the lock was not operated until the level at St-Suliac was 10m. Mooring lines are provided which should be kept taut as the lock fills and afterwards until the turbulence subsides. For opening times see notices in harbourmaster's office at St-Malo or telephone the lock ☎ 96 39 55 66.

Above the lock there is a small marina on the east bank, with a food store open in the summer months.

Between Le Châtelier and Dinan, the best water in the first reach is found by turning easily to port on leaving the lock and steering to pass between the first pair of red and black posts, before the first bend, thereafter between the red posts and the towpath. Note the power line crossing the river by the sewage farm, half a mile downstream of Dinan. The clearance is stated to be 16m, it looks less and it is advisable to keep well to starboard proceeding up-river.

After a period of low rainfall in 1991 the depth was reduced to 1·1m as far as Dinan, and above Dinan was only 1m. It is as well to check on the depth before proceeding up the canal.

The port of the ancient town of Dinan is formed by that part of the canal running through the town, and has quays on either side which are used by barges and *vedettes* from St-Malo and by small motor yachts. There are also short (6m) finger pontoons on the starboard hand. Very crowded in mid-summer.

Facilities

Water and electricity on the pontoons. Showers, toilets and a laundrette in the port office. Restaurants and small food shops on the quay. A steep climb up a narrow cobbled street between mediaeval houses leads to the town where there are all shops, banks, hotels and restaurants. Buses and a rail service to Rennes.

Canal

After sufficient rain the maximum draught in the canal to Rennes is now 1·3m. There is little point in continuing to Nantes, as there is no difficulty in proceeding from Rennes, down the Vilaine river to Redon and on to the sea. There are sixty-five locks from sea to sea, counting the barrages at both ends, and it is necessary to help in working them.

3. St-Briac

Charts
BA *3659*
Imray *C33B*
SHOM *844*
ECM Navicarte 535

Tidal data
See under St-Malo.

General
Lying 7·5M SE of Cap Fréhel, this small natural drying harbour is liable to be confused with St-Brieuc, 25M farther west. St-Briac harbour is formed by the mouth of the Rivière de Frémur. The sand bottom dries 1·3–6·2m LAT, with rocky outcrops along each bank. There are no berths alongside and a yacht must dry out in the middle of the harbour.

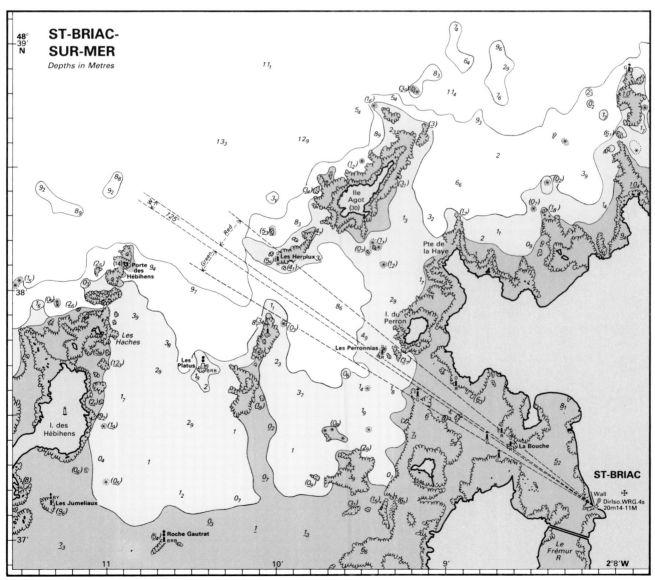

Plan 5. St-Briac-Sur-Mer

St-Briac channel at half tide. The bridge is not visible from the entrance. The leading light column is on the end of the wall just left of the port beacon (centre of picture).

Approach

By day

First identify La Porte des Hébihens, a small rock which lies 0·65M 020° from the large tower on Ile des Hébihens.

From a position about 0·2M N from La Porte des Hébihens (do not approach nearer than 0·1M as drying rocks extend north) bring the port beacon on Les Perronnias (200m SW of Ile du Perron) in transit with the port beacon La Bouche (which appears as the third) bearing 125°, if they can be identified. This line is also indicated by the St-Briac light structure, a small white column at the southern end of a conspicuous wall supporting the road leading to a bridge which is not visible until the river is entered. Follow this line.

On close approach leave Les Perronnias beacon to port and thereafter make good a mid-channel course between the beacons.

By night

From seaward to the NW pick up the directional light (DirIso.WRG.4s) at St-Briac bearing between 122° and 129°. This has a green sector to the south, a red sector to the north and a white sector over the channel bearing 125°. Steer to keep in the white sector, only 1° wide.

On close approach visibility will be necessary to identify the channel beacons as in *By day* above.

Anchorages

In fair weather in about 1m LWS south of Ile du Perron; or pick up a vacant mooring in this area. Yachts which can take the ground can find better shelter on or outside the moorings in the next bay or complete shelter to port beyond La Bouche beacon.

Facilities

An unspoilt small resort with a Vietnamese restaurant, a yacht club, hotels and shops.

St-Jacut pier, looking NE over the drying moorings.

4. St-Jacut

Charts
BA *3659*
Imray *C33B*
SHOM *844, 7130*
ECM Navicarte *535*

Tidal data
See under St-Malo.

General
The village stands on a peninsula between Baie de l'Arguenon and Baie de Lancieux both of which dry. On the eastern side of the peninsula are the small drying ports of Le Chatelet (the winter harbour) and La Houle-Causseul (the summer harbour).

Approach
By day only
First identify La Porte des Hébihens rock (see under *St-Briac*, above). From a position 100m E of this steer to bring it on a stern bearing of 344° then steer to make good 164°, leaving Platus isolated danger beacon 0·15M to port, Roche Gautrat isolated danger beacon 0·15M to starboard.

With Roche Gautrat beacon abeam, steer 190° to leave La Charbotier E cardinal beacon 0·25M to starboard.

When this is abeam alter course for the northerly La Houle-Causseul or for Le Chatelet to the S.

Anchorages
At Le Chatelet, inside jetty 70m long drying 8m at outer end, or on hard sand inshore. Secure but restricted. Tide only just reaches pierhead at MTL.

At La Houle-Causseul in open roadstead where boats moored in photograph. Hard sand.

Facilities
Very pleasant unspoilt village about 1M from La Houle-Causseul and ½M from Le Chatelet. Yacht chandlery, shops and cafés. Market on Fridays.

5. St-Cast

Charts
BA *3659*
Imray *C33B*
SHOM *844, 7130*
ECM Navicarte *535*

Tidal data

Tidal heights
See St-Malo.

Tidal streams
Off Cap Fréhel the ESE-going stream begins at −0525 St Helier (+0205 Dover) and the WNW-going stream begins at −0030 St Helier (−0525 Dover). Both streams attain between 3·5 and 4 knots.

General
The Anse de St-Cast lies immediately southeast of the Pointe de St-Cast, which itself is 4M southeast of Cap Fréhel. The port of St-Cast is 1M north of the village and, while continuing to harbour a number of fishing boats, has also been developed as a holiday resort, with deep-water moorings, catering for yachtsmen. A mole with a slip 80m long alongside is assisted in providing shelter by Bec Rond, a rock, elevation 5m painted white some 150m south of the head of the mole.

St-Cast, looking south. The grey rock Bec Rond is conspicuous above the breakwater head. Photo *Brian J. Green*

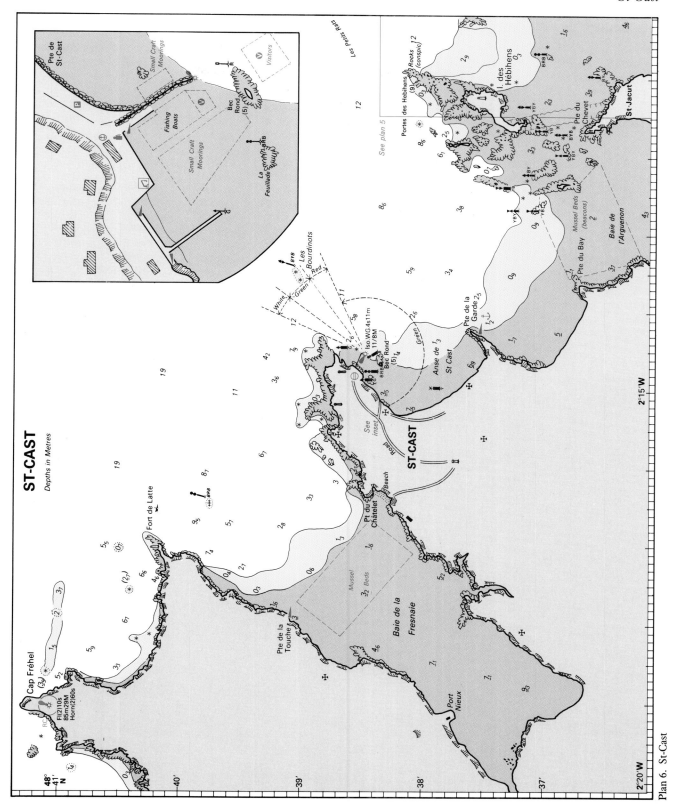

ST-CAST

Depths in Metres

Cap Fréhel

Fl(2)10s
85m29M
Horn2/60s

RC

Fort de Latte

BRB

Pte de la Touche

Pt du Châtelet

Beach

Baie de la
Fresnaie

Mussel
Beds

Port Nieux

Les Petits Rats

Pte de St-Cast

Small Craft
Moorings

Visitors

Bec Rond
(5)

La
Feuillade

BRB

Fishing
Boats

Small Craft
Moorings

P

Les
Bourdinots

BYB

White

Green

Red

Iso.WG4s11m
11/8M

Bec Rond
(5)

BRB

Green

Anse de
St Cast

Pte de la
Garde

See inset

Road

ST-CAST

Portes des Hébihens

Rocks
(conspic)

I. des
Hébihens

BRB

YBY

St-Jacut

Pte du
Chevet

Mussel Beds
(beacons)

Pte du Bay

Baie de
l'Arguenon

See plan 5

2°15'W

2°20'W

48°
41'
N

40'

39'

38'

37'

Approach

By day

Avoid the Bourdinots rocks, which are just over 0·5M northeast of Pointe de St-Cast, marked at the northern end by an E cardinal spar buoy. Enter the harbour between Le Bec Rond port beacon and the pierhead.

By night

Identify the mole head light, Iso.WG.4s11/8M. Approach by one of two white sectors, between 204° and 217° or 233° and 245°. The green sector between these covers the Bourdinots rocks, Le Bec Rond port beacon is unlit.

Anchorages

This harbour, although usually crowded, has the advantage that it provides moorings that can be approached at any state of tide and yachts can remain afloat in 1·4m in the northern section. The first two lines of buoys parallel to the mole provide double-ended moorings for fishing boats. The yacht moorings are situated a short distance south, with some protection from Bec Rond. The harbourmaster is most helpful. In calm weather he prefers visitors to pick up a waiting buoy outside Bec Rond and to come in by dinghy to arrange for a mooring inside.

There is a good anchorage about 0·15M SSE of Pointe de la Garde, 1M to the south, with a landing slip and yacht club adjacent, sheltered from south through west to northwest.

Facilities

On the quay, some shops, a café/bar, chandlers and customs. Water, petrol and diesel at the root of the mole. Cranes of 6 and 12 tons.

The usual shops, hotels and restaurants, a good supermarket and a laundrette will be found in St-Cast about a mile away.

St-Cast moorings at LW, looking NE.

6. Baie de la Fresnaie

Charts
BA *3659*
Imray *C33B*
SHOM *844*
ECM Navicarte *536*

Tidal data
As for St-Cast.

General
A large bay lying about 2M SE of Cap Fréhel. Most of it dries and there is a large oyster bed near the mouth. The SHOM chart *5646* shows a line bearing ESE from Pointe de la Latte, the area south of which is labelled *Zone Dangereuse*. It contains Port-Nieux, a small drying harbour, which lies on the NW side of the bay about 1M from its head. Anchoring in this area is not advised due to the possibility of unswept mines from the Second World War resting on the bottom.

Approach
By day only
The approach from the north is straightforward, after identifying the conspicuous Fort de la Latte on the western headland.

Anchorages
There is an anchorage in 3m sand and mud, very good holding ground, with Fort de la Latte bearing 010°, distant 0·6M. It is presumed that the *Zone Dangereuse* does not refer to anchorages such as this. South of the above anchorage there is a small landing slip with a boathouse, and a number of moorings, on Pointe de la Touche which at the end dries about 3·5m.

Port Nieux, further up the bay, has a quay and a small jetty, with berths alongside which dry 7·8m. As the neap tide rise does not exceed 9m, keel boats would risk being neaped here when the tides are taking off.

200m NW of Pte du Chatelet on the east side of the bay there is an anchorage, open to the northwest, in about 2m. South of the point there are yachts moored off a sandy beach, with a caravan park behind and a road up from the beach leading to La Ville Norme and on to St-Cast. At neaps it should be possible to anchor off the beach to obtain supplies.

Facilities
Except for the above, none, but it is said that a visit to Fort de la Latte is well worth a scramble up the cliffs.

Fort de la Latte on west side of the Baie de la Fresnaie, from the NW.

7. Sables d'Or-les-Pins

Charts

BA *3674*
Imray *C33B*
SHOM *833*
ECM Navicarte *536*

Tidal data

As for St-Cast.

General

A holiday resort in a small bay 4M SW of Cap Fréhel. The bay contains two small drying harbours. In the eastern corner is Port Barrier which is sheltered by a jetty and with a quay which dries 5·5m at the north and 6·5m at the south. Les Bouches d'Erquy, a small natural harbour, lies in the western corner, immediately west of a large sand dune where several small streams run into the bay and which dries 5 or 6m.

Approach

By day only

Identify Ile St-Michel with a diminutive chapel on the summit. There is an unmarked drying rock, Roche Plate St-Michel, shaped like an inverted saucer just over 0·5M NE of Ile St-Michel. The bay should be entered to give this a wide berth and approach could be made with the help of plan 7. Follow line J (*see under Chenal d'Erquy below*) until Plurien belfry is in transit with a conspicuous water tower bearing 177° and is well open to the west of the left-hand large hotel on the *plage* (see photograph). Alter course to follow this line (M) which leaves Roche Plate St-Michel 0·3M to starboard and Rocher Bénard 0·3M to port.

Anchorages

Port Barrier was built for loading stone from neighbouring quarries. One quarry is still active but the stone is now taken away by road, the outer end of the jetty is partly demolished and access is becoming more and more difficult due to the encroachment of shingle. There is a jetty at Les Bouches d'Erquy which is reserved for fishing boats. There is stated to be a good anchorage in offshore winds SE of Rocher Bénard with about 3m ordinary LWS, but beware of Rocher Fournel, 200m offshore farther SE which dries 11m.

The bay, with its extensive sandy beach, has many attractions for a day visit in settled weather. Come in on the transit of spire and water tower bearing 177° and turn to starboard when the chapel on the islet is abeam, thus avoiding an isolated rock, which may have less than 2m over it at LAT, off the middle of the beach. Anchor as close to the beach as tide permits for a landing by dinghy.

Facilities

Sables d'Or-les-Pins has all the amenities of a popular holiday resort.

Sables d'Or-les-Pins, leading marks, out of line, centre.

8. Chenal d'Erquy

Charts
BA *3674*
Imray *C33B*
SHOM *833*
ECM Navicarte *536*

Tidal data

Tidal streams
In the Chenal d'Erquy the ENE-going stream begins at −0540 St Helier (+0150 Dover) and the WSW-going at HW St Helier (−0455 Dover). Both reach 3 knots at springs.

General
This channel lies between Cap d'Erquy and the off-lying rocks which extend 3M to seaward of it. It can be regarded as having a least depth of 3·5m, and should offer no difficulty in daylight and clear weather. Passage by night is now possible under ideal conditions as the two S cardinal buoys to the south of the off-lying rocks are lit.

Approach

By day
Approaching from the east, having passed north of Cap Fréhel and of Amas du Cap, the large rock which lies about 0·4M from it, close the shore until the southern edge of Amas du Cap (HW mark) is touching the end of Cap Fréhel, bearing 077° (line J, see photograph). Steer 257° to hold this stern transit, leaving the Plateau des Justières S cardinal spar buoy 0·4M to starboard.

Chenal d'Erquy leading line, Cap Fréhel in transit with right-hand edge of Amas du Cap on 077°.

When this buoy is just abaft the beam, and Cap d'Erquy bears 230°, alter course to make good 240° (line K), leaving the Basses du Courant S cardinal spar buoy 100m to starboard and Cap d'Erquy 0·3M to port.

If continuing west, when Basses du Courant buoy is abeam alter course to 235° to leave L'Evette cardinal N beacon tower 0·4M to starboard and when Erquy lighthouse (red and white circular tower 10m high on the head of the jetty) bears 084°, alter course to make good 264° so as to keep it on that bearing astern (line L). This line passes well north of Plateau de Jaunes, a group of above-water and sunken rocks lying 4M WSW of Erquy, just off the western edge of plan 7.

By night
Take a position 0·4M north of Cap Fréhel from where Les Justières S cardinal buoy (Q(6)+LFl.6s) will bear 256°, distant 5M and thus below the horizon. Steer 247° for 3M when Cap Fréhel light (Fl(2)10s) will bear 080°.

Then steer the reciprocal 260°, holding the light on 080° and identify Les Justières buoy light.

When the buoy bears 025° and Rohein (green sector) light (VQ(9)WRG.10s10-8M) bears 260°, steer 240° and identify Basses du Courant S cardinal buoy (VQ(6)+LFl.10s) which should then appear fine on the starboard bow distant 1·9M. From here the channel narrows and, should the buoy light not be located at this stage, turn back.

With the Basses du Courant buoy light in sight make good 240° leaving the buoy 100m to starboard.

Continue through the red sector of Erquy light (Oc(2+1)WRG.12s) until in the white sector, when steer 220° through the green sector and into the second white sector 081°-094° to proceed west on a course of 265°.

If bound for Erquy, approach the light in the white sector (111°-120°), leaving an unlit port buoy to port.

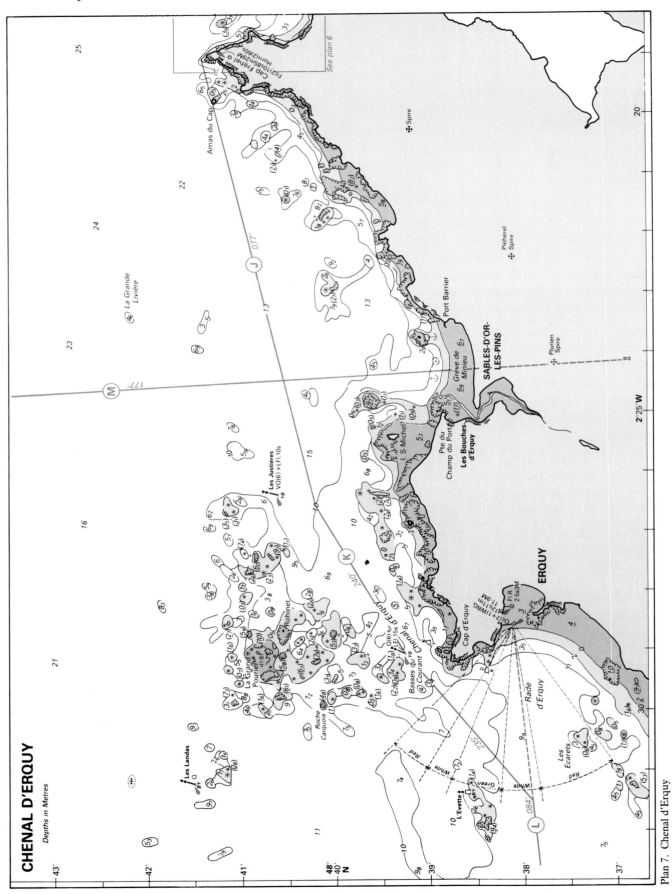

CHENAL D'ERQUY

Depths in Metres

Plan 7. Chenal d'Erquy

9. Erquy

Charts
BA *3674, 3672*
Imray *C33B*
SHOM *833*
ECM Navicarte *536*

Tidal data

Tidal heights (approx)

HW −0020 St Helier, −0515 Dover, +0205 Brest
MTL 6·2m. Index 12A
Heights of tide above chart datum
MHWS 11·4m, MLWS 1·4m, MHWN 8·7m, MLWN 4·1m

Tidal streams

1. For Chenal d'Erquy see above.
2. About 5M west of Erquy the ENE-going stream begins at −0600 St Helier (+0130 Dover) and the WSW at −0010 St Helier (−0505 Dover). Both streams reach 2·8 knots at springs.

Erquy inner mole at LW.

General

A small drying harbour ¾M south of Cap d'Erquy. It consists of two parts, the old harbour to the east which is partly sheltered by a jetty, on the end of which stands a red and white circular lighthouse 10m high, and to the west of this the new *port de pêche* protected by a new rocky mole and having a landing slip 80m long. The village at the harbour and the town ½M to the south of it make a pleasant holiday resort and there is an active sailing club.

Approach

By day

If approaching from the east, sail along line K (*see under Chenal d'Erquy, above*) until Cap d'Erquy is abeam to port distant 0·3M. Then follow the coast round keeping about this distance offshore and leaving Les Trois Pierres port buoy to port.

When Erquy lighthouse bears 090° course may be shaped to enter the old harbour.

Beware of a strong eddy running past the end of the jetty, before and at high water.

If approaching from the north, leave Landas N cardinal spar buoy (see plan 7) to port and L'Evette N cardinal beacon tower, at least 0·2M to starboard. If approaching from the west, pass 1·25M south of Le Rohein lighthouse (white tower with black top, elevation 13m), which is just off the limits of plan 7 to the west, steering to make good 084° for Erquy lighthouse, and leaving Plateau des Jaunes (on the centre of which is a rock which never dries) 0·5M to the south and Plateau des Portes d'Erquy (on which stands L'Evette N cardinal beacon tower) over half a mile to the north.

By night

The best approach is from the west. The southerly white sector of Le Grand Léjon light leads between the Roches de St-Quay and Le Rohein, after which course should be altered to between 081° and 093° to keep in the white sector of Erquy light, Oc(2+1) WRG.12s. The recommended anchorage is on the dividing line between the southern white and red sectors, with the harbour light bearing 081° and Cap d'Erquy bearing 355°.

Harbour and anchorage

There is an anchorage in about 3m LAT sand and mud, good holding ground, with the lighthouse bearing about 100° and Cap d'Erquy bearing 355°. This position is sheltered from NE through to SE but is open to the west, especially to northwest. This anchorage is a long row from the harbour and there is sometimes an uncomfortable swell there. The bottom is gently shelving, so on an ordinary spring tide it is possible to anchor closer to the harbour if soundings are taken and if the weather is sufficiently settled to allow only a margin of 0·5m or so under the keel at LW. At neaps a yacht drawing 2m can lie in a position nearly 0·1M east of the harbour entrance.

The old harbour jetty has a quay and slipway. The outer harbour is for the exclusive use of fishing boats and the inner harbour under the lee of the breakwater is busy during the season with small fishing and hire boats. There are many chains on the bottom which dries in most parts 3 hours after HW. Erquy is a doubtful bet as a harbour, but the anchorage is good under suitable conditions and, near high water a yacht can anchor temporarily close to the harbour whilst her crew go ashore for shopping or a meal. Land at the slip in the old harbour or on the sailing club slip.

Yachts that can take the ground may dry out on hard clean sand abreast the inner harbour wall and the crew can walk a short distance to the shops. However, with any swell from the west, grounding and take off is most uncomfortable.

Facilities

Water tap by the *bureau du port*, which is occasionally occupied by harbourmaster and *douane*, at the root of the old jetty and slip. Free ice from the *halle à marée*. The sailing club, with its own slip, is just west of the root of the old jetty and is the centre of active dinghy racing and sailing. *L'Abri des Flots*, which is the second restaurant on the left, is excellent, but in season it is best to book a table in advance. There are good shops and a garage for petrol in the town, but this involves a ½ mile walk from the port, unless one is given a lift in a car.

Local bus service from the town.

10. Dahouet

Charts
BA *3674*
Imray *C34*
SHOM *833*
ECM Navicarte

Tidal data

Approximately as for Erquy.

Tidal streams

Off Plateau des Jaunes the ESE-going stream begins at −0600 St Helier (−0505 Dover) reaching 3 knots at springs. The W-going stream begins at −0010 St Helier (−0505 Dover) reaching 2·5 knots.

General

The Port de Dahouet is a small drying harbour, with wet basin marina, lying in a gap in the cliffs 5M SW of Erquy. In strong onshore winds the seas break as much as 0·2M offshore and entrance is dangerous.

The harbour bottom is maintained at between 4·5m and 5·5m above chart datum and the minimum depth in the marina is 2·4m.

Approach

By day

With a draught of 1·5m, entry is possible 2 hours either side of high water.

Approach from the north or west. First identify Verdelet, a conical island about 0·2M NW of Pointe de Pleneuf. Then make for a position just north of Dahouet N cardinal buoy, from which Verdelet bears 050° about 1·5M.

With sufficient rise of tide and leaving Dahouet buoy to starboard make good about 120° to leave a red stake to port and La Petite Mouette lighthouse at the entrance about 50m to starboard.

When this is abeam steer to make good 158° until two white stakes to port come into line, then turn to leave them close to port. (These are on the extreme edge of a wall 3m high and a watch should be kept for floating warps attached to them.)

Leaving a starboard concrete beacon to starboard, the quay wall will be seen immediately to port. Keep between this and the centre of the harbour and proceed into the marina, whose sill is at the level of the harbour bottom, 5·5m above datum.

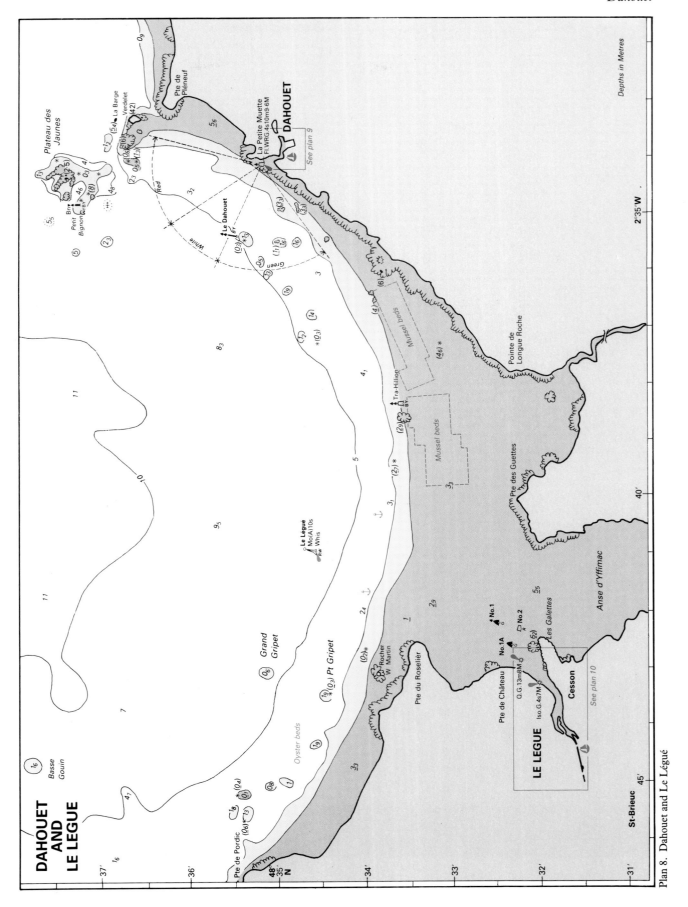

Plan 8. Dahouet and Le Légué

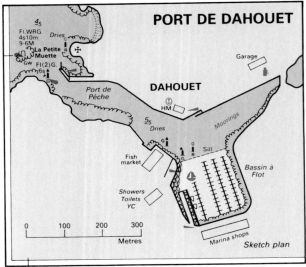

Plan 9. Port de Dahouet

By night

La Petite Mouette lighthouse, Fl.WRG.4s, has a directional light. This has a red sector to the north and a green sector to the south with a white sector over the safe approach, between 114° and 146°. Nevertheless entrance by night would be dangerous for a stranger. A sectored light has been installed on the starboard concrete beacon inside the entrance, Fl(2)G.6s 156°-vis-286°.

Anchorages

In calm weather, anchor in 2m 0·25M NW of La Petite Mouette lighthouse, or closer in on soundings. There are rocks to the south of the line joining La Petite Mouette and Le Dahouet N cardinal buoy.

The harbour is very crowded with fishing boats and small yachts, and space for visitors in the marina is limited. In the outer harbour fishing boats berth two and three abreast alongside the quay. The inner, drying harbour, which is to port beyond the customs house, provides maximum shelter, but is packed with moorings. The wall may be clear and it may be possible for yachts to lie alongside.

On entering the marina, the visitors' pontoon is to starboard and yachts may raft along the outer side. Do not attempt to go between the pontoon and the slipway.

Facilities

Water and electricity on the pontoons. Showers and toilets in the yacht club by the marina. Small food shop, boat yard, small chandlers, 6-ton crane, fuel by long hose from garage at head of inner drying harbour. Winter laying up (floating at springs) is possible. Excellent fish available from the cold store by the marina. Two café/bars, poor shops locally, better shops, banks etc. one mile away at Le Val André.

The harbourmaster is helpful and determined to maintain a family, rather than a commercial atmosphere in the marina.

Dahouet entrance. La Petite Muette GW light tower bearing 164°.
Inner starboard light column (centre) below house, and port beacon clear of rock spit and below pagoda shrine.

Dahouet entrance at LW. La Petite Muette GW light tower left centre with inner starboard light column. End of slipway with two white poles as markers and pagoda shrine on right.

Dahouet visitors' pontoon. The harbour is dry. Note slipway on left.

11. Le Légué (St-Brieuc)

Charts
BA *3674*
Imray *C34*
SHOM *833*
ECM Navicarte *536*

Tidal data

Tidal heights (approx)
HW −0025 St Helier, −0520 Dover, +0220 Brest
MTL 6·4m. Index 12A
Heights of tide above chart datum
MHWS 11·4m, MLWS 1·4m, MHWN 8·7m, MLWN 4·1m

General

Le Légué is the port of St-Brieuc, and lies about 1M from the mouth of the river Le Gouet at the head of the Baie de St-Brieuc. During strong northerly weather the sea breaks right across the head of the bay and no attempt should be made to enter, but the approach is sheltered by land during prevailing west and southwest winds and, with sufficient rise of tide, is easy.

Le Légué, approaching the buoyed channel with Pte de l'Aigle white light tower bearing 235°. A tall building of St-Brieuc on either side of the light tower. The ruined tower is on top of the right-hand end of the green hillock, centre.

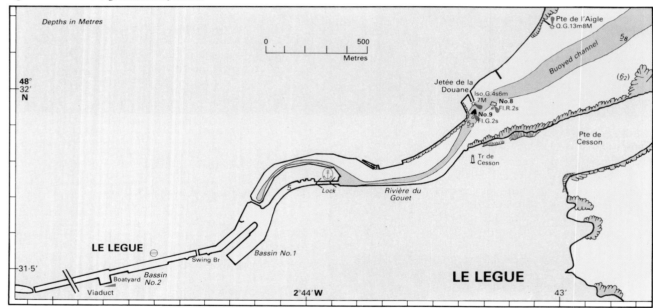

Plan 10. Le Légué

Approach

By day

From the north *see below under Paimpol, Portrieux and Binic.*

Le Légué landfall light-and-whistle (safe-water mark) buoy lies 1·5M NE of Pointe du Roseleir. From this position make good 202° with sufficient height of tide, to leave No. 1 starboard buoy off Pointe du Château close to starboard, thence proceed along the channel marked with small lateral buoys to the lock gates. Vessels can secure to the wall on the south side immediately outside the lock whilst waiting for the gate.

By night

From seaward pick up Pointe à l'Aigle exterior jetty light (Q.G.13m8M). Steer so as to bring this on a bearing of 208° and Le Rohein W cardinal beacon tower light astern. This leads to Le Légué landfall light-and-whistle (safe-water mark) buoy (Mo(A)10s ·—). From thence, with sufficient height of tide and good visibility, make good 202° to pick up unlit No. 1 starboard buoy which leave to starboard. Thence proceed as *By day* above. There are some ten lateral buoys of which three were lit in 1990. In addition the Jetée de la Douane has an Iso.G.4s light.

Anchorages

In settled weather with the wind offshore, a yacht awaiting her tide can anchor in suitable depth south of Le Légué landfall buoy. The lock, which opens between 1 hour before to 1 hour after high water, measures 85m long by 14m wide and the sill is 5m above datum. Inside the lock there are two interconnected basins.

Basin No. 1 is to port about 0·3M from the lock and No. 2, which is formed by a canalised part of the Rivière du Gouet, is entered through a swing bridge about 0·5M from the lock. This bridge is opened not more than twice a day. Yachts should proceed past the swing bridge, to moor to the wall on the starboard side near the viaduct, or under the direction of the harbourmaster. On leaving, fresh water from the river continues to flow into the lock for some time after the gates have opened and it is advisable to have the stern warp ready first.

Facilities

There are cranes of up to 2 tons capacity and mobile cranes are available. Fresh water is not available on the quays. There is a boat yard in Basin No. 2. There are some shops, including a small supermarket, close to Basin No. 2.

Twenty minutes walk up a steep hill, there are larger shops, banks, a number of exotic restaurants, hotels and a laundrette, at St-Brieuc, which is a cathedral town with several fine old timber houses.

Rail service to Brest, Roscoff, Paimpol, St-Malo and Paris.

Local bus service to other ports and flights to Paris twice a day.

Historical

The Baie de St-Brieuc is an area of shallow water which has greatly increased in size during the last 2,000 years. At the time of the Roman Empire, forests and cultivated land existed where there is now nothing but drying sand. The Tour de Cesson was built by Jean IV in 1395 and was blown up by Henri IV.

St-Brieuc, which stands on high ground a mile to the southwest, is an old cathedral town, named after the Celtic monk who arrived with his disciples in the 5th century, and converted the district to Christianity. Much of the cathedral is 13th and 14th century.

Le Légué was formerly a commercial port and a base for a fleet of *goëlettes*, the fine two-masted topsail schooners that fished off Iceland and Greenland. It now caters for small tankers, bulk carriers and general dry cargo ships, as well as a number of resident fishing boats.

12. Binic

Charts

BA *3674*
Imray *C34*
SHOM *833*
ECM Navicarte *536*

Tidal data

Tidal heights (approx)

HW −0030 St Helier, −0525 Dover, +0150 Brest
MTL 6·4m. Index 12A
Heights of tide above chart datum
MHWS 11·4m, MLWS 1·4m, MHWN 8·7m, MLWN 4·1m

General

Binic is an artificial harbour at the mouth of the Rivière d'Ic. It consists of an outer harbour which dries 4m at the entrance and 5m or 6m inside which provides good shelter in winds from north through west to south, and a wet basin which was formerly the Vieux-Port, access to which is through a dock gate 10·5m wide, the sill of which is 5·5m above datum. In the basin the depths vary between 5·5m and 7·5m.

Approach

By day

The outer approach from the east is clear except for Basse Gouin, a rock about 1·5M ENE of the entrance with a depth of 1·6m LAT, and oyster beds, marked by buoys, to the south of it. These should not affect yachts otherwise than as an anchorage. With sufficient rise of tide the inner approach is straightforward.

For the approach from the north *see under Paimpol* and *Portrieux* (pages 57 and 58). When La Ronde W cardinal beacon tower bears 090° with sufficient rise of tide, alter course for the entrance. This leaves an E cardinal spar wreck buoy and L'Ours Seul isolated danger beacon each about 0·25M to starboard.

By night

From east, as in *By day* above. The breakwater light (Oc(3)12s) has an elevation of 12m and a range of 12M.

Anchorages and moorings

The nearest anchorage in which a yacht can stay afloat at springs is with the lighthouse on the end of the northern mole (white circular tower elevation 12m) bearing about 270° distant 1·25M, but see note on Basse Gouin and oyster beds above. From here course may be shaped to enter the port when the tide serves. If there is space, a yacht may berth in the Avant-Port alongside the eastern mole which dries

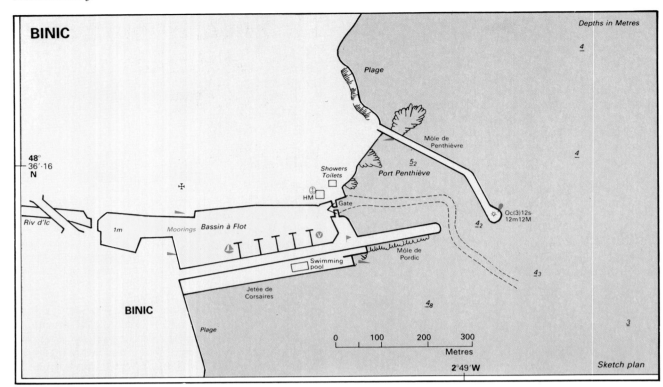

BINIC

Depths in Metres

Plage

Môle de Penthièvre

48° 36'·16 N

Showers Toilets

Port Penthièvre

HM

Gate

Oc(3)12s· 12m12M

Riv d'Ic

1m   *Moorings*   Bassin à Flot

Môle de Pordic

Swimming pool

Jetée de Corsaires

BINIC

Plage

0   100   200   300
Metres

2°49'W

Sketch plan

Plan 11. Binic

Binic approach, with north wall triangle bearing 278°.

4·2m sand and mud. Alternatively, if early on the tide, there is space to anchor in the centre. The dock gate is not operated between about 0100 and 0530, nor when the tides are of an index of about 7 (HW St Helier 8·5m) or less. Otherwise it is opened between 1 and 1¾ hours before HW and must close at HW or within 10 minutes or so. For a day or two either side of neaps the gate may not open at all. The harbourmaster will furnish a time table on request and one is exhibited outside his office. There is a rolling bridge across the E end of the lock which is operated by the harbourmaster. There are marina-type pontoon berths in the harbour and there are berths reserved for visitors, alongside the mole immediately to port inside the basin. There are also berths alongside the north wall.

Binic wet basin entrance at HW.

Facilities

Fresh water is laid on the pontoons, but not the visitors' berths, although a spare resident's berth may be taken temporarily for this purpose. There is also a water point on the north quay, immediately outside the lock. Application for this should be made to the harbourmaster. Toilets and showers in cabins behind the harbour office.

There are banks and shops of all kinds. Mechanic, sailmaker, chandlery, slips and a 20-ton crane. Fuel in the town. Many hotels, restaurants and cafés. Bus service to St-Brieuc for rail connection and flights to Paris.

Despite the restricted access to the basin, in all respects this harbour is preferable to Le Légué from the yachtsman's point of view and the harbourmaster is most obliging. The alternative is of course the marina at St-Quay, which is pricy in comparison but can be entered at any state of tide.

Historical

Binic was the first Breton port to fit out a vessel for the Newfoundland cod fisheries, which had previously been a Basque monopoly. The Binic *terre-neuviens* commonly sold their fish in Marseille before returning home for the winter. The old town is now surrounded by villas and hotels and is a minor holiday resort, with good bathing beaches each side of the harbour. There are also good sands at Grève des Rosaries, about 3·5M southeast, where there is a sailing school and club.

13. St-Quay-Portrieux and Roches de St-Quay

Inner Passage

Charts

BA *3674*
Imray *C34*
SHOM *833*
ECM Navicarte *536*

Tidal data

Tidal heights (approx)
HW −0030 St Helier, −0525 Dover, +0150 Brest
MTL 6·4m. Index 12A
Heights of tide above chart datum
MHWS 11·4m, MLWS 1·4m, MHWN 8·6m, MLWN 4·1m

Tidal streams

1. The offshore streams to the NE of Le Grand Léjon turn SE at −0600 St Helier (+0130 Dover), and NW at +0020 St Helier (−0435 Dover). Both streams reach 3·8 knots at springs.
2. In the Rade de Portrieux the SSE-going stream begins at +0600 St Helier (+0105 Dover), and the NNW-going stream at −0015 St Helier (−0510 Dover). Both streams reach 2·5 knots at springs.

Lights

Ile Harbour (St-Quay-Portrieux) 48°40'·0N 2°48'·5W Oc(2)WRG.6s16m11/8M 270°-R-306°-G-358°-W-011°-R-080°-W-133°-G-270° White square house with small white tower with R top on its roof.
Pointe de Portrieux Breakwater elbow. DirIso.WRG.4s15-11M 159°-W-179°-G-316°-W-320°-R-159°.
Herflux East side of Rade de St-Quay. DirFl(2)WRG.6s 8/6M 115°-G-125°-W-135°-R-145°.
La Roselière E cardinal buoy. VQ(9)10s.

General

A substantial new fishing port and marina with depths of 2·5m below LAT was opened in August 1990. 60% of the finance for this costly project was provided by government and the remainder by the local chamber of commerce. It may be entered at any state of tide and adjoins the northeast wall of the old drying harbour, lying to the west of the Roches de St-Quay, separated from them by the Rade de Portrieux which can be entered either from the north or south.

Approaches

From the north, see under Paimpol, below.

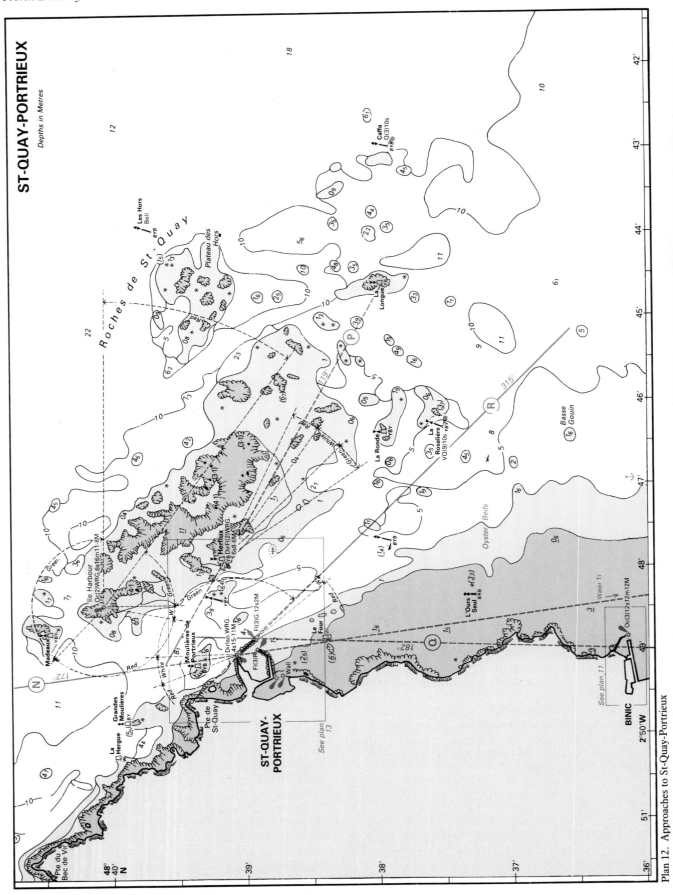

ST-QUAY-PORTRIEUX
Depths in Metres

Plan 12. Approaches to St-Quay-Portrieux

St-Quay Nouveau Port, looking north. Photo *Brian J. Green*

Northern entrance

By day

This entrance has a depth of at least 4·2m as far as the Rade de Portrieux. First identify Madeux W cardinal beacon tower and behind it Ile Harbour lighthouse (a white house with a small light tower on its roof), the northernmost islet of the Roches de St-Quay group. To the west on a headland is the conspicuous signal station or *sémaphore* of St-Quay. It should then be possible to make out the marina breakwater 0·4M south of the headland and Moulières de Portrieux E cardinal beacon tower in front of the breakwater.

A convenient approach is with Moulières de Portrieux beacon in transit with a water tower bearing 172° (line N). The water tower can be identified on the skyline approximately halfway between Pordic spire and the Pointe de Pordic some 4M south of St-Quay. In 1991 the water tower did not appear on any chart. Its position is 48°32'·983N 2°47'·667W.

When Herflux S cardinal beacon tower comes into line with La Longue S cardinal beacon tower bearing 119° (line P) alter course to follow this line for 0·3M, then follow line Q, which is formed by Le Four white beacon tower in line with Pordic belfry, bearing 182°.

When the breakwater head is abeam to starboard course may be altered to enter the marina or the old harbour.

Alternatively, if intending to continue south or to enter Binic, a course of 135° will lead out of the Rade.

By night

Approach in the white sector of the Pointe de Portrieux light, course 170°. *Note* that in the red sector you would be too far to starboard, not to port.

When Herflux light turns from red to white, prepare to alter and steer 120° for Herflux until the white sector of Ile Harbour light is entered, when course may be altered to head for the marina entrance.

Les Noirs E cardinal unlit buoy lies on the eastern edge of the white sector of Ile Harbour light.

Southern entrance

By day

This entrance carries a least depth of 1·4m (2·7m MLWS) along line R, but as it passes close to a 0·3m patch it would be safe for a stranger to regard it as having a least depth of 0·3m (1·5m MLWS). First identify La Ronde W cardinal beacon tower, taking care not to confuse it with La Longue S cardinal beacon tower, which lies 1M farther east.

Approach from the north. The rear leading mark (water tower) is midway between the Moulières de Portrieux beacon tower (front leading mark) and the crane on the breakwater which was operating in 1991. *Sémaphore* on Pointe de St-Quay far right.

Telephoto of leading marks for northern approach to St-Quay.

Approach from the SE. Old, drying harbour entrance far left; new port entrance left of *sémaphore* on Pointe de St-Quay. For approach it should be open to the left of the column on 315°.

Make a position from which La Ronde bears 035°, distant 0·5M, and La Roselière W cardinal pillar buoy bears 090°, distant 0·3M. From here, the leading marks for line R will be in line: the conspicuous white signal station, or *sémaphore* on the Pointe de St-Quay in transit with the eastern arm of the marina breakwater, bearing 315°. This line leaves an E cardinal spar buoy marking a wreck about 0·2M to port and Le Four white beacon tower about 0·4M to port.

When Le Four beacon tower is abeam to port, course may be altered for the marina or the old harbour entrance. If proceeding north, when Le Four is in stern transit with Pordic spire on 182°, turn onto the reciprocal course 002° and hold the transit until Herflux S cardinal beacon tower comes into line with La Longue S cardinal beacon tower bearing 119°.

Then steer 299° for 0·3M, keeping the beacons in stern transit.

When Moulières de Portrieux E cardinal beacon tower is in transit with the water tower on the skyline halfway between Pordic spire and the Pointe de Pordic bearing 172°, steer the reciprocal course 352° until Madeux W cardinal beacon tower is clear abaft the beam.

By night

The southerly white sector of Grande Léjon (Fl(5) WR.20s, see plan 2) leads between the Roches de St-Quay and Rohein W cardinal light beacon tower. When Binic breakwater (Oc(3)12s) bears 253° steer as if entering Binic.

Immediately the Pointe de Portrieux light changes from green to white steer 317° on the edge of this sector, leaving La Roselière E cardinal light buoy to starboard and avoiding two wrecks close to the western edge of the sector.

For entry, on close approach steer for the lights marking the marina entrance.

If intending to proceed north, after Ile Harbour light has turned from green to white, alter to keep the light on 007° in this sector, clearing Les Noirs unlit E cardinal buoy which lies on the eastern edge of the sector.

On entering the white sector of Herflux beacon tower light, turn to port and steer 310° in this sector with the light astern until in the northerly white sector of the Port du Portrieux light.

Steer out of the Rade in this sector on a course of 350°.

Anchorage and harbour

Anchor in 0·7m LAT east of the southern wall of the old harbour with the marina entrance bearing 360°, or as far inshore as soundings permit in order to keep out of the main strength of the tide. The bottom is sand and mud, good holding ground, and at neap tides a small yacht will be able to stay afloat close south of the old harbour entrance. Yachts are not permitted to berth alongside the jetty and the quay in the old harbour, but yachts with legs or twin keels may prefer to lie out in the harbour rather than the marina, on hard sand drying 5m.

Facilities

The marina provides all facilities: fuel, water, electricity, showers, toilets, chandlery, engineers and a restaurant. The cost of construction was high and this is reflected in the berthing charges for visitors. However, for the first three years at least, the second night will be free.

Portrieux-St-Quay is a lively holiday resort with shops, banks, hotels and restaurants. A bus connects with the rail service at St-Brieuc and there are two flights per day to Paris from St-Brieuc airport.

Historical

In former times several of the big *terre-neuviens* would spend the winter in the old port, with their bows well up the beach inside the harbour.

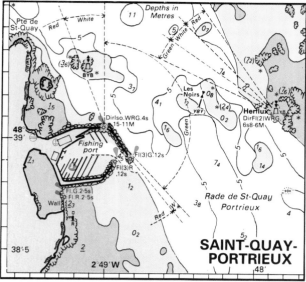

Plan 13. St-Quay-Portrieux

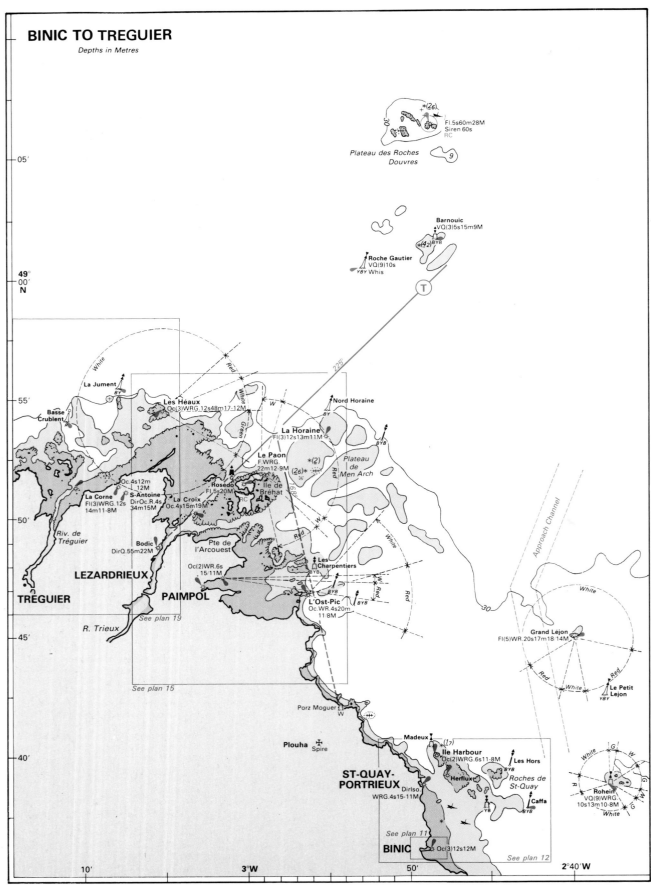

BINIC TO TREGUIER

Depths in Metres

(26)

Fl.5s60m28M
Siren 60s
RC

Plateau des Roches Douvres

05'

Barnouic
VQ(3)5s15m9M
BYB

(42) BYB

Roche Gautier
VQ(9)10s
YBY Whis

49°
00'
N

T

225°

55'

La Jument
BY

White

Red

White Green

W

Nord Horaine
BY

Les Héaux
Oc(3)WRG.12s48m17-12M

La Horaine
Fl(3)12s13m11M

Basse
Crublent

Le Paon
F.WRG.
22m12-9M

(2)

*(26)**

Plateau
de
Men Arch

159°

Oc.4s12m
12M

Rosedo
Fl.5s20m
RC

La Corne
Fl(3)WRG.12s
14m11-8M

S-Antoine
DirOc.R.4s
34m15M

La Croix
Oc.4s15m19M

Ile de
Bréhat

Red

50'

*Riv. de
Tréguier*

Bodic
DirQ.55m22M

Pte de
l'Arcouest

W

White

LEZARDRIEUX

Oc(2)WR.6s
15/11M

Les
Charpentiers
BYB

Red

Approach Channel

White

TRÉGUIER

PAIMPOL

BYB

L'Ost-Pic
Oc.WR.4s20m
11/8M

BYB

W Red

Red

30

Grand Léjon
Fl(5)WR.20s17m18·14M

45'

R. Trieux

See plan 19

Red

White

Le Petit
Léjon
YBY

See plan 15

Porz Moguer
W

Madeux *(17)*

Plouha
Spire

Ile Harbour
Oc(2)WRG.6s11-8M

Les Hors
BYB

White G W

40'

ST-QUAY-
PORTRIEUX

Herflux

*Roches de
St-Quay*

R

G

Dirlso.
WRG.4s15-11M

YB

Caffa
BYB

Rohein
VQ(9)WRG.
10s13m10-8M

G

White

See plan 11

BINIC

Oc(3)12s12M

See plan 12

10'

3°W

50'

2°40'W

Plan 14. Binic to Tréguier

14. Paimpol

Charts
BA *3670, 3673*
Imray *C34*
SHOM *832*
ECM Navicarte *537*

Tidal data

Tidal heights (approx)
HW −0030 St Helier, −0525 Dover, +0155 Brest
MTL 5·5m. Index 12A
Heights of tide above chart datum
MHWS 10·5m, MLWS 0·6m, MHWN 7·8m, MLWN 3·2m

Tidal streams

1. For tidal streams in the outer approaches from north see Ile Bréhat, page 71.

2. For tidal streams in the outer approaches from the south and east off Le Grand Léjon see under Portrieux, page 49.

3. In the northern entrance of Chenal du Dénou, the SE-going stream begins −0420 Brest (+0050 Dover); and the NW-going stream begins +0135 Brest (−0540 Dover). Both streams reach 2·8 knots at springs.

4. At the eastern entrance of the Chenal de la Jument the SSW-going stream (and the SSE-going stream between La Jument and Le Dénou) begins −0405 Brest (+0105 Dover). The NNE-going stream off the entrance of Chenal de la Jument and the NNW-going stream between La Jument and Le Dénou begin +0120 Brest (−0555 Dover). These streams reach 3·5 knots at springs.

5. In the outer anchorage SSE of Ile St-Rion, the SE stream begins about −0405 Brest (+0105 Dover) and the NW-going stream about +0105 Brest (−0610 Dover). Both streams attain 1·9 knots at springs.

6. In the anchorage off Porz Even in the Chenal de la Trinité the SW-going stream begins half an hour earlier than the SSE and SE streams referred to above.

General

The Anse de Paimpol is a large, shallow harbour which dries at MLWS except for a system of deep, winding channels in the northern and eastern parts. These channels offer fairly sheltered anchorage except in easterly winds, but they are mostly a long way from the shore. The outer channels appear difficult on the chart, but add 5·5m for mean tide level and it will be seen that at half tide there is plenty of deep water. Add 7·6m for high water neaps and one can sail almost anywhere except across the rocks marked by beacons. The port of Paimpol, at the head of the harbour, may be approached towards high water; in spite of the soundings shown on charts, the channel of approach is said to dry 4·8m

Paimpol inner basin with training ships *Etoile* and *Belle Poule*.

Paimpol docks, looking north. From RCC Pilotage Foundation *Classic Passages*.

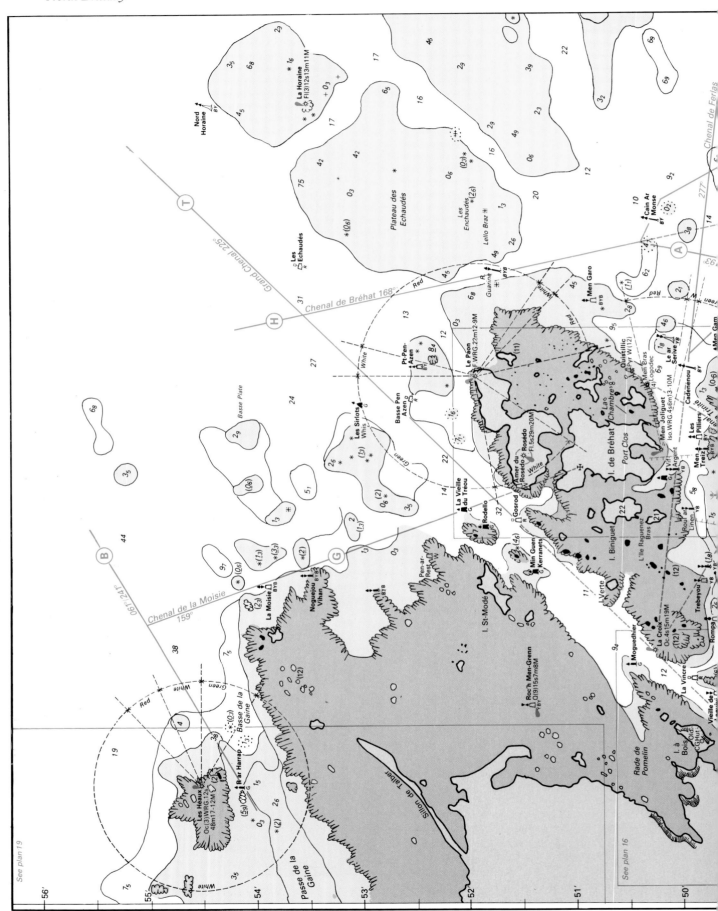

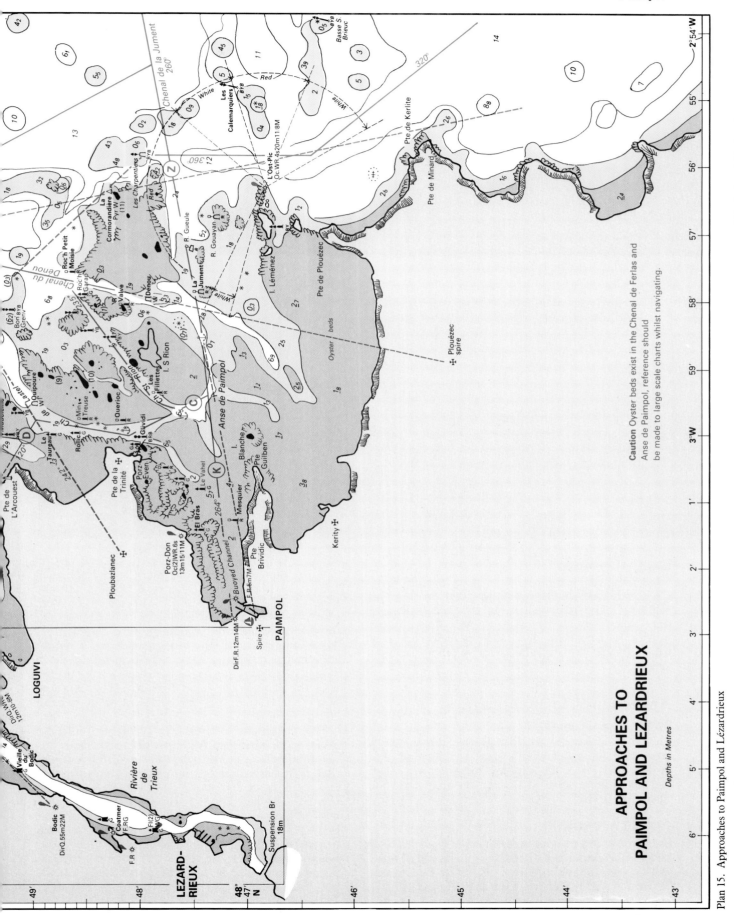

APPROACHES TO PAIMPOL AND LEZARDRIEUX

Depths in Metres

Caution Oyster beds exist in the Chenal de Ferlas and Anse de Paimpol, reference should be made to large scale charts whilst navigating.

Plan 15. Approaches to Paimpol and Lézardrieux

L'Ost Pic lighthouse, bearing 238°.

Leading line for Chenal de la Jument. Paimpol spire over Pointe
Brividic summit on 260°.

LAT only (i.e. to have a least depth of 2·7m at
MHWN). The port consists of two interconnected
wet docks, entered through a lock. These docks
provide a convenient and fairly peaceful berth in
which a yacht can stay afloat with excellent facilities
nearby.

Approaches to anchorage

By day from the north

First make a position with La Horaine lighthouse, a
grey octagonal tower with a black top, bearing 195°
distant 3M. From this position there is a choice of
two initial approaches: the outer approach, and the
Chenal de Bréhat.

OUTER APPROACH

From the above position steer to make good 150°. (If
arrival at Paimpol is planned at or before HW there
will be considerable lift from the tide.) Follow this
course for 8·25M, leaving Men Arch E cardinal spar
buoy 0·3M to starboard. See plan 14 page 54.

When the conspicuous day mark at Porz-Moguer
comes into line with the belfry of Plouha church,
bearing 212°, distant 8·5 and 10M respectively, alter
course to follow this line for 0·75M then alter course
to pick up Chenal de la Jument (line Z, plan 15).
The leading marks for this channel are Paimpol
church spire (taking care not to confuse with Plounez
to the south and Ploubazlanec to the north) in line
with the summit of Pointe Brividic. (This is a low
woody hillock in line with Paimpol town bearing
260°.)

The conditions are seldom favourable for these
marks to be identified from this distance, but L'Ost
Pic lighthouse, a square white tower with a flat grey
roof and red lantern is conspicuous, bearing 250°,
and a course of 260° made good will lead in to the
channel, leaving Basse St-Brieuc E cardinal spar
buoy 1·6M to port, Calemarquiers E cardinal spar
buoy 0·75M to port, Les Charpentiers E cardinal
beacon tower 0·25M to starboard, L'Ost Pic lighthouse, square tower red top, 0·75M to port, Gouayan
port beacon tower 0·3M to port and Roche Gueule
port buoy 200m to port and La Jument beacon tower
150m to port.

CHENAL DE BREHAT

Navigation of this channel by reference to the leading marks calls for good visibility of upwards of 12M but it can shorten the distance sailed by 5M if the Chenal du Dénou is also used. The tide in this channel runs in both directions at up to 5·6 knots at springs, giving, if arrival timed at or before HW, an even greater lift than the outer approach. From the above position steer to follow the leading marks for the Rivière de Trieux Grand Chenal, which are Bodic light structure (see photos, page 67) in line with La Croix lighthouse (painted white towards the northeast, with a red castellated top, elevation 15m) bearing 225°, line T. (See plans 15 and 17.) Follow this line which leaves:

Nord Horaine N cardinal spar buoy 0·8M to port.
La Horaine lighthouse 1·4M to port.
Les Echaudés port buoy 0·5M to port.

0·25M after this is abeam, if the marks can be identified, course should be altered to bring the conspicuous white daymark at Porz Moguer (distant 12M) in line with the white pyramid La Cormorandière, distant 5·5M bearing 168° (line H). This channel passes between:

Roc'h Guarine which dries and is marked by an E cardinal spar buoy (to be left close to starboard).
Lello Bras about 0·5M to port which also dries and is unmarked.

In view of the strong tides in this area it is essential not only to be certain of one's position before entering the Chenal de Bréhat, but to have reference marks from which to check the set as one proceeds.

This channel then leaves Men Garo E cardinal beacon tower 0·5M to starboard. At this point, again depending on the visibility, there is a choice of two inner approaches to the main channel (line K): the Chenal du Dénou, and the Chenal de la Jument.

CHENAL DU DENOU

With local knowledge it is possible to navigate this channel with a least depth of 5·7m, but no adequate marks can be given for the bottleneck at Roc'h Dénou, which is about 120m west of the beacon and outside a 0·6m patch. It is therefore recommended that it should be regarded as having a least depth of 0·6m (i.e. 1·2m MLWS, 3·9m MLWN).

Steer to leave Cain ar Monse N cardinal spar buoy 0·25M to port. From here the leading marks for the channel will be in line; these are Dénou white pyramid in line with Plouézec belfry, bearing 193°. Dénou white pyramid is smaller than and 1·1M WSW of the white pyramid La Cormorandière, with which it can be confused. Follow this line (line A) which leaves:

Bonn-Grenv E cardinal beacon 0·35M to starboard.
Petite Moisie port beacon 120m to port.
Garap starboard beacon 150m to starboard.
Roc'h Valve (elevation 11m, possibly painted white) 0·15M to starboard.

When the latter is abeam, quit the leading line and steer so as to leave Le Dénou pyramid between 100 and 150m to port. It is important to follow the leading marks precisely up to this point, as the channel is bordered by drying rocks.

Then steer to make good 190° until La Jument port beacon tower bears 110° and the leading marks for the harbour come into line. These are a white hut with red top (elevation 5m) at the head of the jetty and a small white tower with red top 0·2M west of the former, bearing 264° (line K).

Leading line for Chenal du Dénou, Dénou white beacon tower and Plouézec spire, in transit bearing 193°.

CHENAL DE LA JUMENT

Leaving Chenal de Bréhat steer to leave Cain ar Monse N cardinal spar buoy 200m to starboard, then steer to make good 150° for 2·7M, leaving the white pyramid La Cormorandière 1M to starboard and Les Charpentiers E cardinal beacon tower 0·9M to starboard. The leading marks for the Chenal de la Jument (line Z) are Paimpol church spire (take care not to confuse with Plounez to the south and Ploubazlanec to the north) in line with the summit of Pointe Brividic (a woody hill in line with Paimpol town). When these are in line bearing 260°, alter course to follow this line, leaving:

Les Charpentiers E cardinal beacon tower 0·25M to starboard.
L'Ost Pic lighthouse, square white tower red top, 0·75M to port.
Gouayan port beacon tower 0·3M to port.
Roc'h Gueule port buoy 200m to port.
La Jument port beacon tower 150m to port.

APPROACH FROM NORTH TO LE FERLAS CHANNEL, BY RIVIERE DE TRIEUX GRAND CHENAL

If the visibility is insufficient to use the Chenal de Bréhat, continue on line T leaving the following marks on the sides shown:

Les Echaudés port buoy 0·5M to port.
Les Sirlots starboard buoy 0·2M to starboard.
Petit-Pen-Azen N cardinal beacon tower 0·5M to port.
Basse des Pen-Azen port buoy 0·2M to port.
La Vieille du Tréou starboard beacon tower 0·25M to starboard.
Rodello starboard beacon (on base of tower covered at HW) 0·2M to starboard.
Rosédo white pyramid 0·3M to port.
Gosrod port beacon tower 0·1M to port.
Min Guen Kerranets starboard beacon tower 0·15M to starboard.

When about 0·2M from La Croix lighthouse, quit line T and steer for Moguedhier starboard beacon (replacing tower destroyed 1991) for about 0·2M, then pick up the marks for line E, which are Coatmer Aval light structure, a small white tower with grey roof 11m high, elevation 16m, in line with Coatmer Amont light structure, a similar tower, but with a pointed roof 9m high, elevation 50m, bearing 219°. This line leaves the following marks on the sides shown:

Moguedhier starboard beacon 120m to starboard.
La Croix lighthouse 180m to port.
Vincre port beacon tower 0·125M to port.

Then steer about 180° to leave Vieille de Loguivi W cardinal beacon tower 100m to port. Continue this course until the first marks for the Ferlas channel come in line to port. These are Rompa isolated danger beacon tower and Les Piliers N cardinal beacon tower, bearing 084°.

LE FERLAS CHANNEL

Steer this course until about 150m from Rompa, when course should be altered to make good 095° leaving Rompa at least 100m to port, as the rock drying 3m is 50m to the south of the beacon, and head for Roc'h Rouray.

After 0·2M alter course to make good 070° and to bring into line the S cardinal beacons on Roul-ar-Linen and Vif Argent. This line leaves Trebeyou S cardinal beacon tower 200m to port and Receveur Vihan S cardinal beacon 100m to port.

Continue on this course until Rompa is in transit with the right edge of Roc'h Levret astern, bearing 259°. Then steer to make good the reciprocal 079°. This line leaves:

Roul-ar-Linen S cardinal beacon 100m to port.
Vif Argent S cardinal beacon 230m to port.
Roc'h Ourmelec N cardinal beacon 0·25M to starboard.
Men Joliguet W cardinal light tower 0·25M to port.
Les Piliers N cardinal beacon tower 0·15M to starboard.

At this point there is a choice of five inner approaches to the main channel (line K). These range from the short and difficult to the long and simple: 1. Chenal de la Trinité (or Chenal de l'Ile Blanche); 2. Chenal de Lastel; 3. Chenal St-Rion; 4. Chenal du Dénou and 5. Chenal de la Jument.

1. Chenal de la Trinité

This channel is the most direct route between Le Ferlas channel and Paimpol. It passes close between unmarked rocks which dry 1·2m and 1·1m LAT and must be regarded as drying 1·2m (i.e. has a least depth of 2·1m MLWN and 4·2m at half tide).

First make a position from which Les Piliers beacon tower bears 270°, distant 0·2M. From here Quistillic white pyramid (elevation 12m) will be open to the right of Men Bras Logodec (a rock which never covers, elevation 4m) on a bearing of 032°.

Steer to make good the reciprocal 212° keeping Quistillic open to the right of Men Bras Logodec since the transit of 035° runs directly over Lel-Ouene rock (drying 2·2m) and Quevelious rock (drying 1·1m). Above half tide they will present no hazard.

This course leaves:

Men Treiz E cardinal beacon 0·14M to starboard.
Roc Château 0·12M to port.
Roc'h Lème E cardinal beacon 0·18M to starboard.
La Madeleine W cardinal beacon 0·1M to starboard.

When La Croix lighthouse (circular tower, white towards the NE, red castellated top, elevation 15m) is in line with the coast on the NW side of the Pointe de l'Arcouest, bearing 300°, follow this line D making good 120° until Le Taureau starboard beacon is abeam to starboard distant 0·3M, when course should be altered to about 195° to leave Le Taureau beacon 150m to starboard.

Then proceed as described under *Chenal de Lastel*, below. When following line D it may be necessary for an observer to stand well above water level in order to see La Croix over the intervening rocks.

Roche Ouipoure white beacon tower marking course alteration to port in Chenal de Lastel. In this position the Porz-Even buildings, open to the right of the beacon bear 208°.

2. Chenal de Lastel

This channel which leads in from the northeast (see plan 15), may be regarded as having a least depth of 1·2m, and is subject to a cross tide. After passing Les Pilliers beacon tower bring La Croix lighthouse in line with the left side of l'Ile Raguenez Bras bearing 277°, then steer so as to make good the reciprocal 097° leaving Cadenenou N cardinal spar buoy 140m to starboard.

When Men Gam E cardinal beacon tower is abeam to starboard distant 0·3M, alter course to make good 136°. This will be heading for La Cormorandière white pyramid in transit with Les Charpentiers E cardinal beacon tower.

When Ouipoure white beacon tower bears 235°, alter course to keep it on this bearing until Ploubazlanec spire bears 242°.

Steer towards it leaving Ouipoure white beacon tower 150m to port.

From here, shape a course for Le Taureau starboard beacon until about 250m therefrom; then make good 185°, which leaves Rollic starboard beacon 100m to starboard; Min Treuse port beacon 60m to port, and Roc Queroic port beacon 130m to port.

Then when Pointe de la Trinité bears 335° alter course to make good the reciprocal, 155°. This line C is also formed by keeping Roc Ar Zel port beacon bearing 155°, and leaves Glividi 200m to starboard, and so into the main channel (line K).

3. Chenal St-Rion

From Les Pilliers beacon tower, proceed as for Chenal de Lastel and continue making good 138° until the leading marks for the Chenal du Dénou (Plouézec belfry in line with Dénou white pyramid) come into line bearing 193°, when course should be altered to keep this transit.

When La Cormorandière white pyramid comes into line with Roc'h Petite Moisie port beacon alter course so as to make good 235°. This line passes midway between Boisseau and Garap rocks, and then midway between Roc'h Vras and the northwestern outlier of Ile St-Rion. Then steer so as to leave Les Fillettes port beacon 75m to port and then for a point midway between Ile Blanche and Pointe Guilben, and so into the main channel (line K) when the tide serves.

4. Chenal du Dénou

Proceed as for Chenal de Lastel continuing to make good 138° from Men Gam beacon tower until the leading marks for the Chenal du Dénou (Plouézec belfry in line with Dénou white pyramid) then continue as described under *Chenal du Dénou*, above.

5. Chenal de la Jument

After passing Les Pilliers beacon tower, bring La Croix lighthouse in line with the left side of l'Ile Raguenez Bras bearing 277°, then steer so as to make good the reciprocal 097° leaving Cadenenou N cardinal spar buoy 140m to starboard, and Cain ar Monse N cardinal spar buoy 0·35M to port.

When this bears 330° alter course to make good the reciprocal and proceed as described under *Chenal de la Jument*, above.

Approaches to anchorage

By day from south and east

Chenal de la Jument may be joined anywhere if approached from the southeast outside the Basse St-Brieuc and Les Calemarquiers, each marked with an E cardinal spar buoy. An approach can be made to the west of these dangers from a position between 0·75 and 1·0M east of Pointe de Minard.

Steering about 320°, course can be shaped to keep Roc'h Gouayan port beacon tower open to the east of l'Ost Pic lighthouse.

When the summit of Plouézec is abeam to port and l'Ost Pic lighthouse is distant 0·25M, course is altered to 360° for Les Charpentiers E cardinal beacon tower, to avoid the rocks which extend 0·1M northeast of the lighthouse.

The northerly course may be held until the leading marks for Chenal de la Jument (Paimpol church spire and the summit of Pointe Brividic) are in line bearing 260°, when course is altered to follow this line (line Z).

Approach from anchorage to port

By day

The channel dries 5m LAT and, after arriving at the anchorage by one of the foregoing approaches, if the height of tide permits the harbour can be approached with the white hut (with red top, elevation 5m) at the head of the jetty in line with a small white tower (with a red top, elevation 12m) 0·2M west of the former, bearing 264° (line K).

This line leaves:

Le Vahel starboard beacon 200m to starboard.
Mesquier port beacon 250m to port.
El Bras starboard beacon 130m to starboard.

Thereafter the channel is marked by buoys and by a port and a starboard beacon where it passes between rocks. The channel tends to be silted towards the northern side, and the southern half is preferable although this is closely bordered by oyster beds. Extensive oyster beds are to be found in all drying parts of the bay outside the main channels.

Turn closely round the end of the Jetée de Kernoa and, to wait for the lock, secure along its western side, avoiding the centre part which submerges at HW.

By night

From seaward to the east, approach in the white sector of Porz-Don (Oc(2)WR.6s), between 269° and 272°, which leads north of La Jument beacon tower. When the Paimpol leading lights come in line (both F.R, the rear being intensified between 261° and 266°), bearing 264°, follow this line until just inside the red sector of Porz-Don, which is the outer anchorage on line K.

If the tide serves follow the Paimpol leading lights into the inner anchorage or the harbour.

Anchorages

It is possible to anchor, clear of any oyster beds, in the Anse de Paimpol wherever there is enough water, but some parts of the channel are rather deep for small craft. Of the following positions, only (3) can be classed as a good cruising anchorage.

1. On line K, with La Jument beacon tower bearing east and the right-hand end of Ile St-Rion bearing north. Towards LWS care must be taken to avoid the 0·7m rock some 250m WSW from this position. This anchorage is not particularly sheltered, and is a very long way from civilisation.
2. NNE of Pointe Guilben, at the head of the deep channel. The most sheltered position has a least depth of 0·5m (i.e. 1·1m at MLWS). The swinging room is restricted. This anchorage is roughly on the following transits:

   a. Le Vahel beacon and Lande de Porz-Don monument.
   b. Kerity church and the western side of the hillock on the end of Pointe Guilben.

   The part of the channel which lies about 0·15M ENE of the anchorage is used by fishing boats which moor head and stern across the stream from half ebb to half flood, and fish for garfish and mackerel with hand lines. In the upper half of the tide there is quite a good dinghy landing in the sandy bay on the north side of Pointe Guilben, and from here there is a footpath to Paimpol 2·4km away.

3. Off Porz-Even in 2·7m with Glividi beacon bearing about 190°, distant 0·1M. Anchor slightly to the east of local moorings.

   Porz-Even, once a harbour for yachts that can take the ground, is now reserved for the use of fishing boats.

Harbour

The berths alongside the western side of the Jetée de Kernoa dry between 4·4 and 5·5m and the centre portion becomes submerged at HW. There is a grid on the NW side of the lock.

The lock is 63m long by 12m wide; the outer sill is 2·7m and the inner 4·2m above datum. Vessels of 3·5m draught can pass through into the basins on all tides. The lock-keepers work on the time of HW St-Malo. When the height is 8·5m or less the lock is operated at HW. With a height of between 8·5m and 9·5m both gates remain open between −0145 and +0030, and for a height superior to 9·5m between −0200 and +0100, HW St-Malo. In 1991 new gates were being installed and these times may be adjusted for 1992.

Facilities

The harbour is divided into two basins. There are floating pontoons for yachts in both basins and that for visiting yachts is marked in No. 2 basin, but other berths can be made available if need be under the direction of the harbourmaster (Sylvie Delaveaud 1991).

Showers and other facilities at the former custom house on Quai Neuf. This is the yacht harbour office. Water and electricity on the pontoons. Fuel berth at the end of the quay between No. 2 basin and the lock leading to No. 1 basin. The east side of the inner basin (No. 1) is used by commercial craft and has cranes. Facilities for yachts were excellent in 1991. There are yacht yards, electrical and marine engineers, sailmaker, and yacht chandlers available, also a dry dock. There are three garages.

Paimpol is a very pleasant old town, with banks, hotels and good shops, Librairie Maritime at Rue de Romsey and an excellent supermarket close to the south of Bassin No. 2. There are restaurants to suit all pockets.

Communications are excellent. Rail connection to Guingamp for St-Malo or Brest. There is an exciting bus service on the winding road near the coast from Lézardrieux and Tréguier to Portrieux and St-Brieuc. The basin is a convenient place in which a yacht can be left temporarily in charge of a caretaker. It has become very popular with British yachtsmen in July and August.

Historical

Paimpol used to be the great base for the Iceland cod-fishing fleet. These craft were either *goëlettes* (topsail schooners) or *dundees* (ketches), and used to be away for the whole six months of summer every year. The cod were taken on hand lines worked from the ship herself, hove-to in deep water. *La Glycine*, the last of the *goëlettes*, made her last voyage to Iceland in 1935.

15. Lézardrieux (Rivière de Trieux)

Charts
BA *3670, 3673*
Imray *C34*
SHOM *832, 882* (new charts in preparation)
ECM Navicarte *537*

Tidal data

Tidal heights (approx)
HW −0030 St Helier, −0525 Dover, +0200 Brest
MTL 5·6m. Index 12A
Heights of tide above chart datum
MHWS 10·2m, MLWS 1·0m, MHWN 7·6m, MLWN 3·5m

Tidal streams
1. For tidal streams in the outer approaches see page 71 and for Chenal de Bréhat, Le Kerpont and Le Ferlas channels see page 72.
2. In Grand Chenal and Rivière de Trieux. In the outer part of the channel outside Pen Azen, the SE-going stream begins at −0405 Brest (+0105 Dover), and the NW-going at +0205 Brest (−5010 Dover). Spring rate reaches 3·75 knots.

To the SW of Pen Azen the SE-going stream turns south towards Bréhat and into the Kerpont channel, and the NW-going stream runs north towards Plateau des Sirlots.

South of Gosrod beacon tower and in the Rivière de Trieux the ingoing stream begins at the same time as the outer SE-going stream and the outgoing at the same time as the outer NW-going stream. Both streams follow the course of the river. Within the river the streams reach 2 or 2·75 knots at springs and 3·75 knots under Lézardrieux suspension bridge. On the south side of Rochers

Donan, before reaching Lézardrieux there is an eddy on the flood stream, so that the stream always runs north here.
3. In the Moisie passage at the northern entrance, the E-going stream begins earlier at −0450 Brest (+0020 Dover), and the W-going at +0120 Brest (−0555 Dover). Both streams reach 3·8 knots at springs.

General

Lézardrieux has always been very popular with yachtsmen. The Grand Chenal can be taken by day or night at any state of tide and in any weather, except with bad visibility or with strong wind over tide conditions, when the approach is rough going. The other approaches require daylight and careful pilotage.

The Rivière de Trieux is most attractive. Navigation is possible up to Pontrieux, 9M from the entrance, where there is a wet dock.

Approaches
(See plan 15)
By day from the north
Rosédo radiobeacon near the lighthouse (*DO* 287·5 kHz) is a useful aid in making the outer approach. First make a position with La Horaine lighthouse, grey octagonal tower with black top, bearing 195° distant 3M. From here steer to follow the leading marks for the Grand Chenal, which are Bodic light structure (see photos) in line with La Croix lighthouse (white tower with red castellated top as seen from NE, elevation 15m) bearing 225° (line T on plan 15). Follow this line which leaves:
Nord Horaine N cardinal spar buoy 0·8M to port.
La Horaine lighthouse 1·4M to port.
Les Echaudés port buoy 0·5M to port.
Les Sirlots starboard buoy 0·2M to starboard.
Petit-Pen-Azen N cardinal beacon tower 0·5M to port.
Basse des Pen-Azen port buoy 0·2M to port.
Vieille du Tréou starboard beacon tower 0·25M to starboard.
Rodello starboard beacon on base of old tower 0·2M to starboard.
Rosédo white pyramid 0·3M to port.
Gosrod port beacon tower 0·1M to port.
Min Guen Kerranets starboard beacon tower 0·15M to starboard.

When about 1M from La Croix lighthouse, quit line T and steer for Moguedhier starboard beacon (replacing beacon tower destroyed 1991) for about 0·75M, (alternatively steer for Ile à Bois with its small coastguard building) then pick up the marks for line E, which are: Coatmer Aval light structure, a small white tower with grey roof 8m high, elevation 16m, in line with Coatmer Amont light structure, a similar tower, but with a pointed roof 6m high, elevation 50m, bearing 219°.

This line leaves the following marks on the sides shown:

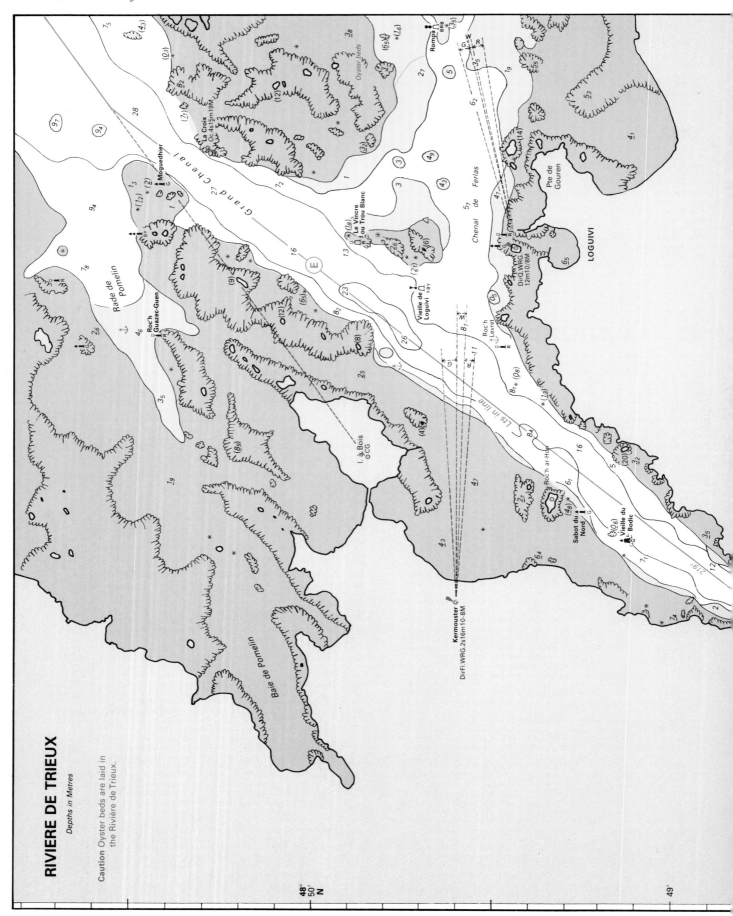

Depths in Metres

Caution Oyster beds are laid in the Rivière de Trieux.

48°
50'
N

49'

64

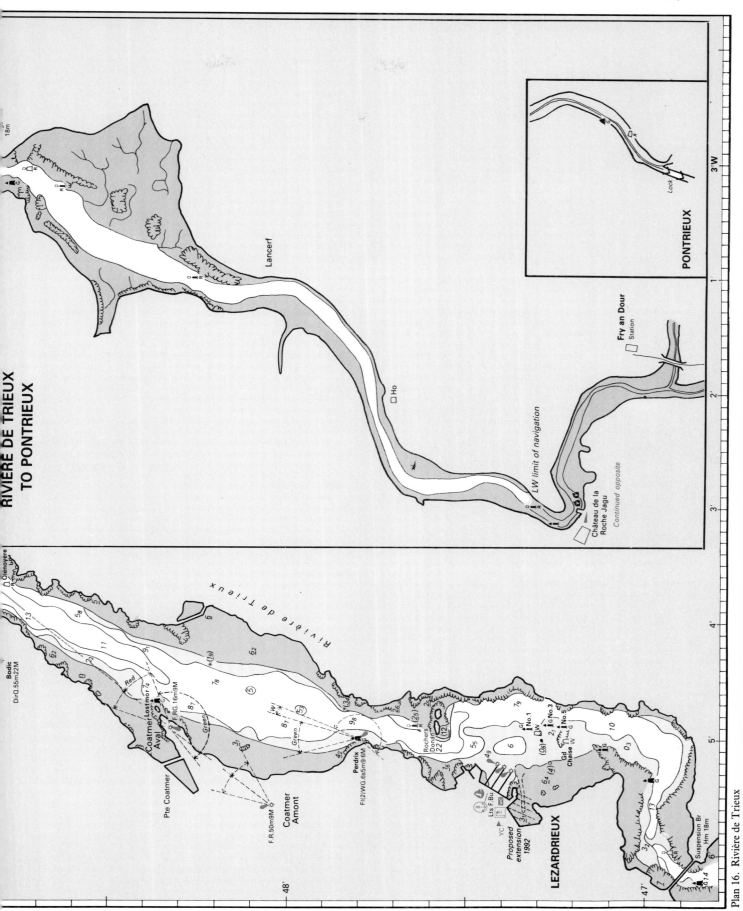

RIVIÈRE DE TRIEUX TO PONTRIEUX

Lancerf

Ho

LW limit of navigation

Château de la Roche Jagu

Continued opposite

Fry an Dour
Station

PONTRIEUX

Lock

3'W

Olenovere

Bodic
Dir 0.55m 22M

Coatmer Aval
Lostmor
F.RG.16m 9M

Pte Coatmer

Red

Green

Green

Coatmer Amont

F.R. 50m 9M

Perdrix
Fl(2)WG.6s5m 9 6M

Rivière de Trieux

Rochers
Donan
22

Lts F. Bu

YC

Proposed extension 1992

LEZARDRIEUX

Gd Chase

G No.1
G No.3
G No.5

Suspension Br
Hm 18m

G 14

Plan 16. Rivière de Trieux

Leading marks for Grand Chenal, La Croix lighthouse with Bodic on skyline to the right.

Close up of La Croix and Bodic.

Le Paon lighthouse and Petit-Pen-Azen N cardinal beacon tower. Telephoto looking SSW from the entrance to the Chenal de Bréhat.

Moguedhier starboard beacon 120m to starboard.
La Croix lighthouse 180m to port.
Vincre port beacon tower 0·125M to port.
Vieille de Loguivi W cardinal beacon tower 200m to port.
Ile à Bois (Custom House Island) 0·1M to starboard.
Vieille du Bodic starboard beacon tower 150m to starboard.
Olénoyère port beacon tower 100m to port.

When the latter is abeam, quit the leading line and proceed up the river on any convenient course, noting the marks and obstructions shown on plan 16, and in particular the following:

a. Le Perdrix light tower, lateral starboard.
b. The prominent Rochers Donan which may be left 30m to port.
c. The quay and the Port de Plaisance.
d. Les Chaises, a rocky middle ground marked by two white beacon towers with three starboard beacons to the east of them, which should be left to starboard, if proceeding upstream of the anchorage.

Half a mile above the quay the river turns sharply to starboard and the channel runs between Bec-an-Arvor starboard and Min Kéraoul port beacon towers. After passing the latter the channel turns to port, marked by two port beacons and passes under the suspension bridge with safe overhead clearance of 18m, leaving to starboard Beg an Ty Meur starboard beacon tower, and to port a port beacon tower. A further pair of beacons closely follow. Above this the channel is not marked.

By day from the east

For the leading marks for the Ferlas channel see under Paimpol, (page 55). When Vieille de Loguivi, W cardinal beacon tower, has been passed, turn into the Grand Chenal and proceed as above.

Les Heaux lighthouse from the northeast.

Leading marks for Chenal de la Moisie, with La Vieille du Tréou starboard beacon tower foreground right.

By day from the west via the Moisie channel

The Moisie channel carries a least depth of 1·3m and is particularly useful as a short cut from Tréguier to Lézardrieux or Paimpol, but is difficult near low water in hazy conditions if the leading marks cannot be seen. It is also liable to be encumbered with lobster/crab pot lines and floats. First make a position from which Les Héaux lighthouse (grey granite tower 53m high) bears 270° distant 1·75M. From here the leading marks on the Ile Bréhat will be in line. These are Rosédo white pyramid and St-Michel chapel, a small building with a red roof and a small red spire at its western end (see photograph), bearing 159° (line G plan 15). Before following this line, check that it passes about 150m east of Roche Moisie E cardinal beacon tower, then follow it closely. It leaves:

La Moisie beacon tower 150m to starboard (note the shoal north of the transit, in the approach to La Moisie and La Traverse rock, drying 2m, which is only 100m to port of the line, NNE of Nougejou beacon).

Nougejou Bihan E card. beacon 50m to starboard.

Pen ar Rest white beacon tower 0·4M to starboard.

Then quit the leading line and steer to leave Vieille du Tréou 100m to starboard and proceed as described under *By day from the north*, above.

By night from the north

If passing to the west of the Roches Douvres, keep in the fixed white sector of Le Paon (F.WRG), bearing between 181° and 196° until the leading lights for the Grand Chenal (line T) come into line. These are: La Croix (front) Oc.4s, and Bodic (rear) Q, bearing 225°. La Croix is intensified 215° to 235° and Bodic from 221° to 229°.

If passing SE of the Plateau de Barnouic, keep in the white sector of Les Héaux Oc(3)WRG.12s, bearing between 247° and 270° until the leading lights for the Grand Chenal come into line.

Note that there are dangers near the edges of both sectors and that, from the deck of a small yacht, Bodic light will dip behind La Croix tower at some point along this line. When this happens, borrow slightly to the west.

When Men Grenn, Q(9)15s (this is WSW of Ile St-Modé, and is a mark to a secondary channel, see plan 15), is abeam to starboard, quit the leading line and steer 235° for about 0·2M then bring Coatmer Aval and Amont lights, both F.R in this sector, into line bearing 219°.

Follow this line (line E) until Olénoyère beacon tower is abeam to port, then quit the leading line and proceed as described under *By day from the north*, above, leaving Perdrix, Fl(2)WG.6s, about 100m to starboard.

Perdrix light in line with Coatmer Aval light F.G sector leads to the anchorage, but passes close to Rochers Donan. The pontoons at Lézardrieux are marked by fixed blue lights.

Anchorages

1. The Rade de Pomelin (refer to plan 16), lying west of Moguedhier starboard beacon, offers a reasonable temporary anchorage in 3·5–4·6m, mud and shells, sheltered from NW through south to east. Further upstream there are many moorings on both sides of the river and they must be taken into account when anchoring.

2. Loguivi. This little drying harbour lies SSE of Vieille de Loguivi beacon tower, and is used mainly by fishermen and pilots. There is a reasonable anchorage outside the entrance in about 7·5m sand and shells, but the tide runs strongly, it is open to the east and contains a number of fishing-boat moorings and *viviers*. There is also an anchorage 0·25M west, between an above-water rock (Roc'h Levret, a mark for the Ferlas channel) and a port beacon. Small craft which can take the ground may prefer to dry out in the harbour itself, but it is usually very full of fishing boats, and yachts are not catered for. Loguivi is a small fishing village with few resources. There is a customs office. Boats from here form part of the fleet of French crabbers that fish for lobster and crayfish off the coast of Cornwall.

3. Ile à Bois. There is a good anchorage SE of the Ile à Bois and about 150m to the NW of line E, in about 4·2m LAT, sand and mud. The edge of the drying bank drops away steeply here, and there is a rock with only 0·1m LAT just southwest of the outermost drying outlier, and it is advisable to take soundings before letting go.

4. There is sheltered anchorage almost anywhere in the river proper, but it is advisable to avoid the wrecks in Perdrix reach and keep clear of the fairway as commercial ships pass up and down. Buoys have been laid by the yacht club in Perdrix reach, available to visitors.

Loguivi at half tide.

5. Lézardrieux. Anchorage is just between the quay and Les Chaises beacons off the extensive drying area on the west side. Permanent moorings are laid in this area and 5 large steel buoys have been laid on the W side of the beacon towers for use by visitors in fore-and-aft, raft moorings. There is probably room to anchor to the east of moorings or farther up the river. In 1991 The marina had

Looking north over Lézardrieux. A marina is intended in the inlet below left of the pontoons. From RCC Pilotage Foundation *Classic Passages*.

some 200 private berths, but a vacant berth could be allocated to a visitor, on application to the marina office. An extension south of the existing pontoons was being prepared by dredging and this, with a sill to maintain the depth at low water, may be in use late in 1992.

6. For other anchorages in this area, see under Ile Bréhat.

Facilities

Water and electricity are laid on to the pontoons, and there is a fuelling pontoon at the root of the northernmost pontoon, with petrol and diesel pumps. Yachts can dry out for a scrub on the south side of the quay. There is a bar and also showers at the yacht club but the times of opening are restricted. A Café du Port is close to the harbour but the post office and shops are at Lézardrieux, nearly half a mile from the marina. This is a small country town with fair facilities, including eating places and a garage. There is a landing place on the small beach just short of the bridge, which is nearer the town, with a water tap at the top of the path. The restaurant Relais Brenner is over the bridge on the east side.

16. Rivière de Trieux
Upper reaches and Pontrieux

Approaches

By day

There is no official chart of the 6M of this pretty river from Lézardrieux to Pontrieux but, unless time is short, navigation should present little difficulty if a start is made from Lézardrieux at low water, when the course of the channel can be seen before the mud covers and there will be plenty of time to enjoy the scenery.

The bridge has a clearance of 18m and, in the broad lake above it, after passing between a pair of port and starboard beacon towers and a pair of beacons, the best water is towards the west bank; thereafter, in general, it is close to the rocky steep-to banks, on the outside of the bends. There is an unmarked wreck on the extensive mudbank on the inside of the last curve to port before the spectacular Château de la Roche-Jagu. Here the river enters a narrow wooded gorge with a sharp bend to port under the *château*.

About a mile and a half farther on there is a junction, keep to starboard here. If one intends to enter the lock at Pontrieux the return journey will be at HW and it is as well, on the way up, to keep observation astern to assist later. In the approaches to the lock there are a starboard and a port buoy; keep at least 4m from them when passing.

Arriving early for the lock, it is best to wait in the bend under the *château* until 2½ hours before HW. The bottom downstream of the lock is rock and stones and unsuitable for grounding. A waiting buoy is situated where the river turns sharply round a port beacon in front of the lock but, if there is a danger of grounding, the advice is to enter the lock and lean against the wall.

The lock is 65m long and 11m wide with the sill 3·5m above datum. HW at the lock is as HW at St-Malo. The lock is operated for entry from two hours before to one hour after HW. It is usual to leave Pontrieux at HW, but the lock-keeper will advise.

Above the lock there are commercial quays immediately on the port hand and a rough wall to starboard. The depth in the basin varies from 2m to 4m due to silting and leaks in the gates.

Anchorage

Sand barges use the river by day and also, using searchlights, by night. Anchor clear of the channel with a riding light. There is sufficient water to anchor on neaps up as far as the Château de la Roche-Jagu and at springs in the lake stretching from the Lézardrieux bridge to Lancerf.

There is a very sheltered anchorage with a visitor's mooring in about 3m LWS in the elbow of the bend below the *château*, out of the channel. The mud bank

Mooring below Château de la Roche-Jagu.

Pontrieux lock at half tide.

Pontrieux. Photo *Peter Thomas*

is steep and care must be taken to avoid being set
onto it on a falling tide.

Inside the basin yachts berth alongside the wall
beyond the commercial quays on the instructions of
the harbourmaster.

Facilities

The port of Pontrieux provides all the amenities of a
formal yacht basin, which is within easy walking
distance of a pleasant country town. The harbourmaster (☎ 96 95 64 66) is most helpful and controls
all movements and berthing. VHF call *Port de
Pontrieux* or *Ecluse de Pontrieux* on Chs 12 or 16.

The wall is 600m long and provides berths for 100
yachts, of which 50 are allocated to visitors. Water,
ice, electricity, WCs and showers by the railway
station on the quay. There is a slipway and a 6-ton
crane on the quay, a 20-ton crane is available. Petrol
and diesel can be supplied by the harbourmaster.
Boats may be laid up afloat or ashore. Trains (5 on
weekdays, 3 on Sundays and *fête* days) with
connections to Paris, St-Malo and Roscoff. This is a
useful place to leave a boat temporarily or for crew
changes. There is an official surveillance three times
a day. Excellent café-restaurant Chez Jacqueline on
the quay (book for evening meal) and the Café de
Viaduc, a converted mill, is pleasantly situated.
Pontrieux is a relaxed and welcoming port to visit.

On the third Sunday in July there is a torch-lit
religious procession and a fun fair in the town. There
are excursions to Château de la Roche-Jagu, which
has a programme of theatrical and musical events
between 1 June and 31 August.

17. Ile Bréhat

Charts

BA *3670, 3673*
Imray *C34*
SHOM *832, 882* (new charts in preparation)
ECM Navicarte *537*

Tidal data

Tidal heights (approx)

HW −0025 St Helier, −0520 Dover, +0150 Brest
MTL 5·8m. Index 11A
Heights of tide above chart datum
MHWS 10·5m, MLWS 1·2m, MHWN 8·0m, MLWN 3·7m

Tidal streams

1. About 2·5M WSW of the Plateau des Roches
   Douvres the ESE-going stream begins at −0250
   Brest (+0220 Dover) reaching 4·4 knots at springs
   and the WNW-going stream at +0310 Brest
   (−0405 Dover) reaching 3·9 knots.
2. Near Plateau de la Horaine and the outer
   approaches off Ile Bréhat the SE-going stream
   begins at −0335 Brest (+0135 Dover) and the
   NW-going stream at +0235 Brest (−0440 Dover).
   Both streams reach 3·8 knots at springs. The
   streams are strong in the whole area between
   Plateau de Barnouic, La Horaine and Bréhat,
   causing severe overfalls when opposed to the
   direction of the wind, especially where the bottom
   is uneven.

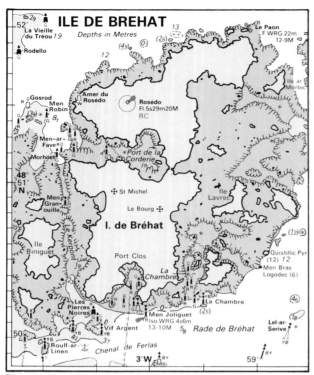

Plan 17. Ile de Bréhat

3. In the Chenal de Bréhat, on the east side of the island, the S-going stream begins at −0405 Brest (+0105 Dover) and the N-going at +0205 Brest (−0510 Dover). Both streams reach 5·6 knots at springs.

4. In Le Kerpont channel, on the west side of the island, the S-going stream begins at −0405 Brest (+0105 Dover) and the N-going at −0205 Brest (−0510 Dover). Both streams reach 3·75 to 4 knots at springs.

5. In the Chenal du Ferlas on the south side of the island the E-going stream begins at −0405 Brest (+0105 Dover) and the W-going at −0205 Brest (−0510 Dover). Both reach 3·8 knots at springs.

General

In spite of its lack of good anchorages at spring tides, this little island at the entrance to the Rivière de Trieux is frequently visited by British yachts. The strong tides and off-lying dangers call for careful pilotage, but the island itself is attractive, with its miniature and colourful rocky scenery and its friendly atmosphere, although it is full of visitors during the season.

For deep-draught yachts that cannot take the ground, it is best visited at neap tides, when small yachts can stay afloat in the sheltered anchorages. At springs, with care, there is restricted anchorage at La Corderie, otherwise the only reasonable anchorages are in the Rade de Bréhat, exposed to strong tides and open to both east and west. By reason of the island's close proximity to other anchorages in the Rivière de Trieux and the Anse de Paimpol, its anchorages can be visited when the tide serves.

Yachts fitted with legs or twin keels will find, with due care, a snug anchorage on sand in the drying harbours.

Approaches

By day from the north

1. The outer approaches and Grand Chenal (line T, plan 15) are given under Lézardrieux (Rivière de Trieux) on page 63, and Paimpol on page 60.

2. If bound for La Corderie, when Vieille du Tréou starboard beacon tower bears N, alter course to port so as to pass midway between Gosrod port beacon tower, leaving it to starboard, and Amer du Rosédo white pyramid (see plan 17).

   Then steer to leave Men Robin starboard beacon about 100m to starboard and then Roc'h Kervarec about 50m to port and Moncello Richard the first port beacon about 100m to port.

   Alter course then to port into the anchorage, passing between a further pair of port and starboard beacons.

3. If bound for Port Clos or La Chambre, there is a choice of four channels:

   a. By the Chenal de Bréhat and Le Ferlas channel (*see under Paimpol, approaches page 59 and page 60 above*).

   b. By the outer approach and Le Ferlas channel (*see under Paimpol, approaches page 58 and page 60 above*).

   c. By the Grand Chenal and Le Ferlas channel (*see under Paimpol, approaches page 60*).

   d. By Le Kerpont channel, which provides an interesting and useful short-cut, but can only be used in daylight and near high water. When the slip at the SW corner of Ile Bréhat is covered the passage is clear for 1·8m draught, this of course has no application if proceeding from north. The tide runs hard through the channel, but is directed along the fairway. Proceed as for La Corderie but instead of altering to port for the anchorage steer so as to pass between Men-ar-Fave port beacon and Morhoet starboard beacon and then leave the following marks on the sides shown:

   Men Granouille starboard beacon about 10m to starboard (This is the narrowest and shallowest part of the channel. When the top of the concrete base of the beacon is awash, there is said to be a least depth of 0·9m in the channel.)

   The isolated rock on the east side of Ile Beniquet 60m to starboard.

   The rock off its southeast corner 100m to starboard. Then follow the deep water round to the north of Les Pierres Noires starboard beacon tower, also taking care to avoid the rocks ESE of it, and so out into the Rade de Bréhat.

By day from Lézardrieux or the Anse de Paimpol

See under Rivière de Trieux approaches and Paimpol – Le Ferlas channel, above.

La Chambre looking NNE near HW.

Port de la Corderie where legs are an advantage.

Ile Bréhat. Looking NNW up Le Kerpont passage.

Port Clos at LW.

Ile Bréhat looking NW. La Chambre anchorage lower right, Port Clos middle left. From RCC Pilotage Foundation *Classic Passages*.

Anchorages

The area in Le Ferlas channel, and at the southern end of le Kerpont, which is enclosed by dotted lines on plan 17, is a prohibited anchorage, owing to telegraph cables.

1. **La Corderie** (plan 17). This small drying harbour is on the west side of the island, with anchorage for yachts of about 1·8m draught in the entrance at springs when La Chambre is not usable at LW. There is good shelter and holding ground within the delightful natural harbour, which dries about 2·4m to give about 1·2m at MLWN. The landing jetty is on the north side.

   Yachts equipped with legs or twin keels can proceed farther east to dry out on the bottom which, except in a few rocky places, is hard sand. In 1991 a power line was laid across the anchorage (see plan), but it is well dug in and does not interfere with the moorings laid in the harbour. However it is advisable to avoid anchoring in this area.

   Yachts of 1·8m draught can anchor between the two port beacons and the starboard beacon SE of the Roche Kervarec, but take soundings to find the best position, as far east as possible to avoid the rush of tide in and out of Le Kerpont. This outer anchorage is somewhat exposed to the west and the northwest, but is said to be better sheltered than it appears. A riding-light is necessary as the entrance fairway is sometimes used by crabbers at night. Land at jetty on the north side or on beaches on the south, as tide permits. Pleasant walk to Le Bourg. Fishermen use La Corderie as a temporary anchorage, taking the ground at low water if necessary.

2. **La Chambre** (plan 17). A small drying harbour, between Ile Bréhat and Ile Logodec, in some ways preferable to Port Clos. At neaps there is about 2·1m of water halfway between the first two port beacons, with excellent shelter, but some of the best positions are occupied by moorings. Small craft with legs will find perfect anchorage in the inner part of the harbour at all tides. As there are moorings in the vicinity, it is best to buoy the anchor. There is also anchorage at neap tides in winds from WNW through N to ENE to the west of the islet on the west side of the approach to La Chambre. It is possible to avoid the tide here, by going as far into the bay as soundings permit.

3. **Port Clos** (plan 17). A small drying harbour on the S side of the island. There is seaweed on the bottom in parts of the harbour, and an ordinary fisherman anchor holds best. At MLWN there should be about 2·4m of water with Men Joliquet bearing 145° distant 130m. Small craft can take the ground alongside the jetty on the west side of the harbour, which dries about 3·3m or, with twin keels or legs, anywhere in the inner part of the harbour in perfect shelter. Port Clos is the harbour to which *vedettes* ply, and they are very active by day taking holidaymakers to and round the island.

Facilities

Bréhat is a pleasant little island with a fair-sized population and many day-trippers in summer. With its mild climate there is much cultivation and sub-tropical vegetation grows in the open air. The village of Le Bourg, halfway between La Chambre and La Corderie, has several shops and restaurants among which La Vieille Auberge is recommended. There is a small but thriving sailing club near the southeast corner of the island.

There is a small restaurant on the west side of the entrance to La Chambre and a very reasonable meal is reported at the Hôtel des Roes at Port Clos.

II. Tréguier to Ile de Batz

The whole of this length of coast is encumbered with off-lying rocks and shoals. In places the coastal dangers extend three miles offshore, and outside them lie the Sept Iles, Plateau de Triagoz, and Plateau de la Méloine, with off-lying shoals of their own.

The shore consists mostly of low cliffs and sandy bays, backed by rolling hilly country, without many distinctive natural features.

Lights and fog signals

Details of the main coastal lights are given below, reading from east to west. Bearings of sectors and leading lines are true, looking towards the light. To convert to magnetic, add the variation, which during the 1990s is about 5·5°W for the area covered in Part II of this book.

The heights of the light structures are measured from the centre of the lantern to the base of the structure. Elevation is measured between the centre of the lantern and MHWS. *See Warning on page 5.*

Les Héaux 48°54'·5N 3°05'·2W Oc(3)WRG.12s48m17-12M 227°-R-247°-W-270°-G-302°-W-227° Grey granite tower 57m high.

Rivière de Tréguier, synchronised leading lights 137°:
Port de la Chaine (front) Oc.4s12m12M White house 5m high.
St-Antoine (rear) DirOc.R.4s34m15M Intensified 134°-140° White house with red roof 6m high. 0·75M from front.
La Corne Fl(3)WRG.12s14m11-8M 173°-G-213°-W-220°-R-052°-W-059°-R-173° White tower red base, 23m high.
Port Blanc-Le Voleur Fl.WRG.4s17m14-11M 140°-G-148°-W-152°-R-160° White tower 12m high.
Perros harbour leading lights for Passe de l'Est 224·5°:
Le Colombier (front) DirOc(4)12s28m18M Intensified 219·5°-229·5° White house 7m high.
Kerprigent (rear) DirQ.79m22M Intensified 221°-228° White tower 14m high (only top visible) 1·5M from front.
Perros harbour Passe de l'Ouest 143·6°:
Kerjean DirOc(2+1)WRG.12s78m15-13M 133·7°-G-143·2°-W-144·8°-R-154·3° White tower, black top, 16m high.
Ploumanac'h-Méan-Ruz Oc.WR.4s26m13-10M 226°-W-242°-R-226°. Square pink tower 15m high.
Les Sept Iles 48°52'·8N 3°29'·5W Fl(3)15s59m24M, but obscured by islands from 237° to 241° Grey tower and dwelling 20m high.
Les Triagoz 48°52'·3N 3°38'·8W Oc(2)WR.6s31m15/11M 339°-R- 010°, white elsewhere. Obscured in places 258°-268° by the Sept Iles. Square grey tower with red top 30m high.

Rivière de Lannion entrance:
Beg Léger 48°44'·4N 3°32'·9W Oc(4)WRG.12s60m13-10M. 007°-G-084°-W-098°-R-129° House painted white towards the west, with red lantern, 8m high.
Locquemeau harbour leading lights 121°:
Front F.R.21m6M 068°-vis-228° Red and white pylon 19m high.
Rear Oc(2+1)R.12s39m7M. White house with gable 6m high. 484m from front.
Primel harbour leading lights 152°:
Front F.R.35m6M 7m high.
Rear F.R.56m6M 4m high Both white with red stripes.
Primel (jetty) Fl.G.4s6m7M White column G top on hut 5m high.
Baie de Morlaix:
Ile Noire Oc(2)WRG.6s15m11-8M 211°-W-051°-G-135°-R-211° (obscured in places) White square tower R top, 13m high.
La Lande Fl.5s85m23M White square tower B top, 19m high. This light forms two transits: 190° with Ile Noire and 176° with Ile Louet.
Ile Louet Oc(3)WG.12s17m15/10M 244°-G-305°-W-244° White square tower B top, 12m high.
Roscoff:
Men-Guen-Bras N cardinal Q.WRG.14m9-6M 068°-W-073°-R-197°-W-257°-G-068° 20m high.
Port de Bloscon (on jetty head) 48°43'·3N 3°57'·6W Fl.WG.4s9m10/7M 206°-W-216°-G-206°. RC *BC* 304·5 kHz 10M.
Ar Chaden S cardinal Q(6)+LFl.WR.15s14m8/6M 262°-R-289·5°-W-293°-R-326°-W-110° (obscured elsewhere) 22m high.
Roscoff harbour synchronised leading lights 209°:
Front Oc(2+1)G.12s7m7M from 078° through E to 318° White column, G top, 7m high.
Rear Oc(2+1)12s24m15M from 062° through E to 242° Square grey tower, white on NE side, 24m high.
Roscoff-Ile de Batz ferry pier F.Vi.5m1M White and purple column, 14m high.
Ile de Batz 48°44'·8N 4°01'·6W Fl(4)25s69m23M Grey circular tower, 43m high. Auxiliary light F.R.65m7M 024°-vis-059°.

Off-lying buoys and marks

In addition to the lighthouses listed above, the following off-lying buoys and marks, some of which are unlit, may be useful when navigating along this coast. Reading from east to west:

La Jument (2M WNW of Les Heaux) N cardinal pillar light and bell buoy
Basse Crublent (3·75M W of Les Heaux) port pillar light and whistle buoy Fl(2)R.6s, radar reflector.

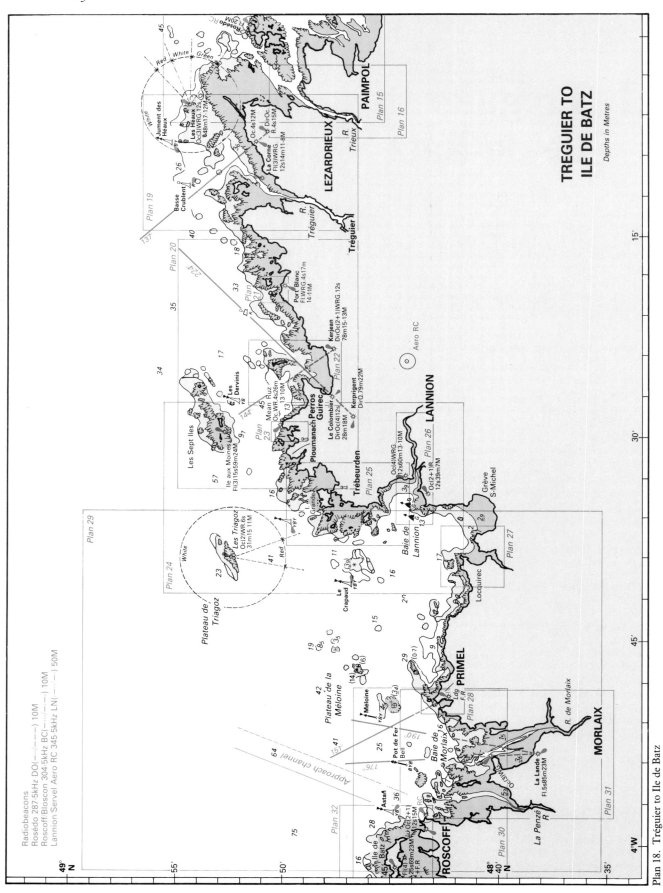

Plan 18.   Tréguier to Ile de Batz

Les Dervinis (1·5M E by S of Sept Iles LtHo). S cardinal spar buoy

Bar ar Gall W cardinal pillar buoy, 3M SE of Les Triagoz lighthouse

Le Crapaud (Basse Blanche) 5·75M S by W of Les Triagoz LtHo). W cardinal spar buoy

Baie de Morlaix:

Plateau de la Méloine A conspicuous rock (Grande Roche, alias Le Neveu) 19m high, stands in the centre of the plateau, in which there are many rocks.

Méloine (3M N by W of Primel) W cardinal spar whistle buoy. This is moored to the NW of Les Trépieds shoals and rocks which are an extension westwards of the Méloine plateau.

Stolvezen (2M N of Ile Louet). Port spindle buoy

Le Pot de Fer (3·5M N of Ile Louet). E cardinal spar bell buoy

Roches Duon (2·5M E by N of Roscoff). White or stone-coloured tower standing on rocks and containing a small room for shipwrecked sailors.

Basse Astan (2·5M E of Ile de Batz LtHo). E cardinal light and whistle pillar buoy

Basse de Bloscon (0·3M S by E of Men Guen Braz). N cardinal pillar light buoy

Aero radiobeacon

Lannion/Servel 48°43'·25N 3°18'·45W *LN* 345·5kHz, range 50M.

18. Rivière de Tréguier

Charts
BA *3670, 3672*
Imray *C34*
SHOM *832, 882* (new charts in preparation 1992)
ECM Navicarte *537*

Tidal data

Tidal heights (approx)
HW −0055 St Helier, −0550 Dover, +0120 Brest
MTL 5·4m. Index 10A
Heights of tide above chart datum
MHWS 9·8m, MLWS 1·1m, MHWN 7·5m, MLWN 3·3m

Tidal streams

1. Outside the river at La Jument and Basse Crublent buoys the E-going stream begins at −0350 Brest (+0120 Dover) and the W-going at +0220 Brest (−0455 Dover). Both streams reach 3·8 knots at springs.
2. In the Passe de la Gaine the ENE-going stream begins at −0450 Brest (+0020 Dover) and the WSW-going at −0025 Brest (+0445 Dover). Both streams reach 2·5 knots.
3. North of La Corne light tower the SW-going stream begins at −0435 Brest (+0035 Dover) and the NE-going stream at +0135 Brest (−0540 Dover). Both streams reach 2·8 knots at springs.
4. In the river the in-going stream begins at −0425 Brest (+0045 Dover) and the outgoing at +0130 Brest (−0545 Dover). Both streams reach 2·4 knots at springs.

General

Although described by one French writer as *un cul-de-sac scabreux* (risky), this river in fact provides a safe and charming anchorage for small craft. Some yachtsmen think it the best on the north coast of France.

The Grande Passe offers a fairly easy approach through the off-lying dangers at any state of tide, and can be taken by day or night, in reasonable visibility.

The river winds through wooded, hilly country for four miles to the old cathedral town of Tréguier, which is the normal limit of navigation. Since the upper part of the river has been buoyed by 13 light buoys, 7 to port and 6 to starboard, the channel is reasonably clear at any state of the tide.

Approaches

Grande Passe. By day

The leading marks for this channel are: the light structures of Port de la Chaine (front) and St-Antoine (rear) in transit bearing 137°. Port de la Chaine is a white house with a small red lantern, 5m high, elevation 12m, and St-Antoine is a white house with

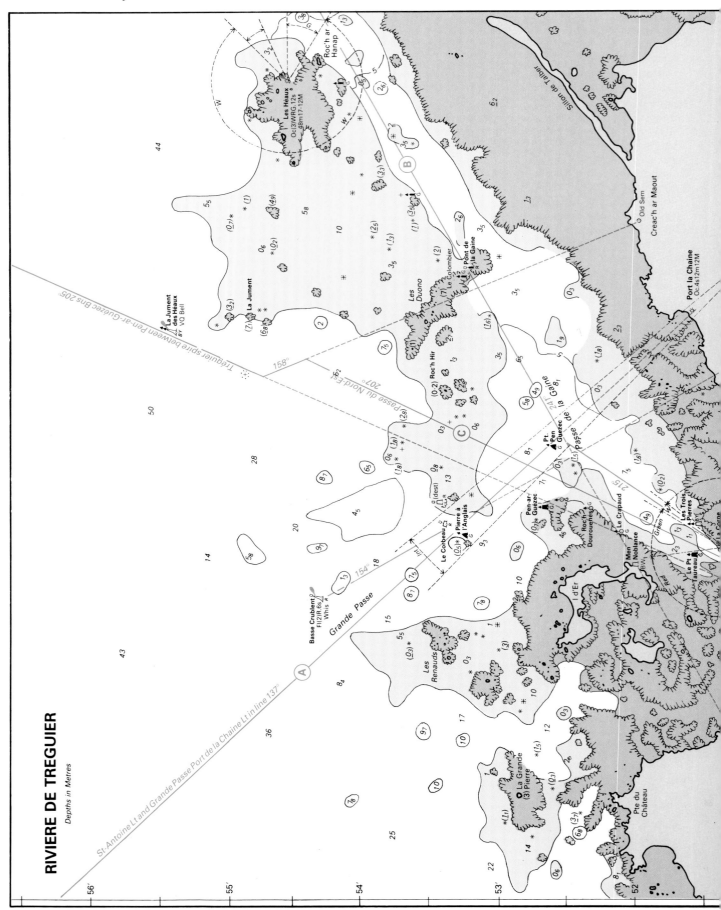

RIVIERE DE TREGUIER

Depths in Metres

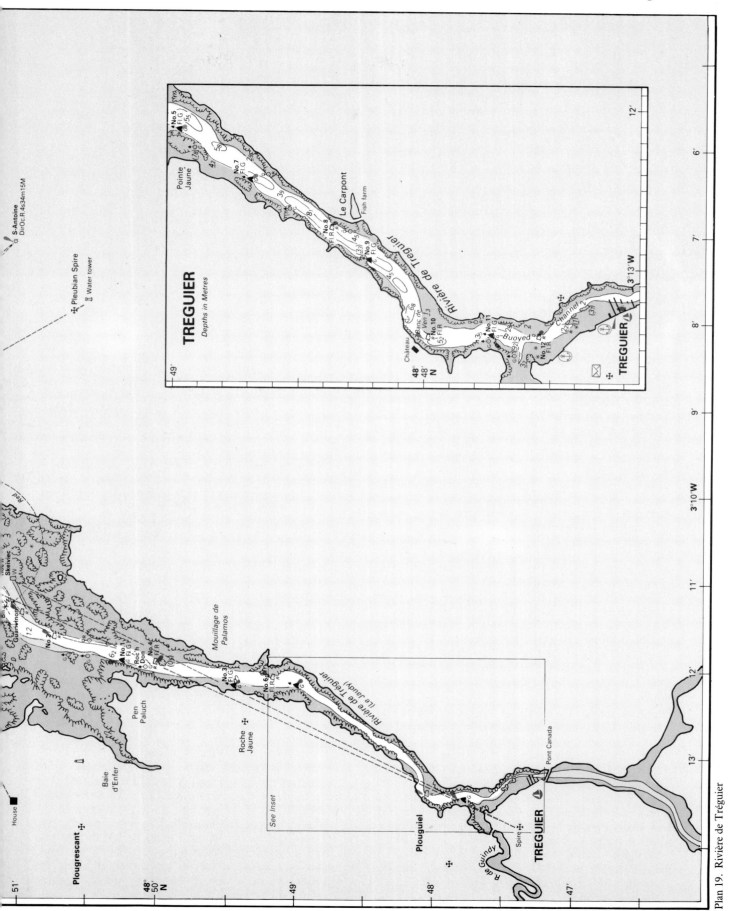

Plan 19. Rivière de Tréguier

Tréguier, initial approach to Grande Passe. From a position SW of Basse Crublent buoy, left foreground, steer with Pleubian spire (front) in transit with Pleubian water tower (rear) on 154°.

a small red lantern 6m high, elevation 34m (line A). Due to other buildings and trees along the shore, these marks are very difficult to pick up in daylight. However with the construction of a water tower at Pleubian an alternative leading line is available.

From a position close SW of Basse Crublent port pillar light and whistle buoy, Pleubian water tower, will be seen to be in transit with Pleubian spire on a bearing of 154°.

Follow this transit which leads between Le Corbeau port buoy (unlit) and Pierre à l'Anglais starboard buoy (unlit). Approaching these buoys, steer to pass midway between them and from here, the light structures of Port de la Chaine and St-Antoine may be seen in transit bearing 137°. Follow this line which leaves Pen ar Guézec starboard buoy (unlit) 150m to starboard.

Beware of the shoal SE of Le Corbeau buoy. Here a yacht must not be to the east of the leading line.

As soon as Pen ar Guézec buoy is abaft the beam, quit the leading line and alter course to 215° keeping the eastern edge of La Corne white lighthouse with a red base in line with Skeiviec white beacon tower. This line leaves the following marks on the sides shown:

Pen Ar Guézec Twin beacon towers 0·35M to starboard. The southernmost tower was damaged and has been reconstructed with a concrete column topped by a beacon pole on the original base. Two starboard beacons on the east side of Ile d'Er, 0·3M to starboard.

Men Noblance black-and-white pyramid, the front mark for the Passe de la Gaine 0·45M to starboard.

Les Trois Pierres N cardinal beacon tower with two green painted cones 110m to port. If entering at very low water, note the Banc de la Pie (1·1m LAT, 2·1m at MLWS) which extends into the channel NW of this tower to within about 60m of the leading line.

When Les Trois Pierres tower is abeam, quit the leading line and steer as if to leave La Corne lighthouse 150m to port, leaving Le Petit Taureau starboard beacon tower 170m to starboard; but when La Corne lighthouse bears about 180°, alter course to leave it 100m to port and Le Taureau starboard buoy 35m to starboard.

When this buoy is abaft the beam, alter course to make good 234° keeping Les Trois Pierres beacon tower touching the west side of La Corne lighthouse as a stern transit. This line leaves:

Skeiviec small white beacon tower, on a rocky shoal which at LW looks like a small island, 0·1M to port.

Laouenan beacon 0·15M to starboard, and leads straight to:

Guarivinon port pillar light buoy; leave this to port.

From this buoy the position of the deep channel can best be seen on plan 19. This channel is marked by 12 lateral light buoys, 6 to starboard and 6 to port, as well as the old lateral beacons, which are on drying rocks.

For the first mile and a quarter the channel lies towards the west side of the river; note in particular the drying rock just upstream of No. 4 port light buoy, off Turkés rock. Thereafter it is roughly in midstream all the way to Tréguier except at the Banc de Ven where it hugs the west bank.

There is a fish farm at Le Carpont 1·5M downstream from Tréguier with floating tanks on either side of the river which can mask the channel buoys.

The corner of the Banc de Ven is marked by No. 10 port light buoy, which should be left to port and given a wide berth near low water. Note the shoal water (1m LAT), as shown on the chart SE of the entrance of the creek, Rivière du Guindy, and the drying banks on each side.

GRAND PASSE

By night

Keeping well to seaward of the off-lying dangers, come on to the leading line formed by the synchronised lights of Port de la Chaine (front) Oc.4s12M and St-Antoine (rear) DirOc.R.4s15M and steer to follow this line bearing 137°. The rear light is intensified 134° to 140° (line A).

For vessels equipped with radar, the Basse Crublent, Pierre à l'Anglais and Pen Guézec buoys are fitted with radar reflectors. The vessel will pass through the red and green sectors of La Corne light Fl(3)WRG.12s (plan 19, pages 80–81) and enter the white sector bearing 213° close to the unlit Pen Guézec buoy.

Alter course to leave this buoy to starboard and steer to keep in the white sector of La Corne between 213° and 220° and keep in this sector until Les Trois Pierres beacon tower (unlit) is abeam to port, and about 0·2M from the lighthouse.

Then alter course about 10° to starboard, so as to pass round the west side of the lighthouse in a shallow curve, leaving it about 100m to port.

When it bears 059° the white sector, between this bearing and 052° will open up (the sectors may be difficult to see when close to the light, owing to the beams passing overhead), and course should be altered to port to keep on the southern edge of this sector in order to leave the unlit Taureau starboard buoy, which is well inside the sector, to starboard.

The southern edge of this sector, on a course made good of 232° leads to Guarivinon port light buoy, which should be left to port. From this buoy the position of the deep channel can best be seen from plan 16 as in *By day* approach, above. The lateral light buoys are on alternate sides of the channel and, to be sure of avoiding the danger upstream of No. 4 and the Banc de Ven to the east of No. 10, it would be as well to record each buoy as it is passed.

Port de la Chaine and St-Antoine, leading lighthouses for the Grande Passe.

Leading marks for Passe de la Gaine on a clear day. Plougrescant church far left.

La Corne light tower with Roc'h Skeiviec white pyramid open to
left and Banc du Taureau starboard buoy to left of yacht far right.

PASSE DE LA GAINE

By day only

This pass can be taken only in daylight and clear
visibility. If the leading line is followed exactly, the
least depth is 0·3m (1·2m at MLWS, 3·6m at
MLWN); but a divergence of 36m from the line will
give 2·1m less water in two places.

At half tide there should be a least depth of 3·3m
for 36m either side of the line and of 2·1m for 100m
each side.

To enter the pass from the east, approach Les
Héaux and identify the Roc'h ar Hanap, which lies
0·25M SSE of the lighthouse and never covers. It is
the outermost of several rocks on this side, and is
steep-to to the southeast. Avoid, if need be, the
Basse de la Gaine (a rock drying 0·3m about 0·4M
east of Roc'h ar Hanap and about 100m southeast of
the leading line).

Make a position from which Roc'h ar Hanap bears
360°, distant 0·2M and a starboard beacon bears
290°. From here the leading marks will be in line
(line B): Men Noblance white beacon tower with
horizontal black stripe, in line with the white wall
beacon with vertical black stripe, bearing 241°. The
rear wall beacon stands below the skyline in a field
just below the first clump of trees about 500 to 600m
west of the prominent Plougrescant church.

Follow this line through leaving the first starboard
beacon 200m to starboard, the second starboard
beacon 150m to starboard, passing between the port
and starboard beacons at Pont de la Gaine, leaving
the former 80m to port and the latter 50m to
starboard and finally Pen Guézec starboard buoy
about 100m to starboard. Then proceed as for the
Grande Passe.

The difficulty about the Passe de la Gaine is that
the wall beacon is over 6M and Men Noblance over
4M from the entrance and, in poor visibility or in the
haze of a summer's day, particularly in late
afternoon, one or both marks cannot be seen.
However in calm conditions it is quite possible to
navigate by Roc'h ar Hanap and the two starboard
beacons on entry, and to steer between the port and
starboard beacons on the Pont de la Gaine, using the
Men Noblance mark which should by that time be
visible.

The tidal streams are strong and the set must be
allowed for. In the outer part of the Passe the east-
going stream is deflected to the northeast, so that
when entering, the tide is foul, although the flood is
fair up the Rivière de Tréguier.

There are also, incidentally, quite heavy overfalls
at certain states of the tide on the shoals, seaward of
Les Héaux.

PASSE DU NORD-EST

By day only

This pass can only be taken in daylight and clear
visibility but, if the leading marks can be seen, it
provides a useful alternative to the Passe de la Gaine
for vessels approaching from the Channel Islands,
particularly in the late afternoon, when it is not
possible to distinguish the marks for the latter, or at
LWS when it has a least depth of 2·3m, as compared
with 1·2m.

Navigate so as to pass 100m northwest of La
Jument (otherwise Jument des Heaux) N cardinal
buoy. From here Tréguier cathedral spire (which is
the right-hand of two spires visible between the river
banks) will be between the two beacon towers on Pen
ar Guézec bearing 205°. The southernmost tower was
damaged and has been reconstructed with a concrete
column topped by a beacon pole on the original base
which is exposed at LW. If not visible, the spire
should be kept open to the left of the one that can be
seen, bearing 205°.

Steer to follow this line for about 0·75M.

When the summit of the middle rock in the Duono
group is in line with the old *sémaphore* building on
the Creac'h ar Maout, bearing 158°, steer to follow
this line for about 0·3M until Skeiviec white beacon
comes in line with the cathedral spire bearing 207°
(line C).

Approaching Tréguier.

Tréguier pontoons. Looking downstream.

Steer to follow this line, leaving:

Pen Guézec starboard buoy 0·2M to port.

Pen ar Guézec beacon towers 0·2 and 0·15M to starboard.

Roc'h Dourouenés starboard beacon 0·1M to starboard.

Le Crapaud starboard beacon 0·15M to starboard.

Les Trois Pierres N cardinal beacon tower with green cones 0·15M to port.

La Corne lighthouse 100m to port.

Then proceed as for La Grande Passe. Owing to the presence of many fishing markers in the area, it might be preferable to quit this line when on the leading marks for La Grande Passe, and to continue as for that channel.

Anchorages

It is possible to anchor in good holding ground almost anywhere in the channel (which is used by coasters), but the following positions are recommended.

a. In mid-channel near the Guarivinon buoy in 5–6m LAT, sandy mud.

b. Towards the west side of the channel between Pen Paluch and Roc'h-Don beacons in 5m LAT, mud.

c. Towards the west side of the channel near the Douane de la Roche Jaune 7·8m LAT, sandy mud. Care must be taken to allow swinging room clear of oyster beds inshore which dry and are steep-to. There is a village half a mile inshore from the quay, where there are shops, a self-service store and telephone. Oysters are for sale near the jetty.

d. In mid-channel near the Gorian buoy No. 6 in 7·5m LAT, mud. This reach of the river is called the Mouillage de Palamos.

e. In mid-channel north of the Banc de Ven in 6·8m LAT, mud.

f. Under the *château*, close inshore opposite Banc de Ven in 5·2m, mud.

g. Anchoring is now forbidden between anchorage (f) and the bridge, and there are no mooring buoys in this reach. A marina has been built below the bridge, having 5 pontoons extending from the W bank. These have fingers on each side for berthing boats up to 12m. There is one berth only for a boat up to 16m at the end of the first pontoon. A notice directs visitors to berth head-on to the current on the second pontoon. The tide runs very strongly under the pontoons and, while the tide is running, if berthed stern-to the tide, one cannot safely vacate a berth without taking lines to the next pontoon or changing berths at slack water.

h. With permission from the harbourmaster for the commercial quay, it might still be possible to take the ground alongside the quay when not required for commercial shipping.

i. When the tide serves, small craft which can pass under the bridge may go a further 3·5M up the river to La Roche-Derrien, where there is said to be a quay that dries 5·7m LAT. The channel dries 5·1m.

Facilities

The marina has berths for 330 boats in between 1·5m and 3m. Water and electricity are laid on to the pontoons. There is a yacht club with lounge, bar, showers and WCs. Fuelling pontoon: apply to the garage opposite the yacht club for service. There is also a sailing school. For boats anchored downstream, there are three main dinghy landings on the town side of the river:

a. At the steps just north of the old custom house. These dry about 2m at MLWS, soft mud.

b. At the slipway and steps at the little promontory at the entrance of Rivière de Guindy, this is rather rough and weedy.

c. At the slipway farther up the Rivière de Guindy, beyond the two bridges. This only dries at extreme LWS.

There are two yacht chandlers, one at the south end of the quay and the other at the north. At HW it is possible to go alongside outside the latter, where stores may be loaded and water is available. *Butagaz* is available here also. Water is also available from a tap at the new public conveniences in the middle of the quay.

The post office is up the main road to the town. There is a good restaurant on the quay and good shops and a laundrette in the town. There is a self-service supermarket in the road from the north end of the quay up to the town. Banque de Bretagne, 200m from the quay.

Bus service to Paimpol and to Lannion railway station.

Historical

Tréguier is a pleasant, quiet old town which traces its history back to the monastery of Trécon, founded by St-Tugdal in the 6th century. The fine church, formerly a cathedral, was founded in the 9th century but mostly rebuilt in the 14th; there is an 11th-century tower on its northern side. The strange granite spire, a sort of honeycomb of irregular openings, was finished in 1787. St-Yves, the 'friend of the poor', lived at Tréguier in the 13th century. A procession from Tréguier cathedral to his birthplace in the nearby village of Minihy takes place each year on May 19th, and is known as the pardon of the poor. Tréguier is the birthplace of Renan.

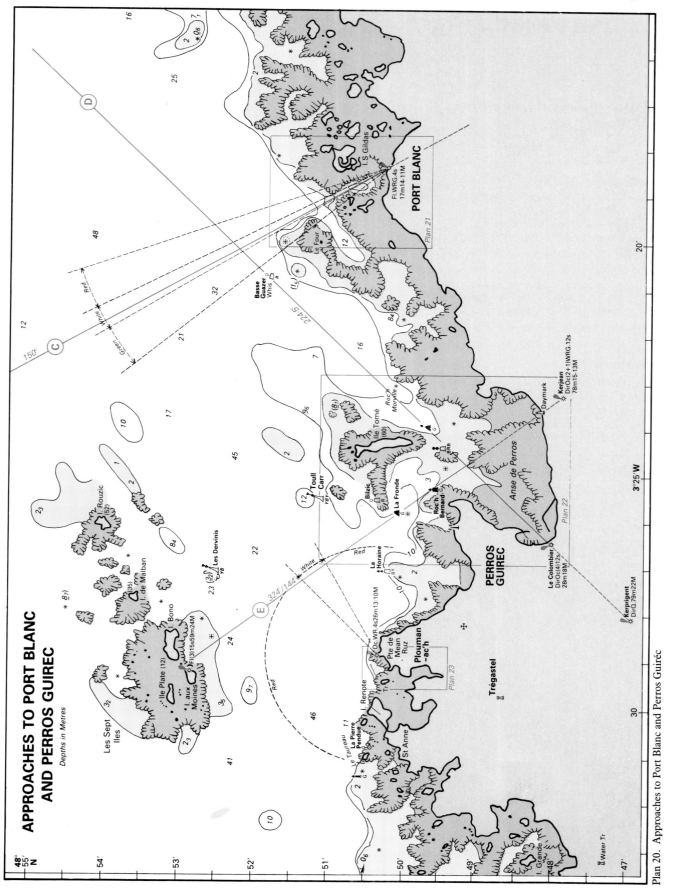

Plan 20. Approaches to Port Blanc and Perros Guiréc

19. Port Blanc

Charts

BA *3670*
Imray *C34*
SHOM *967* (new chart in preparation)
ECM Navicarte *537*

Tidal data

Tidal heights (approx)

HW −0100 St Helier, −0555 Dover, +0120 Brest
MTL 4·9m. Index 9A
Heights of tide above chart datum
MHWS 9·4m, MLWS 0·9m, MHWN 7·0m, MLWN 3·3m

Tidal streams

Off the entrance the east-going stream begins at −0450 Brest (+0020 Dover) and the west-going at −0120 Brest (−0555 Dover). Both streams reach 2·5 knots at springs.

General

This small natural harbour, halfway between the Rivière de Tréguier and Perros, is well sheltered except from winds between NW and NNE which make the anchorage uncomfortable and which, if strong, make the entrance rough (especially on the ebb) and the anchorage untenable. In easterly weather it is more sheltered than the Anse de Perros,

but at high water there is always liable to be a certain amount of swell in the anchorage. The entrance is straightforward but rather difficult to identify, and can be taken by day or night at any state of the tide. The village has few resources, but the rocky island scenery is attractive in fine weather.

Approaches

By day

Owing to the lack of distinctive landmarks, it is not easy to identify the entrance from seaward, but bearings of Plougrescant church, Ile Tomé and of Ile Rouzic, the most easterly of the Sept Iles, will give reasonable fixes for the approach.

Navigate so as to reach a point from which Basse Guazer port whistle buoy bears 218° distant 0·7M (see plan 20). This point is at the intersection of the leading line for Perros (line D) and the leading line for the entrance (line C), originally formed by Le Voleur-Port Blanc lighthouse in line with Moulin de la Comtesse, bearing 150°. The lighthouse, a white tower, with a square window at its half height, was clearly visible in 1991 after the trees surrounding it had been cleared, and a conspicuous white house with a slate roof about 100m to the NE assists identification (see photograph). The *moulin* is ruined and is obscured by trees.

The best means of identifying the entrance is by the Ile du Château Neuf, an islet of bare rock and grass, which is situated on the west side, with a slender white pyramid on its summit (see photograph). The island, being rather steep-to, can be treated, with caution, as a starboard-hand mark. Ile Saint Gildas is a bigger island on the east side of the entrance. It is wooded and also has a white pyramid, which is not nearly as conspicuous as that on the Ile du Château Neuf.

Once these features have been recognised, there is no difficulty in the approach, holding the lighthouse at 150°, line C leads straight into the anchorage, and leaves the following marks on the sides shown:

Basse Guazer port conical whistle buoy 0·7M to starboard.
Le Four white painted rock 0·5M to starboard.
Ile du Château Neuf white pyramid 0·125M to starboard.
Ile Saint Gildas white pyramid 0·25M to port.
Roc'h Huz port beacon 100m to port.

By night

From any direction, navigate so as to reach the line of the leading lights for the east pass into Perros: Le Colombier (front) DirOc(4)12s, in line with Kerprigent (rear) DirQ, bearing 224·5°. This line (D on plan 20), passes close to seaward of the unlit Basse Guazer whistle buoy, and clears all dangers on each side of the entrance to Port Blanc.

Sail along line D in the required direction until the white sector of Le Voleur-Port Blanc Fl.WRG.4s opens up, between 148° and 152°. Steer to keep within this sector which clears all dangers as far as the anchorage.

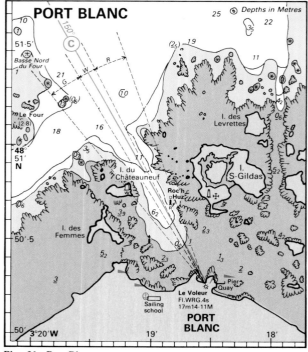

Plan 21. Port Blanc

Port Blanc, Ile du Château Neuf white pyramid bearing 160° right of centre.

Port Blanc entrance. Le Voleur lighthouse, just repainted, bearing 150°(centre). Conspicuous house gable-end catching the evening sun, on shore, left of Le Voleur. Ile du Château white pyramid, far right.

Le Voleur lighthouse and conspicuous house.

Anchorages

23 white visitors' mooring buoys have been laid in the pool; these are well spaced but there should nevertheless be room to anchor clear of them, the bottom being generally sand and shells. The berths at the southern end are the most sheltered. Small craft will be able to lie afloat to the east of the leading line and south of the Ile Saint Gildas pyramid on most tides; for example at MLWN there should be 1·8m of water in a position midway between Ile Saint Gildas pyramid and Port Blanc lighthouse.

Facilities

There is a small quay and slip east of Port Blanc lighthouse but this dries 1·5m LAT. A dinghy landing is possible anywhere round the anchorage on sand and rock. The slip used by the sailing school is in the bay to the west of the lighthouse, and there is a third slip at the extreme west of the bay. Although it dries 3m it is convenient for some shops a short distance inland.

Showers, toilets and drinking water are available at the sailing school building which also contains the harbourmaster's office.

Port Blanc is a small fishing village and seaside holiday resort, with two or three hotels and restaurants. Simple provisions can be purchased, and there is a postbox on the side wall of the Grand Hotel, which is described as modest and good. A taxi can be hired at the café to fetch fuel from a neighbouring village. Shops include a butcher and a baker beyond the western landing mentioned above.

Background

The harbour shelters a few small fishing boats and day boats, all of which lie on drying moorings clear of the pool.

The 16th-century chapel of Notre Dame de Port Blanc stands above the village, and is the scene of a *pardon* held on September 8th and attended mainly by fishermen and sailors.

Anatole le Braz, the author of several classics on Breton traditions and legends, lived at Port Blanc.

One of the local legends tells of a long procession of drowned seamen, led by a woman, which can sometimes be seen landing on the beach of the Ile Saint Gildas in search of fresh water, while the shape of their vessel is dimly visible in the offing.

20. Perros Guiréc

Charts
BA *3670*
Imray *C34*
SHOM *967* (new chart in preparation 1992)
ECM Navicarte *537*

Tidal data

Tidal heights (approx)
HW −0100 St Helier, −0555 Dover, +0120 Brest
MTL 4·9m. Index 9A
Heights of tide above chart datum
MHWS 9·1m, MLWS 0·9m, MHWN 6·3m, MLWN 3·0m

Tidal streams
1. At the Couillons de Tomé buoy, the east-going stream begins at −0435 Brest (+0035 Dover), reaching 3·8 knots at springs and the west-going at +0250 Brest (−0425 Dover), reaching 2·8 knots.
2. In the Passe de l'Ouest the southeast-going stream begins at −0435 Brest (+0035 Dover) and the northwest-going at +0250 Brest (−0425 Dover). Both streams reach 2·8 knots at springs.
3. In the Passe de l'Est the northeast-going stream begins at −0435 Brest (+0035 Dover), reaching 3·5 knots at springs and the southwest-going stream begins at +0250 Brest (−0425 Dover), reaching 3·5 knots.

General

The Anse de Perros is a large shallow bay, most of which dries at MLWS leaving a tongue of deeper water in which a small vessel can lie afloat about 0·4M from the western shore. It provides good shelter in westerly weather, but the anchorage is far from a convenient landing.

The port of Perros was formerly a drying harbour and is in the SW corner of the bay, protected by two stone jetties. The inner part has been made into a wet basin by the construction of a submersible dyke and a dock gate holding a least depth of 7m above datum.

There are two approach channels, one east of Ile Tomé and the other west of it. The eastern channel has leading lights and the western channel a directional sectored light, and both can be taken at night, but towards springs it is necessary to consider the depth of water near the southern ends of the leading lines.

Approaches
PASSE DE L'EST
By day
The leading line (D on plan 20) carries a least depth of 0·3m if followed exactly, but this can be increased to 2·1m by observing the following instructions. The line is formed by Le Colombier, a white house light structure on which the name is shown, 5m high, elevation 28m, and Kerprigent lighthouse a white tower 14m high, elevation 79m, among the trees on the skyline, bearing 224·5°. The marks are difficult for a stranger to pick out at a distance and it may be easier to navigate by the buoys and beacons alone. The leading line leaves the following marks on the sides shown:

Basse Guazer port whistle buoy 0·1M to port.
Roc'h Morville (dries 1·5m), the seaward end of a dangerous unmarked shoal, 0·15M to port.
Pierre Jean Rouzic starboard buoy 50m to starboard.
Durante port beacon 0·25M to port.
Pierre du Chenal isolated danger beacon tower 150m to starboard.
Gribineyer port buoy 100m to port.

0·1M beyond this buoy, the line passes over a 0·4m patch. To avoid this, as soon as Gribineyer buoy is abeam, alter course to 270° and hold it until Roc'h hu de Perros port beacon tower bears 180° then rejoin the line.

Continuing along it, if the tide serves, we leave:
Roc'h hu de Perros port beacon tower 0·125M to port.
L'ost ar C'hraou starboard beacon 50m to starboard.
Gomenénou port beacon tower 0·1M to port, after which course may be altered as necessary to enter the port.

By night
Navigate so as to reach the leading line formed by Le Colombier (front) DirOc(4)12s (intensified 219·5° to 229·5°), and Kerprigent (rear) DirQ (intensified 221° to 228°) (line D), bearing 224·5°.

Follow this line as for *By day* above, except that if Gribineyer buoy and Roc'h hu de Perros cannot be seen, as soon as Kerjean light to port DirOc(2+1) WRG changes from red to white, alter course sharply to starboard to bring this astern and steer so as to keep in the narrow white sector for 150m and then rejoin the line on a converging course of about 215°.

Small fixed lights are exhibited at the entrance to the port; green at the end of the eastern jetty and red on the western jetty.

PASSE DE L'OUEST
By day
Keep well clear of the off-lying dangers on the south side of the Sept Iles and on the north side of Ile Tomé. Note: Les Dervinis S cardinal spar buoy, Couillons de Tomé W cardinal pillar buoy and La Horaine N cardinal beacon tower.

Navigate so as to pass through a point from which Bilzic port beacon tower bears 090° distant 0·2M, from here Nantouar, a white house with a former light tower on its roof, standing near the foreshore, will be in line with Kerjean, a white light tower 16m high, elevation 78m with a conical grey roof, amongst the trees on the skyline, bearing 144° (line E).

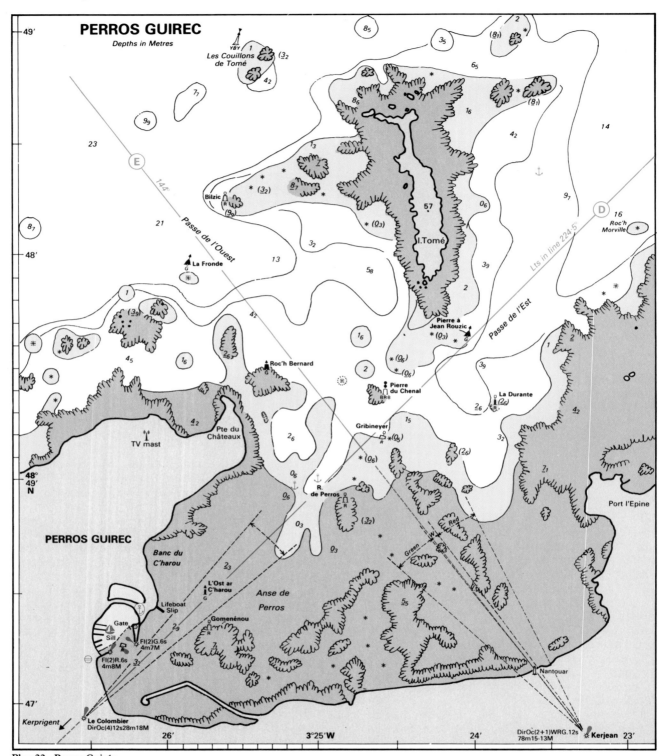

PERROS GUIREC

Depths in Metres

Les Couillons de Tomé

Plan 22. Perros Guiréc

Perros Guiréc, looking south.

Leading marks for Passe de l'Est, in transit, centre, bearing 224·5°.

This line carries a least depth of 0·9m, but is rather difficult for a stranger to pick out at a distance, and it may be easier to navigate by the buoys and beacons alone. Line E leaves the following marks on the sides shown:

La Fronde starboard buoy just 0·125M to starboard.

Roc'h Bernard starboard beacon tower 0·125M to starboard.

Pierre du Chenal isolated danger beacon tower, 0·2M to port.

As soon as Pierre du Chenal beacon tower is abeam, quit the leading line and steer 190° to pick up the Passe de l'Est (line D).

By night

Note that the white sector of Méan Ruz light, Oc.WR.4s, near Ploumanac'h clears all dangers between Les Sept Iles and the mainland. Navigate to pick up the narrow white sector of Kerjean light, DirOc(2+1)WRG.12s, which is only between 143·2° and 144·8° and is flanked by a green sector to the west and a red sector to the east.

Follow this line and proceed as for *By day*, above, taking care to quit the leading line and alter course to starboard just before Le Colombier (front) DirOc(4) 12s comes in line with Kerprigent (rear) DirQ, intensified between 221° and 228°.

Anchorages

1. The Anse de Perros offers good holding ground and is sheltered from southeast through south to northwest. Recommended positions are:

   a. With Roc'h hu de Perros tower bearing 130°, distant 0·16M. Least depth 2·4m (3·3m at MLWS), sand.

   b. With Roc'h hu de Perros tower bearing 120°, and with Bilzic port beacon tower, just open west of Roc'h Bernard tower. Least depth 0·6m

Yachts leaving by the narrow gate. The wall is well covered to the left of the gate.

Perros Guiréc pontoons at low water.

(1·5m at MLWS), sand. With the aid of soundings it may be possible to anchor further to the southwest.

   c. At neap tides, small vessels will be able to stay afloat about 0·2M northeast of C'hraou beacon in 1·8m at low water. There is said to be a slightly deeper runnel near line D, the position of which is variable, but may be found by sounding.

   The disadvantage of all these positions is the long and rather exposed dinghy journey to reach the facilities of the port. Landing may be made on rocks on the shore over ¼M away, but the nearest reasonable landing place, which also carries more water than the outer harbour itself, is at the lifeboat slip, just south of the Banc du C'hraou.

2. The Port de Perros has a large wet basin in which there is a yacht marina. The basin is enclosed by a wall which maintains a level of 7m above datum within and is marked by five red and white poles. The gate is on the east side and it is opened when the level of the tide is at or above 7m.

   The wall is well covered at HW springs but it may not be possible for the gate to be worked at weak neap tides for 2 or 3 days. There are no visitors' berths as such but yachts are directed to one of the pontoons and left to find a vacant berth. The quays outside the basin are used by fishermen, and dry 3 to 4·8m.

3. In westerly weather there is a good temporary anchorage on the southeast side of Ile Tomé, 0·15M offshore in about 3·6m, sand and shells. The island is precipitous and uninhabited.

Facilities

Water and electricity are laid on to the pontoons in the marina. Showers and toilets in the *bureau du port*. There are moorings laid in the northern part of the harbour and a fuelling pontoon is moored just north of the lock, which can supply petrol, diesel and *Butagaz*. There are reasonable shopping facilities, several hotels and restaurants, a laundrette and a post office at the port.

Bus service to Lannion railway station.

It is about a mile uphill to Perros Guiréc town itself, which has all the facilities of a holiday resort. There is an interesting 12th-century church.

21. Ploumanac'h

Charts

BA *3670*
Imray *C34*
SHOM *967* (new chart in preparation 1992)
ECM Navicarte *537, 538*

Tidal data

Tidal heights (approx)

HW −0105 St Helier, −0600 Dover, +0120 Brest
MTL 4·9m. Index 9A
Heights of tide above chart datum
MHWS 8·9m, MLWS 0·9m, MHWN 7·0m, MLWN 3·4m

Tidal streams

Between Ile Rennat and Méan Ruz the east-going stream begins −0435 Brest (+0035 Dover) and the west-going stream begins +0100 Brest (+0610 Dover). Both streams attain 2·8 knots at springs, but are much stronger to seaward towards Les Sept Iles.

General

The entrance to Ploumanac'h lies between dramatic looking rocks about ¼M west of Méan Ruz lighthouse and leads to a beautiful, shallow, almost land-locked bay. Except where there is silting, the sill across the entrance to the inner harbour maintains a depth of 1·5m or more at low water and there are a number of trots of dumbbell moorings for yachts. The moorings just inside the sill are for fishing boats. The remarkable rock formations surrounding the harbour make Ploumanac'h well worth visiting under suitable conditions.

Approaches

Make a position about 0·3M west of Méan Ruz lighthouse and the entrance will be seen clearly. It lies east of the little island of Costaérès on which stands a prominent *château*. The entrance is now clearly marked by conspicuous beacons, six port and four starboard. The fourth port beacon (No. 8) has a

Ploumanac'h, looking south.

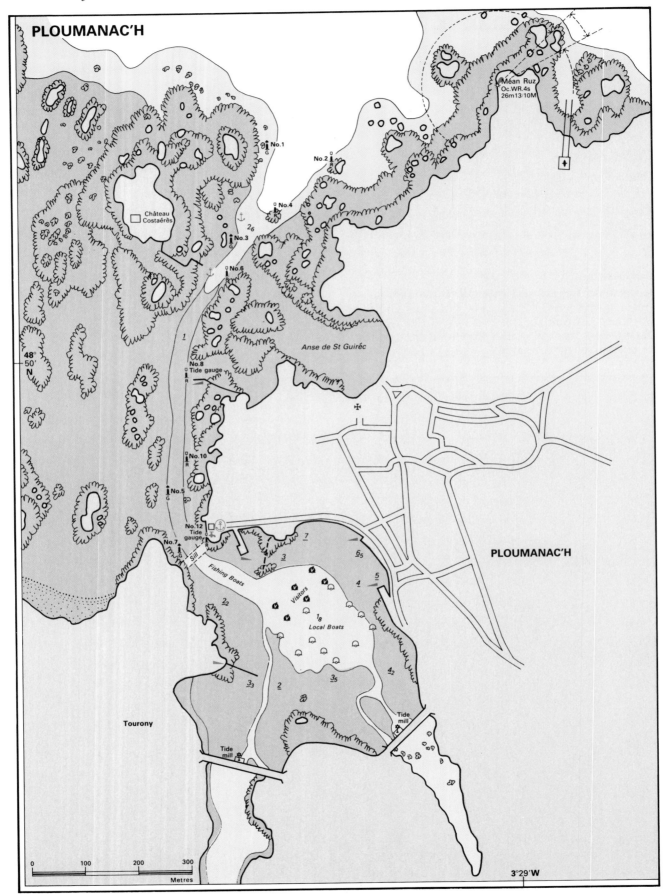

PLOUMANAC'H

Château Costaérès

Méan Ruz
Oc.WR.4s
26m13/10M

No.1
G

No.2
R

No.4

No.3

2.6

No.6
R

Anse de St Guiréc

No.8
Tide gauge
R

No.10
R

No.5
G

No.12
Tide gauge
R

No.7
G

Sill

Fishing Boats

Visitors

Local Boats

PLOUMANAC'H

Tourony

Tide mill

Tide mill

48°
50'
N

3°29'W

0   100   200   300
Metres

Plan 23. Ploumanac'h

Ploumanac'h entrance bearing 208°. Château Costaérès far right.

Approaching the sill. Tide gauge on port beacon is submerged indicating adequate depth for entry.

Moorings at low water from the *bureau du port*. The front row is
for visitors, but there was more water at the third row in. (1991).

depth gauge attached, with red and white divisions of
0·25m. The depth gauge will be submerged at high
water. The beacons sometimes become broken. The
channel leads to a wet basin, depths over the sill
being indicated by a gauge on the port side of the
sill, also submerged near high water. The sill dries
3·25m.

Anchorages

2m can be found inside the entrance east of the islet
on which the *château* stands, with room to swing. At
neaps, with soundings, it is possible to anchor to the
west of the channel northwest of port beacon No. 8.
Care must be taken approaching and leaving as there
are dangerous half-tide rocks adjacent.

Moorings are laid on the port side of the entrance
channel for the use of yachts waiting for water to
enter the basin, however these are often occupied by
fishing boats.

At half tide there should be 1·6m over the sill.
Near high water the gauge covers and there will be
more than 2·75m over the sill. Enter the basin and
secure alongside a pair of white balloon fenders on
aluminium rods, with pick-up lines with red cork
floats. The outer row is reserved for visitors but the
deepest water when the sill uncovers is to be found in
row 'C' (minimum 2m). Either side of this the
bottom shelves and to the SE the moorings are only
suitable for small boats.

Facilities

Toilets and drinking water tap by *bureau du port* at
northern end of sill. Shops, hotels, restaurants and
marine engineers. Good Bathing. No fuel berth, two
garages about 1km SW of basin. Bus to Perros
Guirec and Lannion railway station.

22. Les Sept Iles

Charts

BA *3669, 3670*
Imray *C34*
SHOM *967* (new chart in preparation 1992)
ECM Navicarte *537*

Tidal data

Tidal heights (approx)

HW −0105 St Helier, −0600 Dover, +0120 Brest
MTL 4·9m. Index 9A
Heights of tide above chart datum
MHWS 8·8m, MLWS 0·9m, MHWN 6·7m, MLWN 3·0m

Tidal streams

1. 1M southwest of Ile aux Moines the SE-going stream begins at −0435 Brest (+0035 Dover) and the NW-going at +0130 Brest (−0545 Dover). Both streams reach 4·7 knots at springs.
2. Between the Sept Iles and Plateau des Triagoz the ENE-going stream begins at −0320 Brest (+0150 Dover) and the WSW-going at +0250 Brest (−0425 Dover). Both streams reach 3·8 knots at springs.
3. 1M south of Ile Rouzic (the easternmost of Les Sept Iles) the SE-going stream begins at −0435 Brest (+0035 Dover) and the NW-going at +0130 Brest (−0545 Dover). Both streams reach 2·8 knots at springs.

General

The group consists of four principal islands (uninhabited except for the lighthouse keepers on Ile aux Moines), and many islets. There are many dangers and strong tidal streams within the group but there is no difficulty in entering the anchorage between Ile de Bono and Ile aux Moines under suitable conditions.

Approach

By day

If approaching from the east, first make a position close south of Les Dervinis S cardinal buoy, which lies 105° from Ile aux Moines lighthouse, distant 1·4M. Leaving this buoy close to starboard, with the lighthouse bearing 285°, steer to make good 285°.

If approaching from the west, make an easterly course, passing about 0·5M to the south of Le Cerf and Ile aux Moines.

When the gap between Ile aux Moines and Ile de Bono has opened, and the western end of Ile de Bono bears 345°, alter course to make good 345°. These directions clear the dangers shown on the chart but, as these are marked by reference to LAT they may in practice be ignored at most states of tide, e.g. at MLWN there will be a least depth of 3m over them.

By night

The narrow white sector of Kerjean light, DirOc (2+1)12s, bearing between 143·2° and 144·8° and flanked by a red sector to the east and a green sector to the west, leads on a reciprocal course of between 323·2° and 324·8° into the anchorage very close to the outer rock marked as drying 0m and over the 0·3m rock, but clear of the dangers to the east.

With adequate tide, as in *By day* above there should be no difficulty in approaching the anchorage, or in leaving it. The light on Ile aux Moines Fl(3)15s also helps to pinpoint the anchorage.

Anchorage

The anchorage lies southeast of the gap between Ile aux Moines and Ile de Bono with Ile aux Moines lighthouse bearing about 270° and the west end of Ile de Bono bearing about 360°. There is a mooring buoy in the anchorage which is used by *vedettes* from the mainland and, in any case, is not suitable for yachts.

Anchor between the buoy and the landing slip, which has a beacon at its end. Do not go far directly north of the buoy towards the strand between the two islands as there are two rocks which cover towards high water. The anchorage is protected from the NNE and NE by Ile de Bono and from the W by Ile aux Moines. The strand of sand, stones and rocks which dry out between the two islands, breaks the seas from that direction, but the anchorage must be regarded as a fair-weather one, as it is open to all southerly winds. The anchorage is frequently rather full of yachts in the daytime, particularly at weekends. Land at the slip from which a road leads up to the lighthouse.

Historical and amenities

The only inhabitants of the islands are the lighthouse keepers on Ile aux Moines, although at one time the islands were a resort of corsairs. The old fort on the western side of Ile aux Moines was occupied until 1875, and is worth seeing. There are striking views from the fort over the islets, rocks and inlets of the sea. In season many *vedettes* carry tourists to the island, when a *buvette* is opened on the terrace overlooking the anchorage. The neighbouring Ile de Bono is a bird sanctuary where landing is forbidden.

Ile aux Moines lighthouse bearing 020° with the west end of Ile de
Bono and the anchorage concealed by the sloping headland. Ile de
Malban far right.

The anchorage off Ile aux Moines slip.

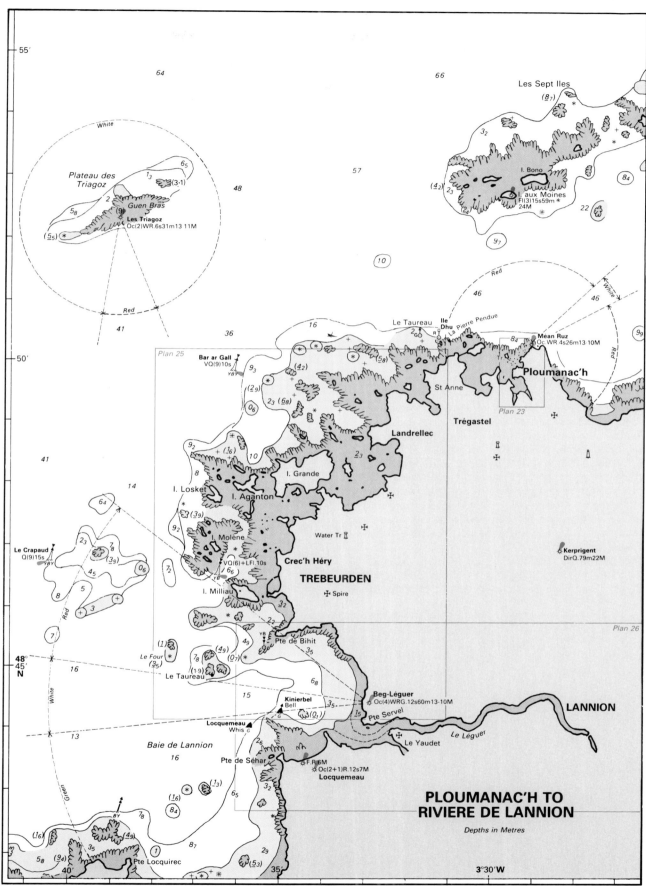

Plan 24. Ploumanac'h to Rivière de Lannion

23. Trégastel Sainte Anne

Charts
BA *3669, 3670*
Imray *C34*
SHOM *967* (new chart in preparation)
ECM Navicarte *538*

Tidal data
See under Ploumanac'h, page 95.

General
This anchorage should not be confused with the seaside village of the same name near Primel. It is situated on the rocky coast about a mile west of Ploumanac'h and less than 3M southwest of the Sept Iles.

Trégastel is worth visiting when cruising in these waters.

Approach
By day only
Make a position 1·5M west of Méan Ruz lighthouse. Observe the prominent overhanging rock La Pierre Pendue (see photograph below) locally known as the *dice* rock. About 0·2M west of this rock is the low rocky Ile Dhu and Le Taureau a dangerous rock which dries 4·5m LAT about 0·2M farther west. This should be marked by a N cardinal beacon but it is frequently washed away. It was in position in 1989 and 1991, but in 1990 only the concrete stump was standing. Its presence should not therefore be taken for granted.

Le Taureau beacon, or its stump, should be identified before attempting to enter, and approach for the first time is therefore easier at half tide or below. Make a position about halfway between Ile Dhu and Le Taureau and note the prominent house ashore, which is shown in the photograph (not to be confused with the rather similar house near Méan Ruz lighthouse). Bring this house to bear between 165° and 170°. Steer to make good this course allowing for any crosscurrent. Then leave:

Le Taureau N cardinal beacon (if existing) 0·125M to starboard.
Ile Dhu port beacon 0·125M to port.
Second port beacon 100m to port.
First starboard beacon 50m to starboard.
Third port beacon 50m to port.

Anchorage
A number of white mooring buoys have been laid and space for anchoring may be difficult to find. Many moorings are occupied by local boats. There is a greater depth to the northwest, less to the east, and soundings should be taken. The anchorage is better sheltered than appears on the chart, from east through south to southwest. As at Port Blanc and Primel there is often a swell if the wind is from a northerly quarter and the anchorage would be dangerous in strong onshore winds. There are no leading lights to facilitate departure at night.

Facilities
Land by dinghy on the sands. There are hotels and restaurants on the front but no shops. Baths can be had (not cheaply) at the Grand Hôtel de la Mer, which has an obliging management who serve excellent meals at a reasonable price. The town of St-Anne is nearly half a mile inland, where there are a post office, garage and shops. Trégastel itself is about a mile farther inland. The bay makes a very pretty little seaside resort, with bathing huts facing wide sands and is almost landlocked at low water. This could be a good place for the family cruising man,

Trégastel from north of Le Taureau beacon and west of the entrance. La Pierre Pendue far left.

Prominent house for entry, right centre, bearing 165°.

provided he is ready to clear out if there is a threat of inclement weather.

Bus service to Lannion railway station.

24. Trébeurden and Ile Grande

Charts
BA *3669*
Imray *C34*
SHOM *7151, 7124*
ECM Navicarte *538*

Tidal data

Tidal heights (approx)
HW +0110 Brest, +0620 Dover
MTL 5·1m. Index 9B
Heights of tide above chart datum
MHWS 9·1m, MLWS 1·3m, MHWN 7·2m, MLWN 3·5m

Tidal streams
1. Northeast of Ile Losket the ENE-going stream begins at −0335 Brest (+0135 Dover) and the WSW-going stream at +0230 Brest (−0445 Dover). Both streams attain 3·8 knots at springs.
2. 0·5M southwest of Ile Losket the N-going stream begins at −0355 Brest (+0115 Dover) and the S-going begins +0200 Brest (−0515 Dover). Spring rate about 2 knots.
3. At Le Crapaud buoy the SE to E-going stream begins at −0405 Brest (+0105 Dover) and the SW to W-going stream at +0220 Brest (−0455 Dover). Both streams reach 2 knots at springs.

General
Until recently Trébeurden and Ile Grande were rarely visited by British yachts, but they deserved more attention as Trébeurden has one of the few deep-water and readily accessible anchorages on this part of the coast and leads to a delightful neap-tide anchorage off Ile Grande. When visited in 1990, the construction of a marina at Trébeurden was well under way and the harbourmaster told me that it would be operating in the summer of 1991. However, all work was halted in the spring of 1991 as a result of environmental objections and the future of the marina depends on decisions taken after a public enquiry.

Trébeurden is situated to the east of the prominent Ile Milliau, at the northern entrance to the bay of Lannion. SHOM *7124* is desirable.

Approaches
SOUTHERN APPROACH
CHENAL DE TOULL AR MEN MELEN
By day only
This is a deep-water channel but there are two rocks awash at chart datum less than 0·5M north of the approach, and rocks to the south as shown on the plan. Make a position 1·25M south of Le Crapaud W cardinal spar buoy, marking the end of Le Crapaud shoals. Identify the conspicuous Ile Milliau some 3M away, bearing about 075°. See photograph on page 106. Make good a course of 070°. When about a mile off the island the Ar Gouredec S cardinal buoy will clearly be seen about 0·3M northwest of the island. Bring this in line with the W cardinal beacon on An Ervennou bearing 061°.

If bound for Trébeurden anchorage steer for the point north of Trébeurden bearing 067° and when 0·1M from Ervennou beacon, alter course to make good 120° into the anchorage.

If bound north, alter course so as to leave An Ervennou beacon 0·1M to starboard when Les Trois Frères E cardinal beacon, northeast of Ile Molène will be in line with the eastern edge of Ile Losket bearing 358°.

Follow this line for about 0·3M until Karreg ar Jantil S cardinal beacon and Karreg ar Merk E cardinal beacon tower are in line bearing 043°.

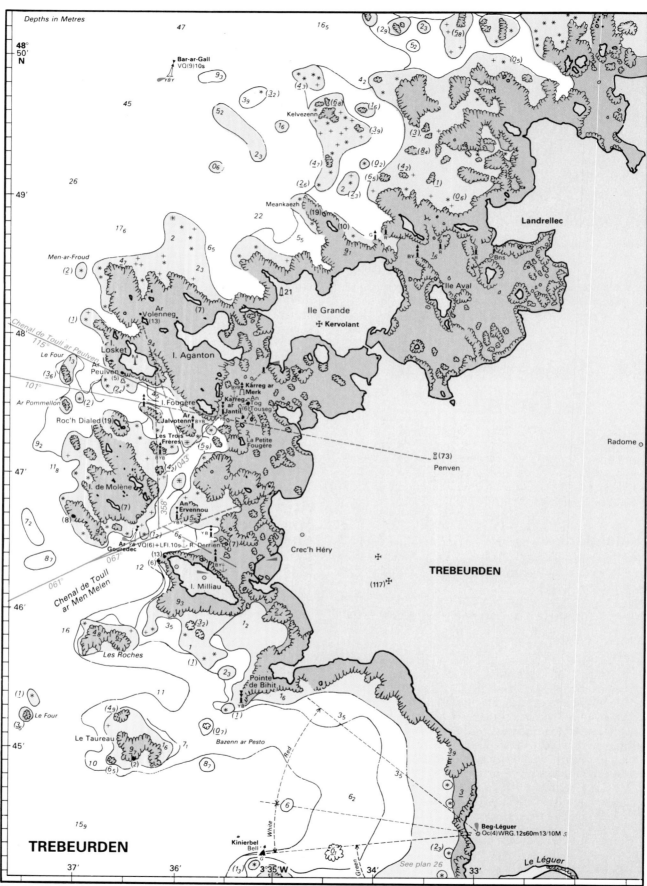

Plan 25. Trebeurden

Trébeurden, looking southeast. Ile Milliau on the right. Radome
on left edge of photograph.

If the tide serves this line can be followed to the Ile
Grande anchorage, but it passes 20m to the
northwest of Karreg Kervareg a rock which dries
2·4m LAT. Leave Karreg ar Jentil close to port and
then borrow to port to be sure to clear another rock
drying 2·4m, 50m east of the line and halfway
between the beacon and beacon tower. Leave Karreg
ar Merk 20m to starboard.

If bound for the northern entrance in order to exit,
follow this transit for 0·2M when Ar Volenneg island
will just be appearing beyond the eastern edge of Ile
Losket bearing 344°. Alter course to follow this
transit leaving, Ar Jalvotenn E cardinal beacon 200m
to starboard and Ar Moc'h Gwenn N cardinal beacon
100m to port, to join the lines directed for northern
approach below.

NORTHERN APPROACH
By day only

The outer approach may be made with Les Triagoz
lighthouse bearing 360°. Identify Ile Losket, which is
steep sided with a number of short white radio masts
on it. Then identify Ar Peulven, a very conspicuous
rock, elevation 5m, painted white on south side,
situated 100m off the southwest corner of Ile Losket.

CHENAL DE TOULL AR PEULVEN
By day only

There are two alternatives:

1. Using an up-to-date SHOM 7124, steer with the
   southern tip of Ile Fougère just open of Ar
   Peulven at 115°, leaving Le Four (dries 3·6m
   LAT) about 300m to starboard. This approach is

deep but, when off Ar Peulven, keep close to this
rock as there is a drying shoal 2·4m LAT only
about 50m SSE of it which must be left to
starboard.

2. Identify Penven water tower which, from a
   position 1M west of Ile Losket will appear just
   south of the conspicuous white radome. With the
   water tower bearing 101° it will be in transit with
   the right-hand end of Ile Fougère and over the
   grey roof of a long white building with two rows
   of windows behind the island.

   Follow this transit, with due allowance for tidal
   set, leaving Le Four and an associated group of
   drying rocks 100m to port and a rock drying 2m
   100m to starboard.

Neither entry should be attempted unless the
marks have been positively identified. The swell
breaking over rocks on either side is disconcerting
and it may be preferable to leave rather than enter by
these passages on a first visit.

In either case when Ar Volenneg appears beyond
the eastern edge of Ile Losket bearing 344° alter
course to make good the reciprocal 164° and proceed
as for southern approach above in reverse.

Alternatively, if bound for Ile Grande, alter to 120°
to pass midway between Ar Jalvotenn E cardinal
beacon and Ile Fougère, turning to join the leading
line described below.

ILE GRANDE, INNER APPROACH

The inner approach to Ile Grande is not difficult
when there is sufficient height of tide, and provides
an interesting and reasonably sheltered anchorage at
neap tides.

Approach from the southwest. North point of Ile Milliau with
disused coastguard station bearing 072°.

Looking north from Ile Milliau. Left, sandy beach on Ile Molène
at half tide. Upper right, channel to Ile Grande.

Looking south over Ile Grande slipway towards Trébeurden near low water.

From a position with Les Trois Frères E cardinal beacon bearing 270° distant 0·2M and Ar Jalvotenn E cardinal beacon bearing 015° distant 0·2M, follow the transit of Karreg ar Jantil S cardinal beacon and Karreg ar Merk E cardinal beacon tower in line, bearing 043°.

If the tide serves this line can be followed to the Ile Grande anchorage, but it passes 20m to the northwest of Karreg Kervareg a rock which dries 2·4m LAT. Leave Karreg ar Jentil close to port and then borrow to port to be sure to clear another rock drying 2·4m, 150m SW of the conspicuous knob An Tog Touseg. Leaving Karreg ar Merk 20m to starboard, proceed towards the pier.

Anchorages

Trébeurden

Anchor in 6m with the northwest edge of Ile Milliau bearing about 235° and Ar Erviniou beacon about 340°. Further east towards Trébeurden the bottom shoals rapidly, drying 1m between the north of the island and Roch Derrien, which is a conspicuous above-water rock. A number of mooring buoys were laid in this area in 1991 which were available to visitors for use at neaps, but the arrangements will probably alter if the marina project is completed. This anchorage is very uncomfortable at HW springs with winds W–SW for about two hours either side. There is a heavy swell from the NW. Shallow-draught vessels can anchor near the slip on Ile Milliau at neaps, the bottom being sand, drying 1·1m. With care it is possible to anchor southeast of

the isolated rock, which dries 4·2m, 100m NNE of the end of the slip and is marked by a N cardinal beacon.

Ile Grande

On a neap tide when the height of HW Brest is 6·1m there is 1·5m at MLWN between Karreg Jentil beacon and Karreg ar Merk beacon tower, and 1·8m close south of Karreg Jentil beacon. These positions are sheltered except when the wind is from the SW between Ile Molène and Ile Milliau, or if there is a swell from that direction. Usually the anchorage is very sheltered, as in this area in a southwesterly weather system the wind seems to blow from the W or WNW. Since swell is most commonly experienced from the NW, the anchorage is comparatively free from swell, being sheltered by islands from this direction. At HW, anchorage is good right up to the pier and boats which can take the ground may do so almost anywhere. See photograph above.

Facilities

There is a landing slip on Ile Milliau, a nature reserve with a well preserved dolmen near the farm buildings.

It is an uphill walk to Trébeurden where there are many hotels and restaurants, with banks and good shopping facilities. There are good beaches, in particular at Ile Molène and, in settled weather, it is an ideal harbour for the cruising man with a young family. If the large-scale SHOM 7124 is carried there are opportunities to explore the neighbouring islands, as well as the HW anchorage at Ile Grande.

At Kervolant, the village on Ile Grande, there are good shops and restaurants. Fuel can be obtained from a garage at Kervolant. Water may be had from a tap at the head of the slip.

Bus service to Lannion railway station.

25. Lannion

Charts

BA *3669*
Imray *C34*
SHOM *7151, 7124*
ECM Navicarte *538*

Tidal data

Tidal heights (approx)

HW +0110 Brest, +0620 Dover
MTL 5·1m. Index 9B
Heights of tide above chart datum
MHWS 8·8m, MLWS 1·3m, MHWN 6·7m, MLWN 3·5m

Tidal streams

1. *For approaches see under Trébeurden and Primel.*
2. Within the Baie de Lannion the streams are weak, attaining only one knot at spring tides and are variable in direction.

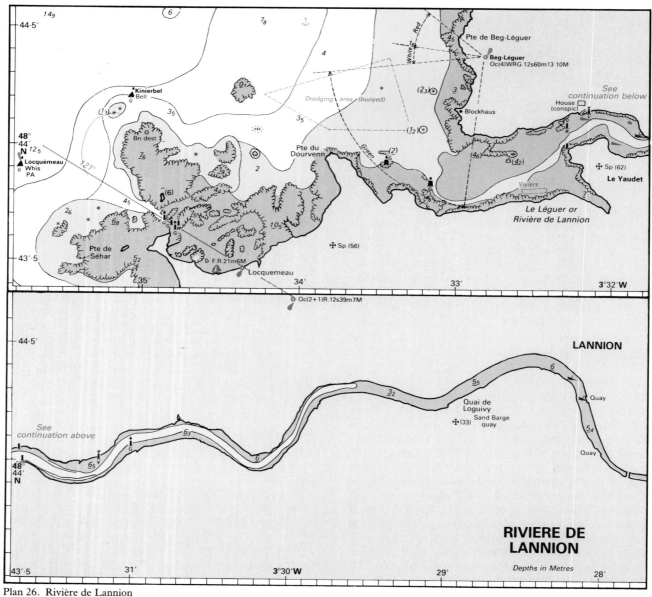

Plan 26. Rivière de Lannion

Lannion river entrance looking east.

General

The port of a large town 4M from the open sea on the Rivière de Lannion, alias Le Léguer, which is narrow and twisting and dries for almost its entire length. With a strong wind between NW and WNW, the sea is liable to break across the entrance, which is then impassable, even at high water. No doubt a large westerly swell makes the bar equally dangerous, especially on the ebb, but the entrance is partly or wholly protected from winds from other directions. The reason why the river is so little used by deep-keeled yachts is that, although there are now deep pools in which to anchor, access to them is tidal and it is off the beaten track from Roscoff to Perros. The navigation is also described as difficult and requiring local knowledge. It is, however, not as difficult as reputed, and the river is exceptionally pretty. Lannion itself is a pleasant country town. In places the channel of the river is marked by beacons and dries 4·8m at Lannion. As a result of dredging for sand, there are now an increasing number of deep pools in which yachts can anchor, even at spring tides.

A scheme to construct a small marina on the south bank at Lannion was under way in 1988, but the project was found to have been abandoned in 1990. On inspection at low water the river bed was seen to be foul in many places, two of the three wharfs had wrecks alongside. The third, upstream near the bridge on the south bank is suitable for a short visit at high water, but several large tractor tyres lying on the bottom would make grounding hazardous. These may well be cleared at some future date.

Approach

By day

The sand dredger at work in the river has formed a narrow channel across the sandbank inside the entrance. However entry should be made between half tide and high water, to allow for deviations. The bar, lying north of Pointe du Dourvenn, no longer dries and, in the absence of swell, is protected from NE through E to S.

Make a position from which Le Crapaud W cardinal pillar buoy bears 360° distant 2M. From here steer so as to bring Beg Léger 'lighthouse' (a white house on the ridge north of the entrance, flanked by trees and not, at first sight, easy to locate) on a bearing of 095°, and then make this good as the course. This leaves:

Le Taureau rocks about 0·3M to port.

Locquémeau starboard whistle buoy 0·5M to starboard.

Kinierbel starboard bell buoy 0·25M to starboard.

The beacon formerly on Kinierbel rocks is destroyed and has not been replaced. When the second starboard beacon tower in the estuary has

Lannion river, slip with sailing club on north bank opposite Le Yaudet. Note sand dredger at work.

opened to the left of the first, course can be altered for the river entrance.

Leave the first beacon tower 150m to starboard and the second close to starboard, then endeavour to follow the channel as shown on plan 26 page 108, keeping about 100m off the southern bank and sweeping round to the NE to head for the slipway and house on the north bank (see photograph), leaving Le Petit Taureau islet about 200m to port.

After Pierre Noire port beacon is passed the channel curves round to starboard and is indicated by a number of boats on moorings. Avoid the wide spit off the south bank as the river curves round Le Yaudet, where small local boats dry out.

Here the river is extremely pretty and the best water farther upstream is found in the bights on the opposite side of the river to the headlands.

In the reach 0·5M beyond Le Yaudet there is a starboard beacon at the bend (see plan 26) where the channel lies on the north side.

In the upper reaches the river is narrow and partially canalised. The first quays to be reached are used by the sand dredger, and a bridge has been constructed downstream of the quay which was formerly most convenient for visiting yachts, making it now necessary to berth for a short stay at HW at the last quay on the starboard side before the bridge. The quay farther downstream on the port side was obstructed in 1990. A yacht of 1·8m draught will take the bottom about 2 hours after HW. The river bottom is mud and rocks and, with other manmade obstructions in places, it would be dangerous to dry out, if a yacht is accidentally grounded on the ebb.

By night

Approach from the north or northwest by keeping to the west of the red sector of Les Triagoz Oc(2)WR.6s bearing between 010° and 020°.

Then pick up the leading lights for Locquémeau: rear Oc(2+1)R.12s7M and front F.R.6M, bearing 122°. Steer to follow this line which leaves Le Crapaud and associated dangers about 0·5M on the port hand.

When Beg Léger light, Oc(4)WRG.12s, changes from red to white alter course and steer towards it in the white sector, which leads into the outer anchorage.

Anchorages

1. Outside, with the wind from N through E to SSW, there is sheltered anchorage in the bay immediately north of the river mouth, known as the Mouillage de Bihit.
2. A yacht can take the ground at Le Yaudet against the outer part of the quay, where it dries about 2·1m LAT.
3. For several years now the bed of the river has been dredged for sand, leaving deep pools suitable for anchorage without obstructing the passage of the sand dredger. These pools can however silt up with time and in 1990 the river was found to dry from a position 0·5M upstream of Le Yaudet slipway. The river is full of moorings from the

The river at LW just below Lannion.

slipway and riverside house on the north shore, beyond the first port beacon, up to well beyond Le Yaudet slip.

a. At the time of *Capelan*'s visit it was possible to anchor upstream of the house and slipway, where there is an active sailing club. At the turn of the tide one must ensure that the yacht swings clear of the moorings and the spit off Le Yaudet.

b. Anchorage was preferred in a pool east of Le Yaudet slipway in 1·2m least water, but again care must be taken to see how the yacht swings and lies during ebb and flood.

The positions of other anchorages may be found by soundings but, as they are in the nature of pools, it is better to obtain local advice from the skipper of the sand dredger who knows where the bottom has been dredged as, in some parts, the bed of the river is rocky and the streams are strong.

The anchorages near Le Yaudet are now excellent as they are not far from the entrance and the river is beautiful.

Facilities

Lannion

Lannion is a large town with banks, good shops, restaurants and other facilities. The restaurant Relais de Bretagne is well spoken of. Petrol and oil from garage near the quay, and water at a hydrant. Customs office. Yacht club. Branch line station. Airport and buses.

Le Yaudet

Land at the slip and walk up the steep hill to occasional mobile shop (sometimes on station in mornings) and two good restaurants. Picturesque little church with a curious statue of the Virgin Mary in bed with the infant Jesus.

Narrows in Toull an Héry approach near HW. The channel and anchorage dry. Enter on a rising tide and only if you can take the ground!

Toull an Héry and Locquirec

Toull an Héry

Toull an Héry is a small drying harbour on the east bank of the Douron river, a mile from the open sea. The channel leading to it is encumbered with shifting sandbanks and the berths alongside the jetty dry 4·8m.

Locquirec

Locquirec is a small drying harbour on the west side of the entrance to the same river. The berths alongside the jetty dry from 4·5m to 6·1m LAT, and there is considerable surf in the harbour with the wind in the exposed quarter.

The Anse de Locquirec lies about 0·5M east of Locquirec, and affords anchorage in 2·7m and upwards, sand, sheltered from west through south to southeast.

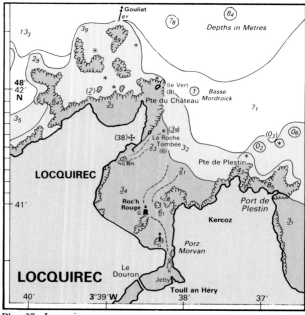

Plan 27. Locquirec

26. Primel

Charts

BA *3669, 2745*
Imray *C34*
SHOM *7151, 7095*
ECM Navicarte *538*

Tidal data

Tidal heights (approx)

HW +0105 Brest, +0620 Dover
MTL 4·9m. Index 8B
Heights of tide above chart datum
MHWS 8·5m, MLWS 1·2m, MHWN 6·7m, MLWN 3·0m

Tidal streams

1. About 6M north of Primel the E-going stream begins at −0300 Brest (+0210 Dover), and the W-going at +0315 Brest (−0400 Dover). The greatest rate of the E-going is attained at about HW Brest and of the W-going at LW Brest, both reaching 2·25 knots at springs; about 1 knot at neaps.
2. *For streams to the west of Plateau des Duons, see under Morlaix.*
3. A local eddy runs inshore between Pointe de Primel and Roches Jaunes (1·5M to the west) during the greater part of the E-going stream in the offing. The eddy NE-going (2 knots at springs) begins at −0450 Brest (+0020 Dover) and SW-going (2·5 knots at springs) begins at −0220 Brest (+0250 Dover).

General

The Anse de Primel is a small natural harbour, which has been improved by the construction of a breakwater and quay. The entrance itself is easily identified and is fairly simple to enter by day or night. In the offing however there are dangers:

Les Trépieds drying rocks about 2·5M to the north, about 0·75M to the east of the leading line, and extending, as the Plateau de la Meloine, 4·5M to the northeast.

Les Chaises de Primel drying rocks which extend for about 2·5M from Pointe de Primel to the northeast.

Les Roches Jaunes which extend for about 2M to the southwest. At high water the harbour is exposed to winds from NW to N by E, and might be dangerous in heavy weather from this quarter, when the sea is said to break right across the entrance, and no attempt should be made to enter. Conversely, any yacht using the anchorage should be prepared to leave on the approach of bad weather from the north. It is uncomfortable if there is any northwest or northerly swell, except possibly under the lee of the breakwater.

Primel looking SSE into the entrance. Small fishing boat entering from left below Roc'h Camm. Larger boat entering from right to leave Ar Zammeguez rock (white patch) to starboard.

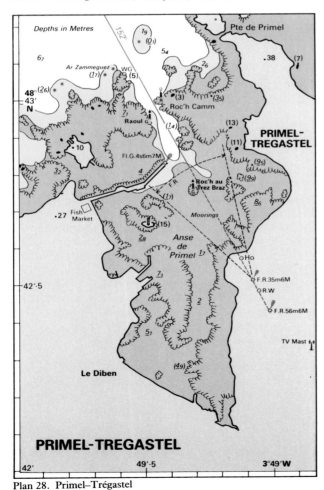

PRIMEL-TREGASTEL

Plan 28. Primel–Trégastel

Approaches

By day

First identify the prominent Pointe de Primel, and then make a position from which this point bears 120°, distant 0·5M. From here bring the leading marks in line at 151°. These are:

1. The lowest is the white chimney of Réprédou Farm (unpainted 1991).
2. The white support with vertical red line of the front leading light, elevation 35m.
3. White wall mark with red vertical line.
4. White wall mark with red vertical line and rear light, elevation 56m.

Follow this line very closely, noting that the submerged dangers lie to port, and leave the following marks on the sides shown:

Ar Zammeguez, a prominent rock with a green and white patch, 30m to starboard.
Cam port beacon 30m to port.
Raoul starboard beacon 15m to starboard.

By night

Approaching south·of Les Meloines from the east or west, keep on the line of the edge of the green and white sectors of Men-Guen Braz Q.WRG at 257°, until the Primel leading lights, both F.R, are in line bearing 151°. This point is slightly east of the intersection of this edge-line and the leading line for the Chenal de Tréguier, Morlaix. The front Primel light has an arc of 34° from 134° to 168°. See plan 28.

Approaching from the north, keep between the two Morlaix leading lines (Grand Chenal and Chenal de Tréguier), until the Primel lights are picked up or, failing this, until Men-Guen Braz (Q.WRG) changes

113

from white to green; showing that, course may be altered to the east along this line to pick up the Primel lights.

When the Primel lights are in line, bearing 151°, alter course to follow this line right through the entrance, leaving to starboard the Fl.G.4s light at the end of the breakwater.

Anchorages

Inside the harbour, the S-shaped pool trends, first slightly to the west of the leading line, then well to the east of it, round Roc'h-an-Trez-Braz starboard beacon. When the depth of water permits, a yacht may proceed farther up the harbour, following the line given by the stern transit Roc'h-an-Trez-Braz beacon in line with the western edge of Pointe de Primel. The following positions are available:

1. On visitors' moorings, a number of which do not dry, east of the starboard beacon, and the fishermen prefer visitors to take one of these to avoid congestion in this small harbour.
2. Moored with two anchors in the dredged area about 50m wide between the elbow in the breakwater and the outer end, in depths of between 0 and +1m LAT (about 1·2 to 2·1m MLWS and 3 to 3·9m MLWN).
3. Secure alongside the breakwater at the outermost of the two projections on the inner face near the light. The innermost elbow is used by fishing boats. Do not attempt to go alongside between the projections, as this part dries and there are rocks and boulders on the bottom.
4. On the leading line off the breakwater in about 9m MLWS.

The harbour is exposed to northerly winds. When anchoring, swinging room is rather restricted and it is advisable to moor if conditions call for a full scope of chain.

There are moorings for local boats, most of which dry, southwest of Roc'h-an-Trez-Braz and it may be possible to borrow one.

Primel leading marks after repainting.

Facilities

Landing: at the slip on the breakwater; at the small slip by the Plage de Primel; on the rocks to the west of the leading line; and at the landing slip at Le Diben on the west side of the harbour. Water tap by freezer building, where *crustacés* are for sale. There are a few shops and hotels at Primel and Le Diben.

27. Baie de Morlaix, Morlaix and Penzé rivers

Charts

BA *3669, 2745*
Imray *C35*
SHOM *7151, 7095*
ECM Navicarte *538*

Tidal data

Tidal heights (approx)
HW (Baie de Morlaix) +0105 Brest, +0610 Dover
MTL 5m. Index 8B
Heights of tide above chart datum
MHWS 8·8m, MLWS 1·2m, MHWN 6·7m, MLWN 3·3m

Tidal streams

1. North of Roches Duon the E-going stream begins −0505 Brest (+0005 Dover), gradually changing clockwise to end +0050 Brest (+0600 Dover) when running SSE. The SSW-going stream begins at +0140 Brest (−0535 Dover), changing clockwise through west and ending NNW at −0535 Brest (−0025 Dover). The SE-going and NW-going streams attain 2·75 knots at springs.
2. In the Grand Chenal and Chenal de Tréguier the ingoing stream begins about −0450 Brest (+0020 Dover) and the outgoing stream about +0105 Brest (−0610 Dover). The spring rates in the Grand Chenal are about 2·5 knots and in the Chenal de Tréguier about 2 knots.
3. In the Rade de Morlaix the streams are weak and variable attaining about 1 knot at springs. The ingoing stream begins about −0430 Brest (+0040 Dover) and the outgoing +0200 Brest (−0515 Dover).
4. In the Rivière de Morlaix to 0·5M above Locquénolé the rate of the ingoing stream does not exceed 2 knots and in the canalised part of the river the stream nearly always runs north.
5. In the Rivière de Penzé the ingoing stream begins about −0450 Brest (+0020 Dover) and the outgoing stream about +0105 Brest (−0610 Dover). In the river the spring rate does not exceed 2·5 knots.

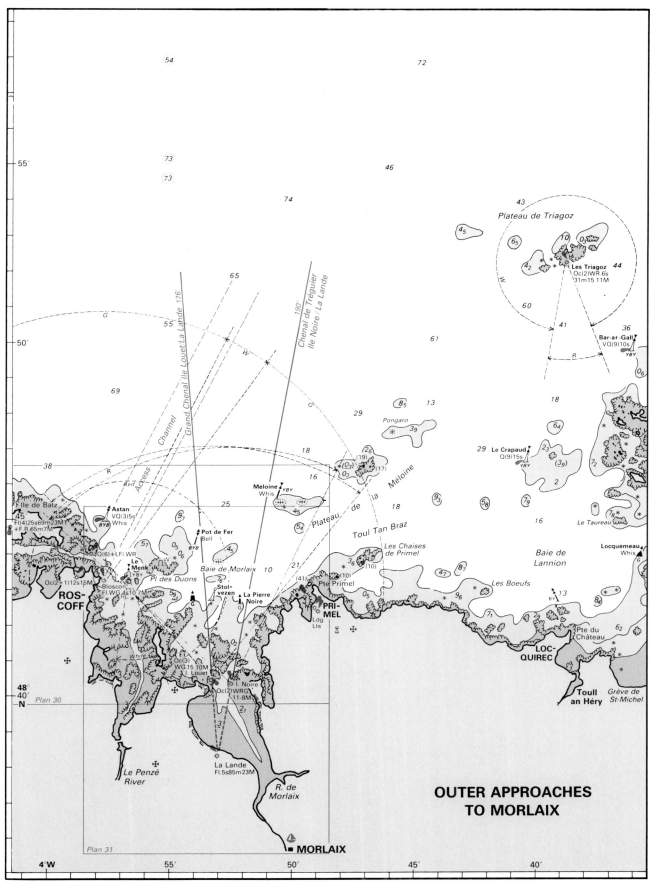

**OUTER APPROACHES
TO MORLAIX**

Plan 29. Outer approaches to Morlaix

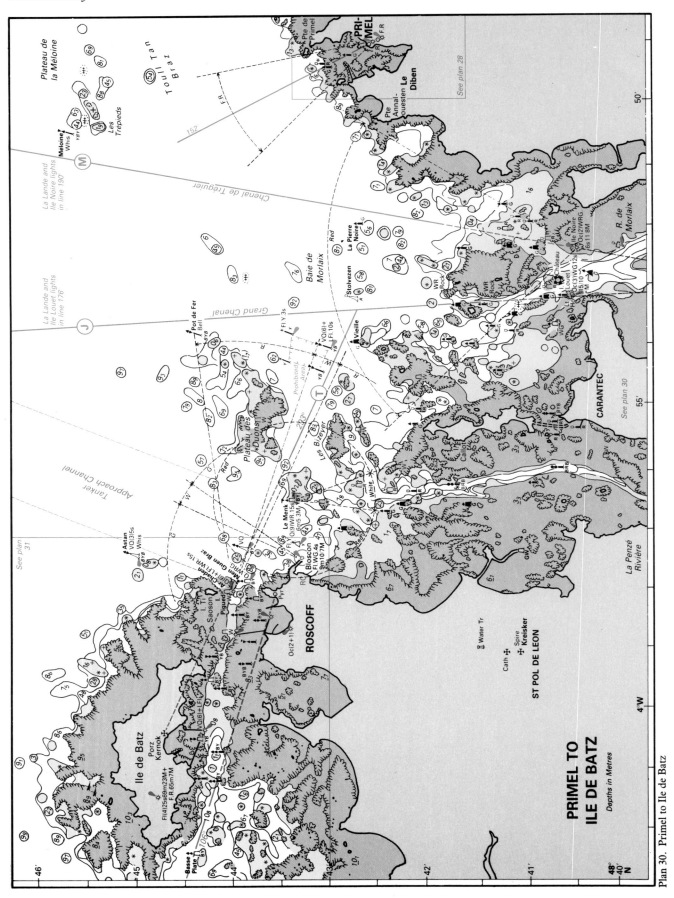

**PRIMEL TO
ILE DE BATZ**

Depths in Metres

Plan 30. Primel to Ile de Batz

General

The Morlaix and Penzé rivers flow into the Baie de Morlaix which is about 6M wide, between (on the east) Pointe de Primel and (on the west) Roscoff and the eastern entrance to the Ile de Batz channel. A vessel approaching from the north has to pass through a 2·5M-wide gap between the Méloine W cardinal spar whistle buoy, marking the western end of the Plateau de la Méloine and Le Pot de Fer E cardinal spar bell buoy, marking the eastern end of the Plateau des Duons.

Both the outer lit channels pass through this gap, as does also the leading line for Primel already mentioned. Approach on a clear night presents no difficulty but in poor visibility, a vessel with RDF facilities, would be better advised to home on Port Bloscon radiobeacon, *BC* 304·5 kHz, on a course of about 225°. This is clear of the tanker track to and from Roscoff, one mile wide, running 202°–022° from the breakwater light. This is about ten miles long, which is the nominal range of the beacon. Approach can then be made as if coming from the Chenal de l'Ile de Batz.

South of the Pot de Fer buoy, between the buoy and La Vieille starboard beacon tower, in a square marked by yellow buoys, is moored a large tanker with a supporting tug. This has been converted into a salmon farm and entry into the area marked out is prohibited. The NE corner yellow buoy is lit Fl.Y.3s. The SE corner is marked by a lit S cardinal buoy.

Approaches

GRAND CHENAL – TO RIVIERE DE MORLAIX
By day

The principal entrance to the Baie de Morlaix is the Grand Chenal due north of Penn ar Lann. This provides two alternative routes to La Rivière de Morlaix and access to the Rivière de Penzé. Navigate so as to pass 0·2M east of the Pot de Fer E cardinal spar bell buoy. This buoy lies about a mile NE of the Roches Duon white beacon tower, 9·7m high. From here follow the leading line 176°: Ile Louet lighthouse in line with Tour de la Lande, line J, (see photo). This line leaves the following marks on the sides shown:

Salmon farm vessel 0·5M to starboard.
Stolvezen port spindle buoy 0·1M to port.
La Vieille starboard beacon tower 0·4M to starboard.
La Fourche starboard beacon 0·3M to starboard.
Le Gouesles a rock painted white and red 0·1M to port.
Le Ricard starboard beacon tower 55m to starboard.
La Morlouine starboard beacon 45m to starboard.
Les Cahers a rock painted white and red 0·1M to port.
Calhic starboard beacon tower 0·15M to starboard.

When Calhic tower bears about 290°, quit the leading line and steer about 160° so as to leave:

Le Corbeau starboard beacon tower 100m to starboard.
Le Taureau port beacon tower 100m to port.

Then pass midway between Ile Louet and the Château du Taureau. From here steer to leave Barre de Flot, starboard buoy marking a 0·3m rocky shoal, to starboard and proceed into the river. If bound for the Penn Lann anchorage leave the Barre de Flot buoy 250m to port.

GRAND CHENAL AND CHENAL OUEST DE RICARD – TO RIVIERE DE MORLAIX
By day

Proceed as for Grand Chenal, passing 0·2M east of Pot de Fer E cardinal spar bell buoy and follow the leading line 176°, Ile Louet–Tour de la Lande (line J), for a further mile until the salmon farm vessel is abaft the beam to starboard.

In the bay to the west of Penn ar Lann the two small white painted rocks of the Pierres de Carantec will, from this position, be in transit with a white wall mark (not always very clear) on the shore behind (line K) bearing 188°.

Baie de Morlaix, leading marks for the Grand Chenal. Ile Louet lighthouse in transit with La Lande on the skyline, centre, bearing 176°. La Lande is hard to identify from a distance and the channel is wide enough to make an approach using the beacon towers and islets on either side. Left to right: Ile Noire lighthouse, Château du Taureau, La Lande and Ile Louet, Pennar Lann point (with white pyramid), Ricard starboard beacon, and part of Ile Ricard.

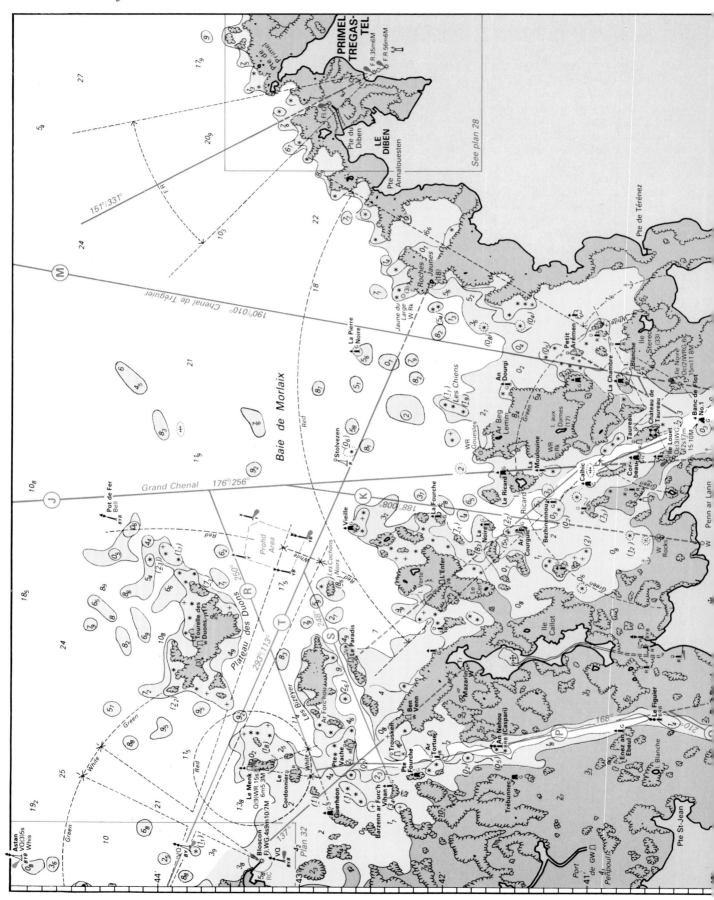

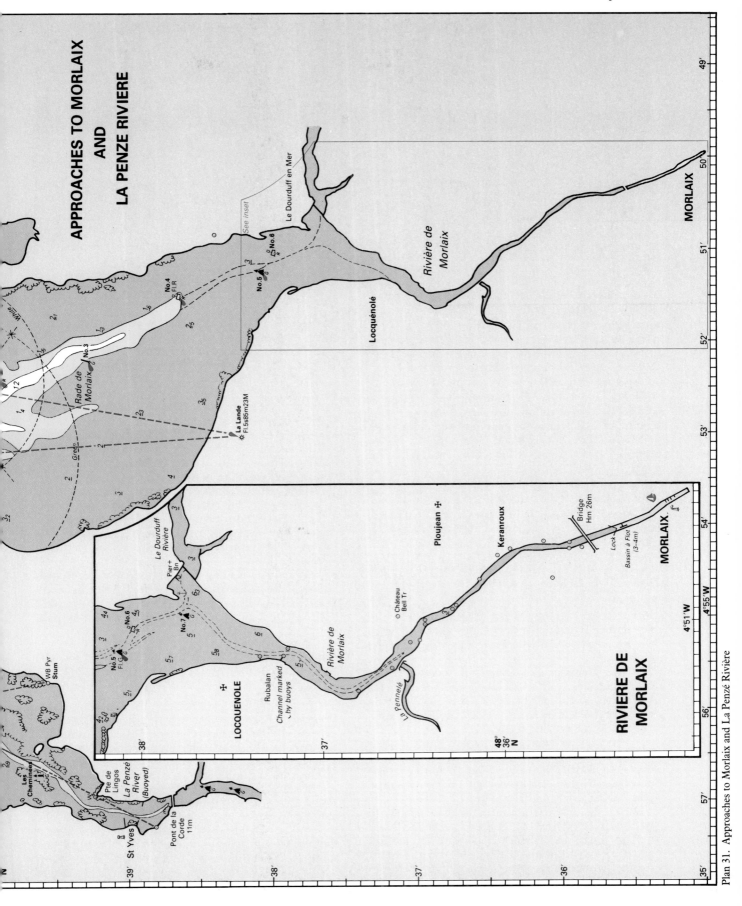

APPROACHES TO MORLAIX
AND
LA PENZE RIVIERE

Le Dourduff en Mer

See inset

No.6

No.4
Fl.R

No.5

White

No.3

Rivière de Morlaix

Rade de Morlaix

Locquénolé

La Lande
Fl.5s85m23M

Green

MORLAIX

Le Dourduff Rivière

Pier
Bn

No.6

No.7

No.5
Fl.G

LOCQUENOLE

Rubalan
Channel marked
by buoys

Rivière de Morlaix

Ploujean ✝

Château
Bell Tr

Keranroux

La Pennelé

RIVIERE DE
MORLAIX

Bridge
Hm 26m

Lock

Bassin à Flot
(3–4m)

MORLAIX

4°51'W

4°55'W

W/B Pyr
Stum

Les Cheminées

St Yves

Pte de
Lingos

La Penzé
River
(Buoyed)

Pont de la
Corde
11m

Plan 31. Approaches to Morlaix and La Penzé Rivière

Carantec, looking south. Chenal Ouest de Ricard leading marks left centre, Kergrist white mark is seen over the left-hand white painted rock of the two Pierres de Carantec. The correct transit is 188·5°.

Alter course to starboard to follow this line which leaves the following marks on the sides shown:

Stolvezen port spindle buoy 0·2M to port.
La Vieille starboard beacon tower 0·2M to starboard.
La Fourche starboard beacon 135m to starboard.
La Noire starboard beacon 135m to starboard.
Ar Courguic starboard beacon 135m to starboard.

Just before reaching Ar Courguic alter course to make good 139° to follow the stern transit: Trépied Jaune (alias L'Enfer) white beacon tower in line with Le Paradis white beacon tower bearing 319°. At low water Le Paradis is almost hidden by rock. This line leaves:

Bezhinennou starboard beacon 135m to starboard.
Calhic starboard beacon tower 0·125M to starboard.

As soon as Ile Louet is brought on with La Lande again, alter course to make good 160° and proceed as for the Grand Chenal.

GRAND CHENAL AND CHANNELS TO THE RIVIERE DE PENZE – FROM THE NORTH

By day only

1. Proceed as for Grand Chenal, passing 0·2M east of Pot de Fer E cardinal spar bell buoy and following the leading line 176° (Ile Louet–Tour de la Lande, line J).

   When Tourelles des Duons white tower bears 273° alter course to make good 250° heading for Guerhéon starboard beacon tower and passing north of the salmon farm vessel's prohibited area, marked by yellow buoys (line R).

   When Le Cordonnier port beacon tower is abaft the beam, 0·15M to starboard, alter course to make good 167° heading directly for Trousken port beacon tower, and leaving La Petite Vache port beacon tower 0·125M to port.

   When the latter is abeam alter to starboard to pass midway between La Petite Fourche starboard beacon tower and Trousken port tower, to find and then to follow the leading line for the river: Roc'h Pigued white pyramid and Amer de Stum black-and-white daymark (line P), bearing 168°.

Follow directions for Rivière de Penzé, (see page 124).

2. Proceed as for *Grand Chenal* as above but continue on the line until the S cardinal light buoy on the SE corner of the salmon farm prohibited area has been identified. Steer to round this buoy leaving it close to starboard and steer 290° until midway between this SE corner buoy and the S cardinal buoy on the SW corner. In this position Barzenn ar Forc'h Vihan starboard beacon will bear 248°.

   Steer to make good 248° heading directly for this beacon (line S). There are two isolated rocks in the channel, one drying 0·3m LAT southeast of Les Biseyers, 80m north of the line, and the other, drying 2·6m, southwest of Les Biseyers 120m north of the line. Les Cochons Noirs, Le Paradis and Les Grandes Fourches are all steep-to on their northern sides and, apart from a 5·9m patch over a rock at the east end, there is a least depth of 12m LAT.

   When the leading line for the river is reached, Roc'h Pigued white pyramid and Amer de Stum black-and-white daymark (line P) bearing 168°, follow directions for Rivière de Penzé (see page 124).

GRAND CHENAL AND CHANNELS TO RIVIERE DE PENZE – FROM THE SOUTH

By day only

To proceed from the Rivière de Morlaix to the Rivière de Penzé proceed north either by the Grand Chenal or the Chenal Ouest de Ricard until just north of La Vieille and Stolvezen buoys, when the Ile Pigued W pyramid (just north of Ar Chaden) comes in line with the spire of Notre Dame de Bon Secours on Ile de Batz bearing 293° (line T), then turn to follow this line until it meets one or other of the lines mentioned above and continue as appropriate. The spire is not at all easy to identify as it is almost hidden behind a copse, however the line runs just south of the southern boundary of the salmon farm which, should it remain on station, provides a useful mark.

Baie de Morlaix, leading marks for Chenal de Tréguier. Ile Noire lighthouse in transit with La Lande light tower, on the skyline and hard to identify unless it has just been repainted. Bearing 190·5°.

GRAND CHENAL – TO RIVIERE DE MORLAIX

By night

With reference to the following lights:

Les Sept Iles Fl(3)15s59m24M
Les Triagoz Oc(2)WR.6s31m15/11M
Men-Guen Braz Q.WRG.14m9-6M
Ile de Batz Fl(4)25s69m23M
La Lande Fl.5s85m23M
Ile Louet Oc(3)WG.12s17m15/10M
Ile Noire Oc(2)WRG.6s15m11-8M

Navigate to keep well clear of the Roches Duon and the Plateau de la Méloine, both unlit, and to bring Ile Louet into line with La Lande bearing 176° (line J). Follow this line very closely until just past Calhic beacon tower, when the Ile Noire light will change from red to green.

Then alter to make good 160° and proceed as for daylight entry, leaving Château de Taureau beacon and fort to port.

CHENAL DE TREGUIER – TO RIVIERE DE MORLAIX

By day

This channel should be used only when the tide serves as it contains isolated rocks drying 1m (awash at MLWS). If approaching from the north, navigate so as to pass 0·25M west of Méloine W cardinal whistle buoy, on the western edge of the extensive Plateau de la Méloine. From here a course made good of 190° leads straight along the leading line (M) formed by Ile Noire lighthouse (front), white square tower 13m high, elevation 15m, and Tour de la Lande lighthouse (rear), white square tower black top 17m high, elevation 85m.

If approaching from the northeast, to the south of the Plateau de la Méloine, proceed as for *Primel, Approaches, By day* above, then navigate to make a position 0·2M east of La Pierre Noire starboard beacon.

From here make good a course of 190° along the leading line (M) mentioned above. This line leaves the following marks on the sides shown:

Pierre Noire starboard beacon 0·2M to starboard.
An Dourgi (Tourghi) starboard beacon 0·2M to starboard.
Petit Arémen port beacon tower 0·1M to port.
Grand Arémen starboard beacon tower 0·1M to starboard.
La Chambre starboard beacon tower 100m to starboard.
Ile Blanche port beacon tower 100m to port.

When Ile Blanche tower is abeam to port, quit the leading line and steer about 240° for 0·15M until La Chambre beacon tower and Petit Arémen beacon tower are in line on 031°, then alter course to make good the reciprocal 211°, keeping on this line as a stern transit; this leads to the Rade de Morlaix No. 1 starboard buoy (named La Barre de Flot).

CHENAL DE TREGUIER – TO RIVIERE DE MORLAIX

By night

With reference to the lights listed under *Grand Chenal* above, navigate to keep well clear of the Plateau de la Méloine and the Roches Duon, both unlit, and to bring Ile Noire Oc(2)WRG.6s11-8M (in R sector) and La Lande Fl.5s in line bearing 190·5° (line M), then make good a course to follow this line.

When almost midway between La Chambre beacon tower and Ile Blanche beacon tower, the Ile Louet light, Oc(3)WG.12s, will change from white to green. At this point quit the leading line and alter course to make good 215° for the Rade de Morlaix No. 1 buoy (named La Barre de Flot) which is unlit.

Anchorages

Baie de Morlaix

The favourite anchorage for yachts is between La Barre de Flot and Pen Lann, with Ile Louet bearing about 340°. This position has a depth of about 9m

Ile Louet bearing 125°. HW channel, marked by beacons, from Carantec bay leaving Ile Louet to port. From left to right: Corbeau G beacon tower, Château du Taureau, Ile Noire white lighthouse, Ile Louet, Grand Cochon WG beacon tower (white from this side), white pyramid on Penn ar Lann and Roc'h Gored.

Château du Taureau and Ile Louet from the west. Ile Noire lighthouse (unpainted on the west side) far right.

28. Morlaix – estuary and river

Approaches

From Pen Lann to the river entrance one mile north of Locquénolé, the fairway is deep and is marked by seven numbered port and starboard buoys. La Barre de Flot, starboard buoy No. 1, is unlit, but has a large radar reflector beneath its cone. The next four on alternate sides of the channel are lit.

The mean course is about 155°. Upstream of port buoy No. 4, the channel dries at LAT. Half a mile above Locquénolé it may dry 2m and further upstream it can dry 4m or 5m.

After port buoy No. 7, opposite to Le Dourduff en Mer, the channel is well marked by a succession of port and starboard buoys leading close to Locquénolé and Rubalan on the west bank, off which local shallow-draught craft are moored on each side of the fairway. Care must be taken not to miss a buoy obscured by a moored boat. Occasionally one or other of the buoys south of Locquénolé may be absent.

Above Rubalan the river curves to port and the buoys are replaced by port and starboard beacons for the next half mile, but for the last mile up to the lock it is very narrow and the best water is indicated by the conspicuous pairs of transit marks on the shore.

The lock leading to the basin is 63m long, 16m wide, the lower sill is 2m and the upper 3·1m above datum giving approximately 3m at MHWN. The gates open 3 times each tide: 1½ hrs before, at HW and 1 hr after. The bridge below the lock has a clearance of 26m (SHOM) at top of spring tides. Whilst waiting for the gates to open, go alongside the

and is well sheltered from westerlies but somewhat exposed from other quarters at high water, so that a yacht sometimes rolls in the anchorage, particularly on the ebb. There is a good dinghy landing at all states of tide at, or near, the northeast corner of Penn Lann. From here a footpath climbs the hill and joins the road to Carantec, which lies a mile farther west. Three mooring buoys in deep water are reserved for visitors.

In settled weather and neap tides, yachts sometimes anchor near the Pierres de Carantec.

In easterly weather and neap tides, small yachts may anchor close south of the Pointe de Térénez about 1M to the east of Ile Noire, where there is said to be 2·1m at LW neaps.

Inside the estuary it is possible to anchor in good holding ground on either side of the fairway, but there is no reasonable landing for dinghies at low water.

Morlaix estuary and river, looking south. From left to right: Ile Noir lighthouse to left of river mouth, Château du Taureau, Ile Louet, Pen ar Lann (*pointe*). Compare with plan on page 118.

quay on the west side, about 150m from the outer gate. Yachts may safely dry out in this position but not nearer to the lock gate, where there are rocks which dry.

The alternative position in which to dry out (which is perhaps better) is below the weir alongside the middle arm of the lock quay on its east side where there are steps and soft mud bottom. Depths in the basin, which is over half a mile long, vary from 2·4m to 5·4m alongside the quays. The southern end of the basin is now a marina with pontoons on the east side.

Visitors may also lie alongside the quays in certain places at slightly less charge. The original pontoon at the south wall is now reserved for local yacht club members.

Facilities

The basin is situated near the centre of Morlaix, with small shops nearby on the west bank, and the principal shops about a quarter of a mile beyond towards the high railway viaduct which dominates the town. Freshwater points near roots of pontoons (supply your own hose), also rubbish bins. Diesel, petrol and oil on quay. The yacht club by the quay is open to visitors, and showers and toilets are available by the harbour office.

Yachts are absolutely secure at Morlaix, so far as weather is concerned, and arrangements can be made with the harbourmaster to leave them there if one has to return to the UK for any reason. The water in the basin appears to be fresh.

Morlaix is one of the biggest towns in Brittany, and has all services and facilities which may not be available in smaller ports such as doctors, dentists, banks, opticians (quick repairs), photographic dealers (quick developing) and first-rate shops of all kinds. There are many restaurants of which Hôtel Europe is the largest and probably the best. The Auberge des Gourmets serves a good meal at a reasonable price, but it is situated up the hill about a hundred yards below the station.

There is a train/bus service to Roscoff, and a good train service to Brest and Paris and also connections with St-Malo or Dinard, though the latter are slow, as one or two changes may be involved.

Rivière de Morlaix, looking upstream towards road bridge over La Pennelé stream. The buoys and leading marks must be closely followed as the channel moves.

Historical

Morlaix is an historical town. At the time of the Roman occupation there was a fortress and the town was called Mons Relaxus. In the Middle Ages it had many warlike connections with England. The Fontaine des Anglais on the east bank of the river marks the place where, in 1522, 600 English who had disembarked to attack the town were surprised while asleep, and killed. Ten years later it was actually captured by the English, but in 1542 the merchants of the town built the Château du Taureau, to discourage any further raids.

29. Carantec – Rivière de Penzé

Charts

BA *3669, 2745*
Imray *C35*
SHOM *7151, 7095*
ECM Navicarte *538*

Approaches

By day only

From a position 150m east of the head of Bloscon breakwater the leading marks, Beneven, a white pyramid, and Tourelle Mazarin, a white beacon tower on the northern tip of Ile Callot, will be in transit on 137°. Follow this transit until the marks for the river are in line leaving:

Guerhéon starboard beacon tower 230m to starboard.

Basse du Cordonnier, a rocky patch drying 1m, 100m to port. Two rocks drying 1m, 150m to starboard, and a rock drying 0·5m, 50m to starboard, present a danger near LWS.

Looking west from anchorage north of Carantec. From left to right: Kreisker tall spire, St-Pol de Leon twin spires and conspicuous water tower.

Continue on this course until La Petite Vache port beacon tower is abeam 200m to port when alter to starboard and steer for Petite Fourche starboard beacon tower until the river leading marks are in line. For approaches from the Baie de Morlaix see page 118.

Having arrived on the leading line for the river: Roc'h Pigued bottle-shaped white pyramid in line with Amer de Stum black-and-white daymark bearing 168° (line P on plan 31), follow this line. These marks may not be easily identified from a distance and to start with it may be easier to keep Ar Tortu port beacon in transit with Caspari BRB beacon on 170°, after which deviations are necessary at the beacons. The following marks should be left on the sides shown:

Barzenn starboard beacon 250m to starboard.

Trousken port beacon tower 130m to port.

La Petite Fourche starboard beacon 150m to starboard.

Ar Tortue port beacon 20m to port (but note that, if beating in, there is an alternative course with a channel 200m wide leaving the beacon well to starboard, avoiding, if necessary, the small rock 180m to the northeast of it 0·8m LAT).

An Nehou (or Caspari) isolated danger beacon (lying about 0·25M ENE of Trébunnec starboard beacon tower) 50m to starboard or 150m to port, making the necessary alteration in good time to avoid the small rock, 0·5m, about 100m north of this beacon and two drying about 0·3m about 50m southwest of it.

Trébunnec starboard beacon tower about 0·2M to starboard.

From here continue on the leading line, but if this is still not identified the deep channel is shown on each side by large numbers of withies marking oyster beds. These withies cover round about half tide, but they are not heavy enough to cause any damage if accidentally touched. Continuing, leave:

Enez an Ebeul starboard beacon (east of Penpoull) 140m to starboard.

Le Figuier isolated danger beacon 50m to starboard.

When this beacon is abeam alter course to about 200° for 0·3M then about 210° to follow the leading line (Q) given by Lingos small bottle-shaped white pyramid and a white rectangular mark on a wall at St-Yves. This line, leading on the southeast side of the channel, would leave Les Cheminées starboard beacon 100m to starboard.

Carantec slip, dries. The Jezequel boatyard is behind the slip.

On approaching Les Cheminées quit the leading line and steer between the beacon and the first of the port buoys.

Thereafter the river is marked by small port and starboard plastic buoys. The cone or can sections of these are very similar in shape and several have been knocked off their floats by the flat-bottomed, steel oyster barges. There are oyster beds on each side of the channel marked by withies.

There is a least depth of about 0·9m (2·1m at MLWS) up as far as the old ferry slips. Here the river is full of double ended moorings. Towards high water shallow-draught vessels can continue upriver for a further mile above the Pont de la Corde bridge to the town of Penzé, where there is a quay which dries 4·8m.

It should be noted that after *Capelan*, with a mast height of 13m, lost her aerial negotiating the bridge one hour after HW the minimum headroom shown on BA and SHOM charts was reduced from 15m to 11m!

Anchorages

There are now numerous moorings between Les Cheminées and Lingos beacon but room is left to anchor clear of them. There is better shelter farther up the river southwest of Lingos pyramid in 3·6m MLWS, or just south of the old ferry in about 1·8m MLWS, mud. Many moorings have been laid. It is suggested that you choose a vacant one. There is a landing-hard each side of the river at the old ferry, available at all states of the tide. The noise of traffic over the Pont de la Corde may be troublesome. The holding ground in the lower reaches has been reported poor.

Facilities

Penzé

Penzé has all the facilities of a small town. There are no facilities at St-Yves, but there appears to be a restaurant/bar by the east side of the bridge and oysters may be purchased on both sides of the river.

Penzé river, looking upstream to St Yves. *Capelan* has turned to starboard off the leading line (Pointe de Lingos white pyramid in transit with white mark upstream of St-Yves) to enter the buoyed channel. The Pont de la Corde (11m clearance!) is round the next curve to the left.

Carantec

There is a stone jetty and slip which dries about 4·6m and two yacht yards which face the estuary. The one nearest the jetty is owned by the cheerful family Jezequel who build beautiful wooden yachts. *Capelan* dried out comfortably for the night on her bilge-keels alongside the jetty.

The town is about a 15-minute walk from the landing where there are good shopping facilities, a night club and a number of hotels and restaurants. The sandy beaches north of Kergrist farm are popular with local holidaymakers. Milk, eggs and poultry can sometimes be had from farms between Carantec and Pen Lann. Between half ebb and half flood the Ile de Callot is accessible on foot from Carantec across the Passe aux Moutons.

Historical

On the Ile de Callot stands the pilgrimage chapel of Notre Dame des Victoires, founded in the 6th century to commemorate a victory over Norse pirates. On August 15th every year seamen from the surrounding districts come to pay their devotions.

St-Pol de Léon is an ancient cathedral town which lies about one mile west of the landing at Pen Poull. It has played a leading part in the history of Brittany. Its name is a corruption of St-Paul Aurelian, its first missionary, who came from Wales in AD 530. The cathedral is entirely medieval, partly 12th century, and its twin spires form one of the most distinctive landmarks in the district.

Close to the south of the cathedral can be seen the thin spire of Kreisker, 109m high, which was apparently built in competition with that at Caen to be the tallest spire in France.

30. Ile de Batz and Chenal de l'Ile de Batz

Charts
BA *3669, 2745*
Imray *C35*
SHOM *7151, 7095*
ECM Navicarte *538*

Tidal data

Tidal heights (approx)
HW +0055 Brest, +0605 Dover
MTL 4·7m. Index 8B
Heights of tide above chart datum
MHWS 8·5m, MLWS 1·2m, MHWN 6·4m, MLWN 3·3m

Tidal streams
HW slack water at the entrance to Roscoff occurs −0005 Brest (+0505 Dover). One mile NE of the Ile de Batz, and in the channel itself, the E-going stream begins at −0435 Brest (+0035 Dover) and the W-going stream begins at −0110 Brest (−0605 Dover). Both streams reach 3·75 knots at springs. NE of the Ile de Batz, the directions of the streams are SE and NW.

General
As with Ile Bréhat, visiting Ile de Batz is very pleasant in the early morning, or evening when the tourists are on the mainland. It appears as one large market garden where, as you walk along a road, you may expect to be offered vegetables from the basket of a smiling islander.

The Chenal de l'Ile de Batz provides a short cut to the Baie de Morlaix for vessels coming from the west and vice versa, as well as giving access to Roscoff and Porz Kernock. With the exception of two rocks, one of which dries 0·8m at LAT, the central part of the

Canal de l'Ile de Batz, looking west. Identify features on plan, pages 128-9.

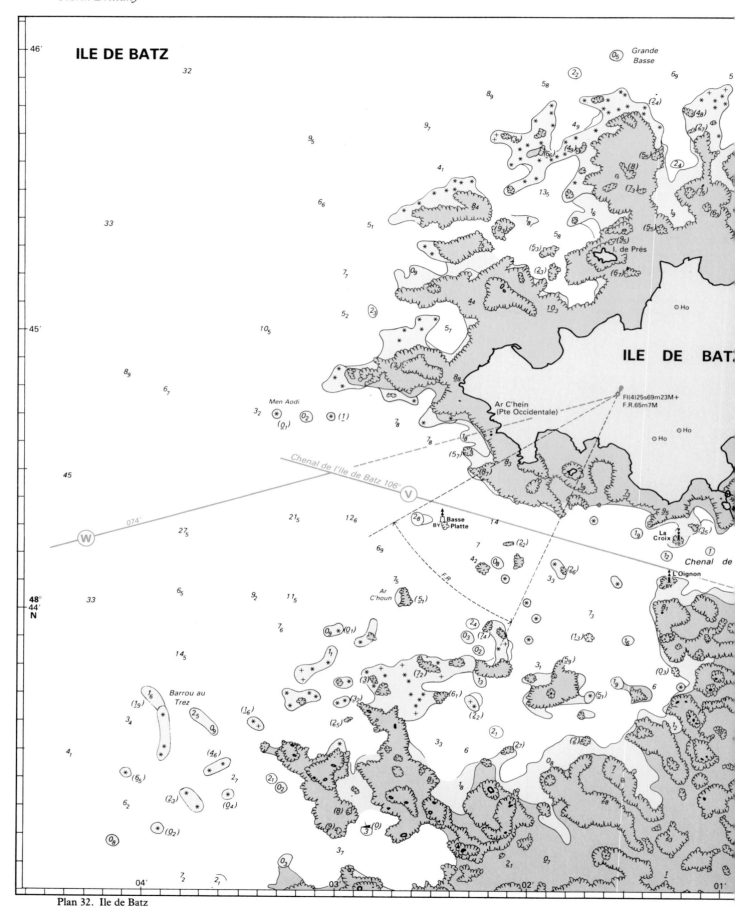

ILE DE BATZ

Plan 32. Ile de Batz

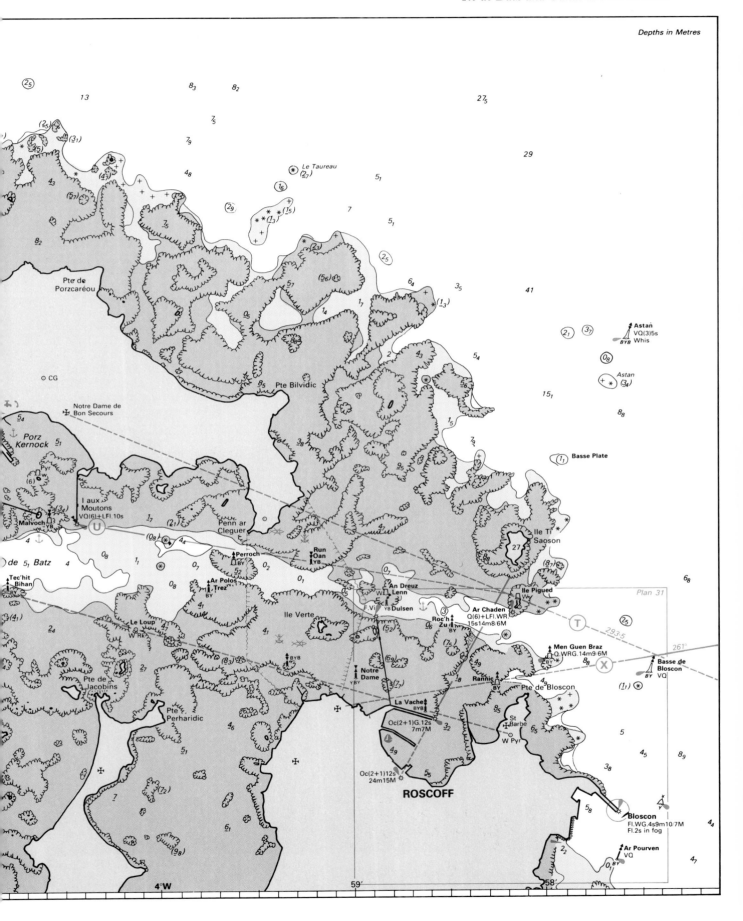

Depths in Metres

ROSCOFF

129

channel carries a least depth of 0·1m (1·3m at MLWS), but owing to the strong tides and lack of satisfactory leading lines it would be unwise for a stranger to rely on being able to keep exactly to the recommended track, even under power.

At half tide there is plenty of water, and enough for a yacht of twenty tons to work through under sail. In fresh or strong westerly winds against a W-going spring tide, the water is rough west of Perroch beacon tower.

Approaches

CHENAL DE L'ILE DE BATZ – FROM THE WEST
By day only

Approaching from the north, keep over 0·8M west of Ar C'hein (Pointe Occidentale) until Basse Plate N cardinal beacon tower bears about 110°, then steer so as to leave it 100m to starboard. When passing west of the Ile de Batz with a flood tide take care not to be set on to the dangers west of the island, shown on plan 32.

Approaching from the west, keep Ile de Batz lighthouse, a grey tower 40m high, elevation 69m, bearing 074° (line W) until Basse Plate beacon tower bears about 110°, then steer so as to leave it 100m to starboard as above.

From here steer to make good 106° along line V which is formed by Le Loup, a small steep rock with a white patch painted on its northern end, in transit with St-Barbe, a white pyramid just to the south of the conspicuous St-Barbe chapel. (These marks are difficult for a stranger to identify from a distance, but it is possible to navigate by the fairway marks alone.)

Continue along line V until l'Oignon N cardinal beacon is abeam to starboard, 100m distant, and La Croix S cardinal beacon is abeam to port distant 0·125M. At this point alter course to port and steer 090° for Perroch N cardinal beacon tower, leaving:

Tec'hit Bihan N cardinal beacon 0·1M to starboard.
Malvoch S cardinal beacon tower and **Ile aux Moutons** S cardinal beacon about 0·15M to port.

When Ile aux Moutons ferry slip beacon bears due north, alter to port and steer 080° for Pen ar Cleguer, the southernmost point of the Ile de Batz passing between two rocks, the northern one drying 0·8m at LAT. These rocks should not present a hazard at half tide or above.

When Run Oan S cardinal beacon comes into line with Ile Pigued white pyramid on 100°, alter course to follow this line (U) leaving Perroch N cardinal beacon tower 100m to starboard.

When about equidistant from Perroch and Run Oan, alter course to leave Run Oan 80m to port. Then head for the Roscoff/Batz ferry pier violet beacon, leaving it 50m to starboard.

Entering Batz channel from the west. Leading marks in line halfway between yacht and church spire. Le Loup rock in line with Sainte Barbe white pyramid on 106°. Ste Barbe chapel is on the green clump of bushes and the pyramid is just to the right of the clump.

Next, steer so as to leave Duslen (An Dreuz Lenn S cardinal beacon about 50m and Duslen white tower 110m to port.

When Duslen S cardinal beacon is abeam, steer towards Ar Chaden (S cardinal) lighthouse, leaving Roc'h Zu N cardinal beacon 100m to starboard and finally Ar Chaden lighthouse 30m to port.

Steer from here so as to leave Basse de Bloscon N cardinal buoy 150m to starboard then, if bound for Morlaix or the east, bring the S cardinal light beacon on the centre of Ile Pigued in line with Notre Dame de Bon Secours spire (if it is still visible over a copse of trees) on Ile de Batz on a stern bearing of 293° and make good 113° to follow this line (T) which leads close to the south of the salmon farm prohibited area and then pick up the leading lines, either for the Chenal Ouest de Ricard or the Grand Chenal as desired, and follow these (lines J or K).

If bound for the Rivière de Penzé then steer to make good 165° with Guerhéon starboard beacon tower fine on the starboard bow.

When the white beacon towers Ben venn and Mazarin on Ile de Callot come into line (line N) bearing 136° follow this line until Petite Vache port beacon tower bears 045°, thus avoiding a rock drying 0·2m 100m to starboard. Then turn to starboard and steer 235° to reach the leading line for the Rivière de Penzé: Roc'h Pigued and Amer de Stum black-and-white daymark on 168° (line P).

Caution This passes near to rocks awash or drying 1m LAT, i.e. covered 0·2m MLWS, 2·4m MLWN.

CHENAL DE L'ILE DE BATZ – FROM THE EAST
By day only

The approach to the eastern entrance may be:

a. From the NE between the Roches Duon and Astan (plan 31).
b. From the ESE and the Grand Chenal, between the Roches Duon and the dangers to the south of them, by following the line: Ile Pigued pyramid in line with Notre Dame de Bon Secours (if visible above a copse of trees), bearing 293·5° (line T on plan 31.) This line passes close to the south of the salmon farm prohibited area.
c. From the SSE and the Rivière de Penzé, from a position in which Trousken port beacon tower bears about 180° distant 0·5M, make good 317° carefully following the stern transit of the white beacon towers Ben venn and Mazarin on Ile de Callot (leaving rocks awash or drying up to 1m, 100m or more on either side) until Guerhéon beacon tower bears 180°, then steer to leave Basse de Bloscon N cardinal pillar buoy 150m to port then proceed along line T as (b) above.

In all the above cases, having reached a position about 150m east of the Basse de Bloscon buoy, identify Ar Chaden lighthouse (S cardinal) and approach it on a bearing of about 295° (see plan 32). This line leaves Men-Guen Braz lighthouse (N cardinal) about 0·125M to port.

Steer a course to pass 50m south of Duslen (An Dreuz Lenn) S cardinal beacon and 120m south of the white beacon tower of the same name, leaving:

Ar Chaden lighthouse about 30m to starboard.
Roc'h Zu N cardinal beacon 100m to port.

When Duslen S cardinal beacon is abeam, alter course for the trumpet-shaped violet-and-white beacon (F.Vi light) at the end of the long ferry pier, which looks like a bridge and a slipway.

Pass close to the beacon and alter course again so as to leave Run Oan S cardinal beacon 80m to starboard.

Then when this beacon is 150m distant bring it into line astern with Ile Pigued white beacon on 100° and follow this line (U) steering 280° leaving Perroch N cardinal beacon tower 100m to port.

Entrance to Batz channel from the east. Church spire bearing 250°.

This line, if followed too far, leads on to the S cardinal beacon on the end of the Ile aux Moutons ferry slip and passes directly over a rock drying 0·8m LAT and having 0·4m over it at MLWS. This rock is 0·25M from Ar Polos Trez beacon on a bearing of 320°. Below half tide it could be considered a hazard and may be avoided by steering 262° for l'Oignon N cardinal beacon when Ar Polos Trez N cardinal beacon bears 160°, with due allowance for tidal streams.

When Ile aux Moutons long ferry slipway S cardinal beacon bears due north steer to leave:

Malvoch S cardinal beacon tower 0·1M to starboard.
Tec'hit Bihan N cardinal beacon 0·1M to port.
La Croix S cardinal beacon 0·125M to starboard.
L'Oignon N cardinal beacon 100m to port.

Just before l'Oignon is abeam, pick up the stern transit of Le Loup, a small steep rock with a white patch painted on its northern end, in line with St-Barbe white pyramid, just south of the conspicuous chapel, bearing 106°.

Make good a course of 287° to follow this line (V). This leaves Basse Plate N cardinal beacon tower 100m to port.

If bound north, follow this line for a further mile in order to clear the dangers on the west side of the Ile de Batz.

If bound westward down the coast, follow this line until the Ile de Batz lighthouse, a grey tower 40m high, elevation 69m, bears 074°. Then alter course to make good 254° so as to keep it on that bearing astern. This line (W) clears all dangers for the next 10M.

Anchorages
CHENAL DE L'ILE DE BATZ

It is possible to anchor almost anywhere in the channel where there is enough water, but all such anchorages are exposed to winds from certain quarters, are subject to a strong tidal stream and thus are uncomfortable with a weather-going tide.

Anchorage is prohibited owing to cables, in an area bounded by a line almost due south from Pen ar Cleguer and on the east by a line running about NNW from the Roscoff ferry beacon.

Porz Kernock drying harbour on Ile de Batz, looking north.

The following positions are frequently used:

1. Between Ar Chaden lighthouse and Duslen beacon tower. E of this a white metal buoy has been laid. At spring tides it may be necessary to anchor in deep water in the strong stream, at neaps it is possible to find a more sheltered position northward with the aid of soundings and clear of the rocks indicated on the plan.

   In northerly weather this is uncomfortable at HW. Moorings with two white plastic buoys are laid here.

2. There is an anchorage to the southwest of Malvoch beacon tower (avoiding the 0·1m rock shown on the chart) and at neaps south of Ile aux Moutons, but these can be uncomfortable in fresh westerly winds. Replacing the visitors' moorings in the channel south of Ile aux Moutons there are now a number of moorings, with small red buoys, in constant use by fishing boats.

The island

Porz Kernock

In 1986 a pier and slip was constructed in the north-west corner of the drying harbour to accommodate a flat-bottomed ferry for transporting produce from the island to Roscoff. At the same time a large area of the harbour was bulldozed flat and clear of rocks, making an excellent, fully protected, anchorage for yachts that can take the ground.

Entrance

With sufficient water, leave the S cardinal beacon column marking the outer end of the Ile aux Moutons ferry pier and slip 15m to starboard and steer NNW to leave the white pyramid on Ile Kernock 60m to port, taking care to avoid small mooring buoys and floating fish boxes.

Anchorage

Steer to a suitable anchorage clear of moorings between the new produce-ferry pier and the old quay in the northwest corner of the harbour. Anchor bow and stern, inspecting the bottom before grounding, as it is no longer as clean as in 1986.

Facilities

A tour of the island reveals two supermarkets as well as a baker and other small shops. There are bars and a restaurant on the front, next to a small hotel which will provide a shower and an excellent meal at a moderate price. Water tap by the telephone box on the front, near the quay.

When storm bound in 1988 *Capelan* and her crew spent a very comfortable few days in this harbour.

31. Roscoff and Bloscon

Charts

BA *3669, 2745*
Imray *C35*
SHOM *7151, 7095*
ECM Navicarte *538*

Tidal data

Tidal heights (approx)
HW +0055 Brest, +0605 Dover
MTL 5·1m. Index 8B
Heights of tide above chart datum
MHWS 8·9m, MLWS 1·3m, MHWN 7·0m, MLWN 3·5m

Tidal streams

HW slack water at the entrance to Roscoff occurs −0005 Brest (+0505 Dover). One mile NE of the Ile de Batz, and in the channel itself, the E-going stream begins at −0435 Brest (+0035 Dover) and the W-going stream begins at −0110 Brest (−0605 Dover). Both streams reach 3·75 knots at springs. NE of the Ile de Batz, the directions of the streams are SE and NW. For other streams see under *Baie de Morlaix*, above.

General

Although Roscoff has the disadvantage of a harbour which dries out it is nevertheless an interesting and convenient port for the visiting yachtsman. A plan to build a sill across the entrance and dredge the harbour is meeting with local opposition as it is felt that this and the subsequent introduction of marina pontoons would destroy the character of this ancient port.

Approaches

From a distance use the directions for the *Chenal de l'Ile de Batz*, page 127. There are two alternative inner approaches which can be used with sufficient rise of tide.

PASSE A L'EST DE BENVEN
By day or night

From a position 150m west of Ar Chaden as already described, turn to bring the front and rear leading lights and structures, in line bearing 209°. The front light is Oc(2+1)G.12s, on a white column 6m high, elevation 7m, on New Mole. The rear light is Oc(2+1)12s. The two lights are synchronised.

Follow this line closely until the end of the eastern jetty is abeam to port, then steer as necessary to enter the port.

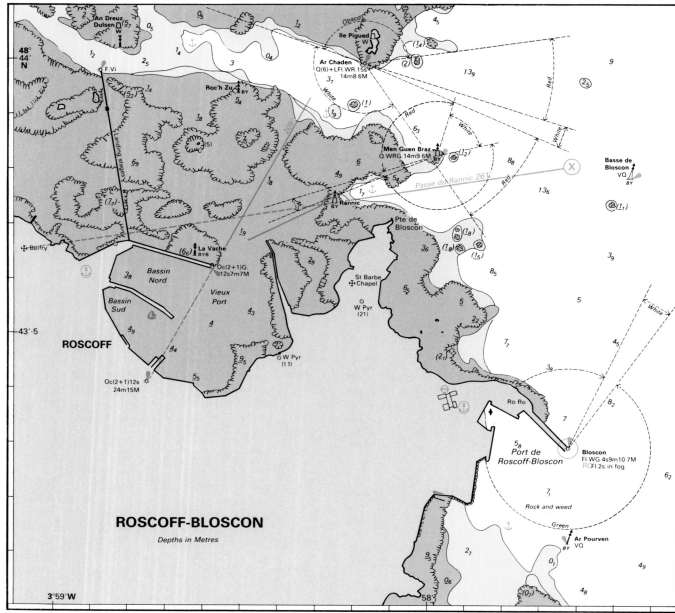

Plan 33. Roscoff–Bloscon

PASSE DU RANNIC

By day only

From a position 100m north of Basse de Bloscon buoy, steer along the line formed by Rannic N cardinal beacon tower and Roscoff belfry, bearing 261°. (This is line X on plan 33.) This line leaves Men-Guen Braz lighthouse (N cardinal) 100m to starboard, after which course should be altered slightly to starboard round Rannic tower leaving it about 30m to port, thus avoiding the rocks which lie 130m NW of Rannic and which dry approximately 5·4m.

Then bring Rannic tower into line astern with Men-Guen Braz lighthouse and follow this transit until past the end of the eastern jetty, when course may be altered to enter the port.

Anchorage and harbour

While waiting for sufficient rise of tide to enter Roscoff the choice of anchorage must depend on the direction and strength of the wind and, in particular, on whether it is springs, or neaps when there is more choice.

a. Between Ar Chaden and Duslen beacon tower, described on page 133. Two white mooring buoys are laid in this reach. These are very exposed and do not always watch (stay above water) at HW but would be convenient while waiting for the tide to enter Roscoff.

b. In about 1m LAT just east of the Roscoff leading line with Roc'h Zu N cardinal beacon bearing 285°; but note the existence of a rock which dries 1m, only 100m east of this position.

Roscoff entrance, viewed from the left of leading line, (lighthouse
in line with BW vertical stripes on breakwater head on 209°).

Roscoff inner harbour, visitors lie against wall (centre of picture).

c. East of Rannic beacon tower, having approached using directions for Passe du Rannic above.

Both (b) and (c) should be used with caution.

d. The visitors' anchorage in Bloscon is only 1·5M distant and is out of the tide.

The outer harbour, Le Port Neuf, has good berths alongside its N and W sides, drying from 2·4–3m LAT on hard bottom. It is however reserved primarily for fishing boats. The steps are in constant use by *vedettes* and other local craft. With the harbourmaster's agreement, it is preferable to lie alongside the second or third ladder where a yacht of 1·8m draught takes the bottom just after half tide. If these are occupied, one may have to berth against the quay without a ladder, which is awkward at low water. It provides excellent HW berths for shopping, but for a long stay, visitors are expected to use the inner harbour.

The inner harbour dries from 3·6m to 5·1m LAT. The old jetty is rather rough, but there are excellent berths for yachts alongside it which may be unoccupied, even if the outer harbour is full. The harbourmaster warns against using halyards from the masthead to ensure that a fin-keeled yacht leans to the wall when taking the ground. He recommends that this be effected by the use of warps, since the wall is high.

The eastern part of the harbour cannot be used for berthing. It is said that there is liable to be a heavy surge in the harbour if there is any swell in the offing; presumably this occurs in strong NE winds or northerly winds at high water springs. The inner harbour may then provide better shelter.

Facilities

The facilities for yachtsmen at Roscoff are good. Water in bulk can be obtained from the hydrants on the quays on application to the harbourmaster, or from a tap in the toilets near the *bureau du port*, across the road at the shore end of the old jetty.

Fuel is obtainable from the pumps on the outer end of the outer breakwater. First obtain a *carte* from the Cooperative Maritime by the lighthouse or from the harbourmaster if he is available.

Tickets for the municipal showers, by the roundabout, can be obtained from the Maison du Tourisme, behind the roundabout, open from 0900 to 1900.

On landing leave the big sheds housing the sailing school (which will provide local advice) to the right and enter the main road. Turning left down the Rue Gambetta one will pass the Restaurant du Centre (a *pension* supplying well cooked meals at a modest price), a photographer, a butcher, a baker and several small shops.

In 1990 bonded stores could be obtained by arrangement with the customs from Monsieur Larher's shop. A chandlers, Comptoirs Maritimes, is near the rear leading lighthouse on the south side of the old harbour and there is a capable marine engineer and a sailmaker. Repairs to wooden vessels can be undertaken.

The road turning right from the quay leads to the church. On this road will be found shops of all kinds, banks and hotels including the Talabardon which has a good restaurant. The aquarium on the northern front has specimens of marine life found in the Chenal de l'Ile de Batz; it is worth seeing.

There is a railway station providing a train or bus connection with Morlaix. From nearby port Bloscon there are frequent ferry services to and from Plymouth and weekly sailings to Cork.

Historical

Mary Queen of Scots landed at Roscoff in 1548, when she was five years old, to be married to the Dauphin in Paris. Here also came Prince Charles Edward Stuart in a French privateer, after the battle of Culloden and after narrowly missing capture by English ships in the channel.

The church has a remarkable Renaissance tower and spire (1550) decorated with carvings of ships and pieces of ordnance. The *pardon* of Sainte Barbe takes place on the third Monday in July.

Port de Bloscon

Charts
BA *3669, 2745*
Imray *C35*
SHOM *7151, 7095*
ECM Navicarte *538*

Tidal data
See under Roscoff.

Tidal streams
East of the end of the jetty these are weak, S at −0300 Brest and N at +0300 Brest, reaching a maximum of 1·1 knots at springs.

General
An unattractive artificial harbour half a mile south of Basse de Bloscon N cardinal buoy, and about twenty minutes walk to Roscoff. Considerable reclamation work has been carried out to provide parking space for vehicles. The port is intended primarily for commercial shipping and the car ferries mentioned under Roscoff.

Approach
By day
Make a position 0·25M east of Basse de Bloscon buoy; in poor visibility this can be assisted by homing on Port Bloscon radiobeacon, *BC* 304·5 kHz. From here steer to give the end of the jetty a fair berth, to allow for ferries leaving, and when the way is clear turn to starboard and enter harbour.

Bloscon, looking NE from site of proposed fishing harbour and marina.

By night

Visually, or with the assistance of the radiobeacon, bring the breakwater light to bear 215° which is in the centre of its white sector, 210° to 220°; elsewhere it is green.

Make good 215° until Basse de Bloscon N cardinal light buoy is abeam to starboard, then proceed as for *By day* above, leaving a buoy Fl.Y.4s close to port.

Anchorage

Yachts may anchor in the south of the harbour, clear of the ferry's swinging ground, but north of a N cardinal light buoy marking a drying shoal, Ar Pourven. Visitors' moorings were removed after a British yacht broke adrift in 1991, and yachts now anchor at the owner's risk. However there is a plan to construct a marina and fishing harbour to the south of the present anchorage. Here, in the future, fishing boats and yachts may remain afloat at low water and the charm of the ancient port of Roscoff will be retained.

Facilities

Land at the slipway at the southern end of the ferry terminal car park. There is a water tap outside the terminal toilets and a one mile walk to Roscoff town. Do not be fooled by the board advertising *SUPERMARKET 500 metres* to the south. It is a much extended half kilometre.

III. Ile de Siec to Ouessant

The coast of the mainland, from Ile de Siec to Pointe de St-Mathieu, is heavily encumbered with off-lying rocks and shoals, in places reaching nearly 3M offshore. Farther offshore there are no dangers except for the island of Ouessant and the maze of rocks and small islands lying to the southeast of it. Ouessant itself has a coastal belt of off-lying dangers extending to a maximum of 1·5M at its southwest corner.

The shore consists of mostly low cliffs and rocky bays backed by hilly country without many distinctive natural features. The only reliable marks for daylight identification are radio masts, water towers and lighthouses, particularly the Ile Vierge tower, which is said to be the tallest light structure in the world and can be positively identified by the presence of the disued 30m-high tower alongside it.

The western part of the area has a reputation for bad visibility, at one time due partly to the smoke produced by the local industry of kelp burning. Nevertheless it provides some of the most interesting harbours in the whole of Brittany, which can be visited when conditions are suitable.

Caution The western part of this area is often subject to a heavy swell from the Atlantic. Under certain conditions the sea will occasionally break over isolated shoals with as much as 38m of water over them. Such shoals occur in many places outside the tinted areas on the plans in this book, but can be located from the official charts.

Lights and fog signals

Details of the main coast lights are given below, reading from east to west. Bearings of the sectors and leading lines are from the ship looking towards the light, and are expressed in degrees true. To convert to magnetic, add variation, which during the early 1990s is about 5·5°W in the area covered by Part III of this book. The heights of the light structures are measured from the lantern to the base of the structure. Elevation is measured between the centre of the lantern and MHWS. *See Warning on page 5.*

Ile de Batz Fl(4)25s69m23M Grey circular tower 43m high Auxiliary light F.R.65m7M 024°-059°.

Moguériec leading lights 162°:
Front, jetty light, Iso.WG.4s9m11/6M 158°-W-166°-G-158° White tower G top 10m high.
Rear F.G.22m7M 142°-vis-182° White support G top 11m high.

Pontusval (Pointe de Beg-Pol, NW of port) Oc(3)WR.12s 16m10/7M 056°-R-096°-W-056° White square tower with B top and white house, 15m high.
Ile Vierge 48°38'·4N 4°34'·1W Fl.5s77m27M Siren 60s. RC *VG* 314 kHz 70M. Grey circular tower 83m high, with old lighthouse square tower about 30m high (painted white to seaward) close NW of it.
L'Aber-Wrac'h leading lights for Grand Chenal 100°. Rear intensified about 090·5°-110·5°.
Ile Wrac'h (front) Q.R.20m7M White square tower with orange top, dwelling, 15m high.
Lanvaon (rear) DirQ.55m12M over an arc of about 18° either side of the leading line, intensified about 10° either side. White square tower, orange top, 27m high.
L'Aber-Wrac'h harbour DirOc(2)WRG.6s5m13-11M 125·7°-G-127·2°-W-128·7°-R-130·2°. Thin white concrete tower on N side of N breakwater.
Corn Carhai 48°35'·2N 4°43'·9W Fl(3)12s19m9M White octagonal tower, B top, 20m high.
Portsall Oc(3+1)WRG.12s9m16-13M 058°-G-084°-W-088°-R-058° White column R top to N of village, 7m high.
Le Four 48°31'·4N 4°48'·3W Fl(5)15s27m18M Siren(3+2) 75s. Grey circular masonry tower, 28m high.
L'Aber-Ildut DirOc(2)WR.6s12m25/20M 081°-W-085°-R-087° Small rectangular white building, 5m high.
Les Plâtresses 48°26'·3N 4°50'·9W Fl.RG.4s17m6M 343°-R-153°-G-333°-obscd-343° White tower, 23m high.
Le Faix 48°25'·8N 4°53'·9W VQ.16m8M N cardinal beacon tower 21m high.
Les Trois Pierres 48°24'·7N 4°56'·8W Iso.WRG.4s9-6M 070°-G-147°-W-185°-R-191°-G-197°-W-213°-R-070° White column 15m high.

Chenal du Four
Leading lights for N part of channel 158·5° intensified:
Kermorvan (front) Fl.5s20m22M Reed 60s White square tower, 20m high.
St-Mathieu (rear) Dir.F.54m28M Intensified 157·5°-159·5° RC *SM* 292·5 kHz 20M. White square tower red top, 37m high.
La Grande Vinotière Oc.R.6s15m5M R octagonal port beacon tower 24m high.
Corsen directional light for centre part of channel Dir.Q.WRG.33m12-8M 008°-R-012°-W-015°-G-021° White hut 3m high.

Chenal de la Helle
Leading lights 137·5° Rear intensified 2·5° each side of transit:
Kermorvan (front) As above.
Lochrist (rear) DirOc(3)12s49m22M Octagonal white tower R top, 17m high.
St-Mathieu (same tower as above) Fl.15s56m29M.
Plougonvelin radio masts 3 F.R situated 0·7M SE of Kermorvan.

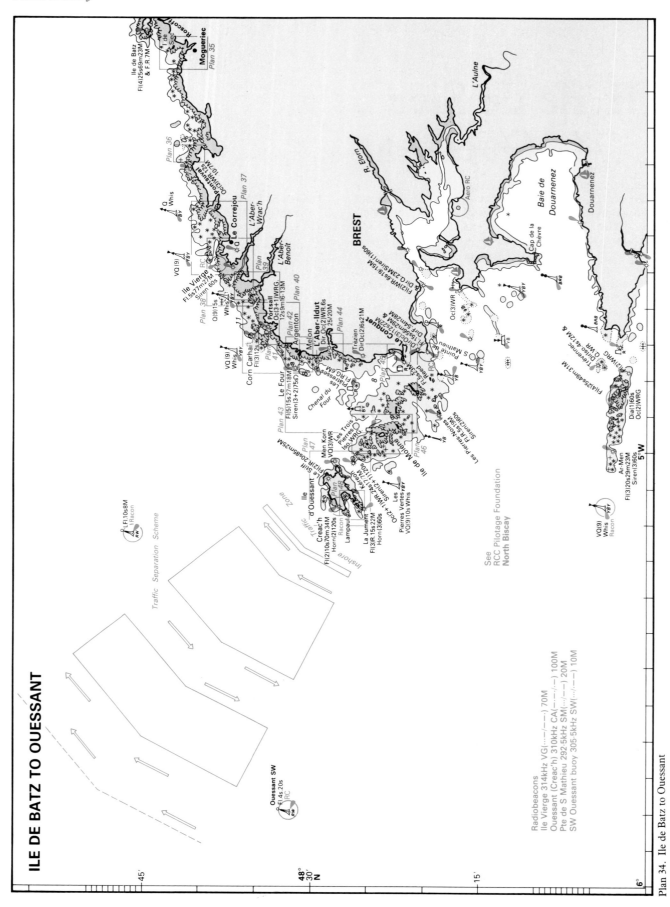

ILE DE BATZ TO OUESSANT

Plan 34. Ile de Batz to Ouessant

Ouessant

Le Stiff 48°28′·5N 5°03′·4W Fl(2)R.20s85m24M Two adjoining white towers, 32m high.

Créac'h 48°27′·6N 5°07′·8W Fl(2)10s70m34M 255°-vis-247° Horn(2)120s RC *CA* 301 kHz 100M. Circular tower painted in B and white bands, 55m high.

Nividic 48°26′·8N 5°09′·1W VQ(9)10s28m9M 290°-vis-225° Octagonal white tower, red bands, with helicopter platform, 36m high.

La Jument 48°25′·4N 5°08′·1W Fl(3)R.15s36m22M 241°-vis-199° Horn(3)60s Octagonal grey tower with red top, 48m high.

Men Corn 48°28′N 5°01′·4W VQ(3)WR.5s21m8/8M 145°-W-040°-R-145°. Obscured 058°-119°. E cardinal beacon tower 29m high.

Kéréon 48°26′·3N 5°01′·4W Oc(2+1)WR.24s38m17/7M 019°-W-248°-R-019° Horn(2+1)120s. Grey circular tower 41m high.

Ile de Molène
Directional light for northern entrance:
Breakwater DirFl(3)WRG.12s6m9-7M 183°-G-190°-W-192°-R-203° Column on breakwater, 5m high.
Directional light for eastern entrance:
Breakwater DirFl(2)WRG.6s9m9/7M 252·5°-G-259·5°-W-262·5°-R-269·5° Column on breakwater, 5m high

Off-lying buoys and marks

In addition to the lighthouses listed above, the following off-lying buoys and marks may be useful when making passages along this coast:

Basse Plate N cardinal beacon tower (1M SW of Ile de Batz lighthouse, unlit).

Port de Pontusval, Toullcoz E cardinal spar buoy (unlit). 1·2M N of entrance.

Amann ar Rouz (4M WNW of Pontusval lighthouse). Tall N cardinal pillar light-and-whistle buoy, Q.8M.

Lizen Ven Ouest W cardinal pillar buoy VQ(9)11M Whistle, radar reflector. 2·2M NxE of Ile Vierge.

Libenter (3M WSW of Ile Vierge lighthouse). W cardinal pillar buoy, Q(9)15s8M Whistle, radar reflector.

Petite Fourche (3·25M SWxW of Ile Vierge lighthouse). W cardinal spar buoy (unlit).

Grande Basse de Portsall (2M NW of Corn-Carhai lighthouse). W cardinal pillar buoy, VQ(9)10s Whistle, radar reflector.

Basse Paotr Bihan (1·5M W of Corn-Carhai lighthouse) W cardinal spar buoy (unlit).

Le Lieu (0·7M W of l'Aber-Ildut lighthouse). Port beacon tower (unlit).

Pierre de Laber (1·0M W by S of l'Aber-Ildut lighthouse). Starboard beacon (unlit).

Ouessant SW lanby Fl.4s RC *SW* 305·5 kHz 10M

Inshore marks

The following conspicuous pair of marks should be noted:

Radio mast 48°38′·3N 4°21′·1W Occasional F.Or.
Water tower 48°39′·25N 4°22′W.

32. Ile de Siec and Moguériec

Charts
BA *3669*
Imray *C35*
SHOM *7151*
ECM Navicarte *538*

Tidal data

Tidal heights (approx)
HW +0050 Brest, +0600 Dover
MTL 5·2m. Index 8B
Heights of tide above chart datum
MHWS 8·2m, MLWS 1·2m, MHWN 6·7m, MLWN 3·3m

Tidal streams

1. In the northern approach from the direction of the Ile de Batz the streams are rotary clockwise and vary in different positions both in direction and strength. It may be broadly stated that the NE-going stream, which runs for some 8 hours, begins at −0505 Brest (+0005 Dover) soon attaining the spring rate of 2·4 knots, weakening and turning ENE to east in the last 2 hours. The SSW-going stream begins at +0255 Brest (−0420 Dover) and runs for 4 hours through SW to NW. The spring rate is 1·4 knots except in its second hour, when the rate is doubled.

2. In the western approach between Ile de Siec and Roc'h Haro, some 2M to the west, the ESE-going stream begins −0435 Brest (+0035 Dover) and the WNW-going stream begins +0125 Brest (−0550 Dover), the former reaching nearly 2 knots and the latter 1 knot at springs.

General

Ile de Siec and Moguériec may be coupled as they are close together and have the same approaches.

Approaches

By day

First make a position from which Ile de Batz lighthouse bears 065° distant 2·9M (point X). Here the leading marks for Moguériec harbour are in line bearing 162°. These are a green and white beacon tower on the jetty and, on the land behind, a white tower with green top, having elevations of 9 and 22m respectively. In some lights it might be difficult to see the front mark but an additional mark on the line is Sibiril church spire which can be seen against the skyline. It is in wooded country and is the first spire to the left of the conspicuous water tower south of Moguériec.

Turn to make good 162° and follow this line leaving Golhédec (just west of and, at low water,

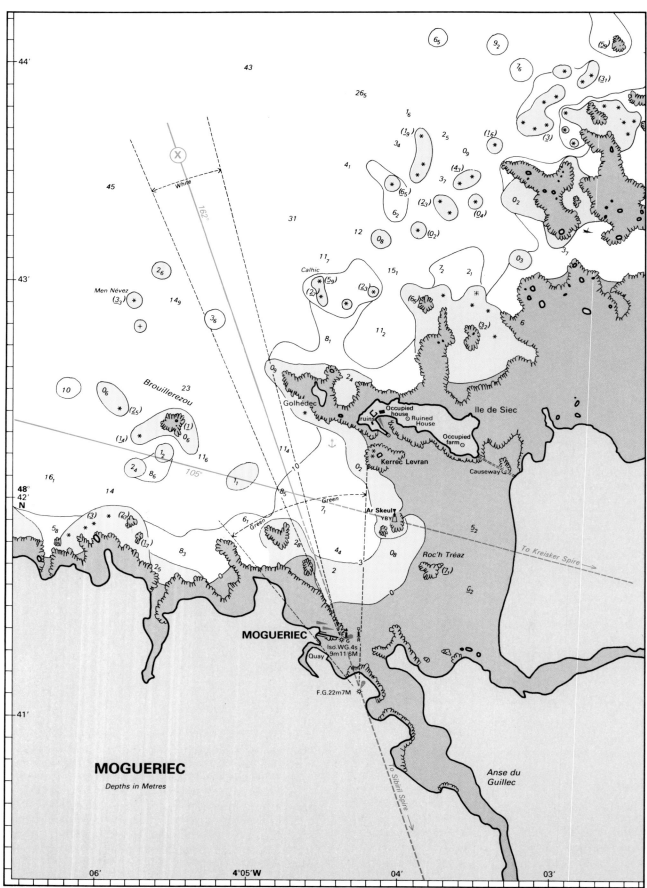

Plan 35. Moguériec

MOGUERIEC

Depths in Metres

Looking south. Ile de Siec foreground left, Moguériec breakwater above black rock on right-hand point of Ile de Siec.

Ruin on Siec in transit with end of jetty on 053°. Kerrec Levran rock far right.

connected to Ile de Siec) 0·2M to port, and various dangerous drying rocks 0·3M to starboard.

As an alternative, a vessel coming from the west can pick up the line Ar Skeul (W cardinal beacon tower) and Kreisker spire (to the right of the twin spires of St-Pol de Leon cathedral) bearing 105° and follow this until Moguériec lights come into line, then proceed as above. This leaves a rock drying 1·4m only 180m to port and crosses a 1·1m patch.

From the north, if proceeding to the Siec anchorage, after passing Golhédec bear east and come in with a conspicuous ruin over the end of the harbour jetty on 053° (see photograph). South of the jetty is the pile of rocks some 300m long, east–west, known as Kerrec Levran.

If proceeding to Moguériec (with sufficient rise of tide) hold on the transit until 0·5M off the break-water lighthouse when bear to port to bring it bearing 170°, then steer to pass between the star-board beacon off the end of the breakwater and the port beacon.

Moguériec breakwater head bearing 200° with rear leading
lighthouse left of picture.

The harbour at low water. *Capelan* on visitor's mooring, behind
4th lamp post from the right.

By night

Steering on a safe course towards or away from Ile de Batz light (Fl(4)25s), pick up the rear light (F.G) which has a range of 7M and is visible over an arc from 142° to 182°, and the front light which is Iso.WG.4s with the white sector between 158° and 166°, that is 4° either side of the alignment. Turn to follow the line. Close approach to the anchorage or the harbour might be difficult for a stranger. It should not however be difficult to make departure by night, by steering a compass course from the anchorage into the white sector of the front light and then following the transit.

Anchorage

The anchorage at Ile de Siec is south of the western end of the island and the exact position depends on the state of the tide. At springs there is 7·3m sand and shells with the end of the island jetty bearing 075° 0·25M, but with the aid of soundings a yacht can find a position nearer to the jetty where it is more sheltered. On a neap tide (6m at Brest) there is 2·1 to 2·4m midway between the island and Kerrec Levran with the main rock bearing about 160°. This rock is clearly identifiable at high water, but there are blocks of rocks which dry out close N and NW of it, so that care must be taken to find the narrow strip between these rocks and those off the island, which gives limited swinging room. The water is generally transparent and the bottom close to the east of this position is rocky and weed covered so that visitors may prefer to anchor farther west on sand and in water which rapidly deepens.

The small harbour itself is protected by a low breakwater. Along the inside runs a rough jetty, the outer half of which is a slipway, running down to the end of the breakwater where it turns back for a few metres, the end drying over 2·4m LAT. The harbour seems quite well protected and small fishing boats lie there on double-ended moorings, drying out clear of the jetty on a small area of sand. A visit at high water is well worthwhile and yachts can lay alongside the inner half of the jetty-cum-slip. On entering, look out for floating lines and fishing floats. The bottom consists of loose boulders and a bilge-keeler could suffer damage to the rudder if this should touch first on taking the ground.

Moguériec harbour

The harbour lies on the west side of the mouth of the river Guillec. At low water the stream turns west into the harbour, running round a large mound of soft sand and out along the wall.

On the middle of the sand mound in 1990 were two visitors' moorings which provided very comfortable berths for a bilge-keeler. Should a swell enter the harbour the keels will ground and take off without pounding. However, a walk ashore produces a distinct sinking feeling!

Ile de Siec harbour at HW.

Facilities

The island has no resources and appears to be deserted at night, but it is joined to the mainland by a causeway (which is probably dry at halftide).

Moguériec is a most attractive and friendly fishing village. The quays were being extended and there were half a dozen large fishing boats alongside in 1990.

There is an *alimentation* 200m from the harbour, two hotel/bars and a restaurant by the quay. There is a water tap behind the public convenience on the quay. There are excellent beaches.

Historical

During the Second World War, two British airmen parachuted into the sea nearby and, as a reprisal for help given to them by the inhabitants, all the buildings on the island were blown up by the occupying forces.

A recently heard version of this history is that arms and explosives were being landed for the Resistance and cached on the island, causing a predictable reaction on discovery.

33. Pontusval

Charts

BA *3668*
Imray *C35*
SHOM *7150*
ECM Navicarte *539*

Tidal data

Tidal heights (approx)

HW +0050 Brest, +0600 Dover
MTL 4·7m. Index 7B
Heights of tide above chart datum
MHWS 8·3m, MLWS 1·1m, MHWN 6·5m, MLWN 2·9m

Tidal streams

1. 5M seaward of Pontusval the east-going stream begins at −0250 Brest (+0220 Dover) and the west-going stream at +0315 Brest (−0400 Dover). Both streams reach 2·8 knots at springs.
2. Inshore the streams turn earlier. Off Aman ar Ross, 4M west, the east-going stream begins at −0405 Brest (+0105 Dover) and the west-going at +0215 Brest (−0500 Dover). Both streams reach 2·8 knots at springs.

General

Many cruising men will have passed Pontusval on their passages between Roscoff and l'Aber-Wrac'h, without attempting entry, as the approach looks forbidding if there is any swell or sea running. However in southerly winds there is a deep-water anchorage in the entrance and small yachts which can take the ground find shelter, except from northerly winds, drying out in the pretty and almost land-locked harbour.

Approaches

By day only

Dangerous rocks and shoals extend for up to 1M north of this coast and it should not be approached more closely, until one is sure of one's position. The most conspicuous landmarks from offshore are a large water tower to the SW and a radio mast 311m high (see photograph). The next mark to identify is Pointe de Beg Pol lighthouse, square tower and white house 13m high, elevation 16m. This, in line with the radio mast, bears 185°. Then identify Basse Toullcoz E cardinal buoy which lies 053° distant 1·3M from this lighthouse.

Pontusval, looking south. An Neudenn beacon tower foreground centre, with white motorboat entering right of tower. Radio mast arrowed.

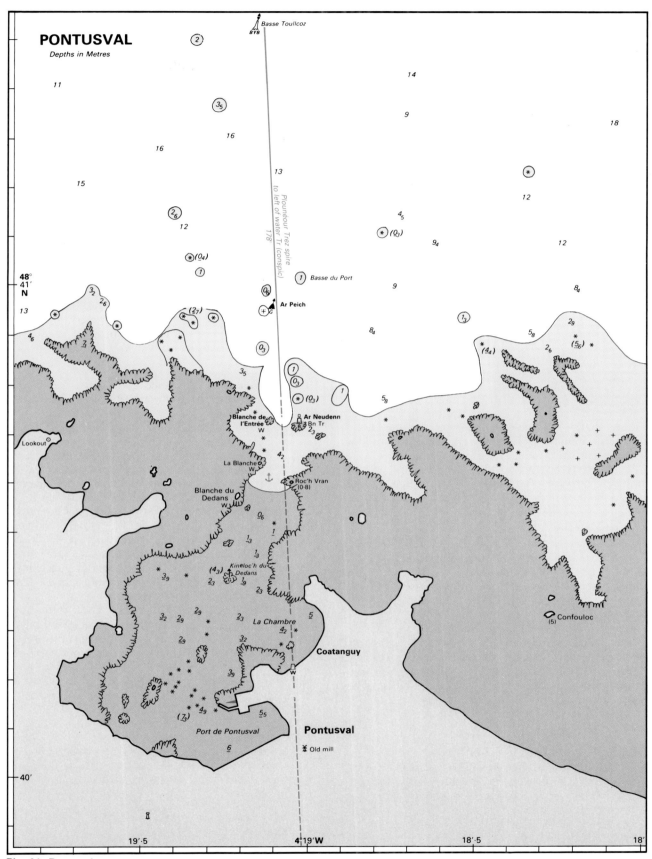

Plan 36. Pontusval

Entry leading marks in transit on 178°.

Approach this buoy from the north and leave it close to starboard. It is on the leading line and the leading marks will be seen in line, bearing 178°. They are: Plounéour-Trez spire in transit with the white beacon on the east side of the harbour.

Ar Peich starboard buoy will then be fine on the starboard bow and An Neudenn port beacon tower fine on the port bow. Follow this line 178° leaving:

Ar Peich starboard buoy close to starboard.
An Neudenn port beacon tower 50m to port.

On the starboard side of the channel is the first of a line of three rocks which, in a good year, are painted white. They were unpainted in 1990 but were unmistakable for all that. 220m past An Neudenn tower and slightly to port of the transit is the above-water Roc'h Vran (elevation 0·8m).

When entering there is the first white painted rock (Blanche de l'Entrée) and two others to be left to starboard farther in (La Blanche and Blanche du Dedans). South of La Blanche the channel shoals rapidly and a yacht can only proceed farther with adequate rise of tide.

Anchorage and harbour

The deep-water anchorage in 4m, with rather restricted swinging room, is defined by the first and second white painted rocks to starboard with An Neudenn beacon tower and Roc'h Vran to port. There are rocks close on each side which are awash or dry 0·3m at low water.

At neaps a yacht can sound her way and anchor or pick up a visitor's mooring farther in, finding about 2·7m at low water. The anchorage is indifferent except in offshore winds with no prospect of a shift of wind to or swell from a northerly direction, when it can become dangerous.

The harbour itself can be entered near high water but no precise instructions can be given as there is a rock in the centre named Kineloch du Dedans which dries 4·3m LAT, marked by a starboard beacon.

The approximate way in is to bring An Neudenn on a NNE bearing and to steer SSW, borrowing to starboard as necessary to avoid the fringes of the rock on the east side. Then when the houses on the headland to port bear east, alter course to west (leaving Kineloch du Dedans to starboard), steer into the anchorage on the west side and borrow a mooring or anchor if there is space, buoying the anchor (sand bottom), near the small craft moorings.

This anchorage is well protected from west but dries over 3m LAT. La Chambre, drying 4·2m LAT, situated on the east side also provides an anchorage for small craft, but there are occasional outcrops of rocks on the bottom. At Port de Pontusval there is a quay and a slip with rocks on its north side and sand on its south side but it is still dry at MTL.

Facilities

There are good shops, a number of holiday hotels, banks and post office at Brignogan, ¼M walk from the beach at the south side of the harbour.

34. Le Correjou

Charts

BA *3668*
SHOM *7150, 7094* (western approach only)

Tidal data

Tidal heights (approx)

HW +0030 Brest, +0540 Dover
MTL 4·7 m. Index 7B
Heights of tide above chart datum
MHWS 7·9m, MLWS 1·2m, MHWN 6·4m, MLWN 3·0m

Tidal streams

1. In Chenal Occidental the ESE-going stream begins at −0515 Brest (−0005 Dover) and the WNW-going stream at +0110 Brest (−0605 Dover). Both 2 knots.
2. In Chenal Oriental the NE-going stream begins at −0445 Brest (+0025 Dover) and the SW-going stream at +0125 Brest (−0550 Dover). Both 2 knots.

General

Like Pontusval this harbour provides anchorage for deep-keeled yachts in settled southerly weather and better shelter for yachts capable of drying out. This harbour should only be approached in good visibility and settled weather. There were omissions in both the BA and SHOM charts available in 1990. It is hoped that the new editions will be corrected and that in particular the two rocks, Carrec and Petit Cromm will be reinserted.

Approaches

FROM THE NORTH – CHENAL ORIENTAL

By day only

From a position about 1·3M west of Aman ar Ross N cardinal pillar whistle buoy, identify Plouguerneau belfry, which is about 0·25M west of a prominent water tower. Bring this to bear 189°, then identify Mean Van, a small rock drying 7·1m (BA and SHOM), which may have a beacon (an inconspicuous metal spike in 1990), on this bearing and lying about 0·25M to the east of a much larger above-water rock, Lizen Du shown on plan 5.

Turn on to this transit and follow it, leaving to port Karreg Hir port cylindrical buoy until about 0·3M north of Men Yan and when Penven rock is abeam to starboard, distant 0·2M.

Le Correjou, looking south. The Croms centre foreground, behind them two fishing boats, not beacon towers.

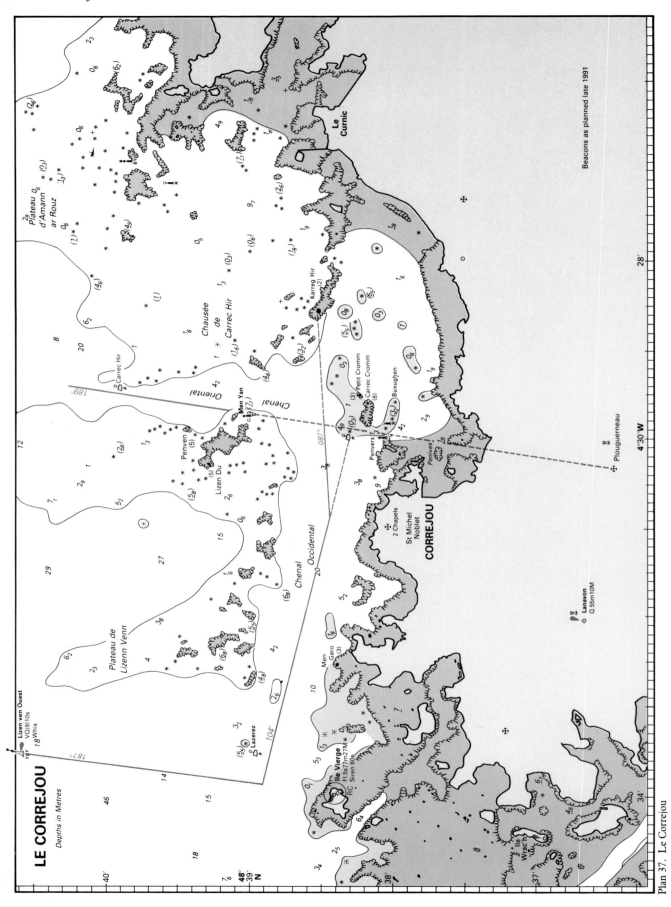

LE CORREJOU
Depths in Metres

**48°
39'
N**

Lizen ven Ouest
VQ(9)10s
18 Whis

Lazerez
R

Plateau de
Lizenn Venn

Carrec Hir
R

Carrec Hir

Plateau 0₆
d'Amann
ar Rouz

Chausée
de
Carrec Hir

Oriental

Chenal

Men Yan

Penven (5)

Lizen Du

Chenal
Occidental

Karreg Hir (2)

Le
Curnic

Petit Cromm
Carrec Cromm
Buxughen

Penvers

Penvers

CORREJOU

2 Chapels
St Michel
Noblet

Men
Garo (3)

Ile Vierge
Fl.5s77m27M
RC. Siren 60s

Ile
Wrac'h

Lanavon
Q.55m10M

Plouguerneau

Beacons as planned late 1991

Plan 37. Le Corréjou

Ile Vierge, bearing 190°.

Then quit the leading line and steer to make good 178°, heading for a point midway between the two pinnacles of Carrec Cromm. This line passes between two 1m LAT patches and must be regarded as having such minimum depth.

When 100m north of the northeast pinnacle, alter course to port so as to leave it 100m to starboard on the same course. This leaves Baxughen drying rock 200m to starboard. Continue to make good 178° until the southern chapel of St-Michel Noblet bears 280° then turn on to this heading into the anchorage.

FROM THE WEST – CHENAL OCCIDENTAL
By day only

This channel is wider than the Chenal Oriental and may be preferred. From a position close west of Lizen Ven Ouest W cardinal buoy Ile Vierge lighthouse bears 187°. Make good this course for the lighthouse until Lazerez port buoy is abaft the beam to port bearing about 080° then alter course onto 104° and identify the two pinnacles of Carrec Cromm and Le Petit Cromm (elevation 8m and 3m) on this bearing.

This course leaves Men Leac'h (or Men Garo), a conspicuous cottage-loaf-shaped, above-water rock 0·28M to starboard. Identify the two chapels with a cross on a pointed rock between them on the headland north of Le Correjou. The right-hand chapel is of St-Michel Noblet. Confirm identification of the Cromms and when the chapels are abeam steer 087° for Karreg Hir rock (elevation 2m) to leave the port buoy marking the entrance to the local fishermen's channel to the west of the Carrecs to starboard.

With Carrec Cromm abeam alter to starboard to leave Petit Cromm 150m to starboard.

When Petit Cromm bears 270° steer 180° until the southern chapel, St-Michel Noblet, bears 280°, then turn onto this heading into the anchorage.

The local fishermen's channel west of the Cromms may not be well enough marked in 1992 to attempt its passage.

Anchorage

Note An *Ancienne Zone Minée* is marked on SHOM *7150* and is mentioned in the BA *Channel Pilot* (*NP 27*). The area is enclosed by a pecked line running along the 48°40′N parallel with lines to the shore on the meridians of 4°23′·5W and 4°32′W. Mines in this area may still be resting on the bottom and anchoring is discouraged without first obtaining advice from local fishermen.

A possible anchorage is southeast of Penvers Island in 0·6 to 2·9m sand.

Amenities

Small fishing harbour with sailing school. Dinghy landing at quay.

35. L'Aber-Wrac'h

Charts
BA *1432, 3668*
Imray *C35*
SHOM *7094, 7150*

Tidal data

Tidal heights (approx)
HW +0030 Brest, +0540 Dover
MTL 4·7m. Index 7B
Heights of tide above chart datum
MHWS 7·9m, MLWS 1·2m, MHWN 6·4m, MLWN 3·0m

Tidal streams
1. Offshore 5M seaward of Le Libenter the east-going stream begins at −0300 Brest (+0210 Dover) and the SW-going at +0310 Brest (−0405 Dover). Both streams reach 2·8 knots at springs.
2. Off Le Libenter and in the Grand Chenal de l'Aber-Wrac'h and probably close in to Ile Vierge the streams turn earlier. The east-going or ESE-going stream begins at −0500 Brest (+0010 Dover) and the west-going or WNW-going stream begins at +0110 Brest (−0605 Dover). The outer streams attain 3·7 knots and the Grand Chenal streams 2·8 knots at springs.

General

L'Aber-Wrac'h is perhaps the best anchorage between Tréguier and Brest, and is much used by yachts bound to or from the Chenal du Four.

The river can be entered by day or night at any state of the tide, but calls for reasonable visibility in order to pick up the leading lines whilst keeping clear of the many off-lying dangers. Approach may be easier by night, but not in bad visibility, as it is necessary to be able to pick up Lanvaon light

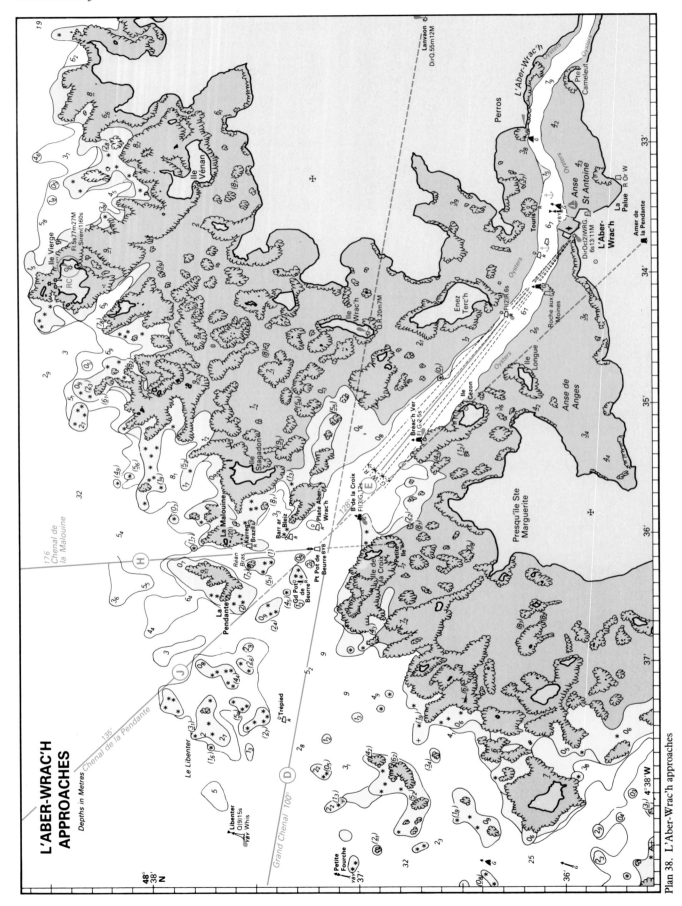

L'ABER-WRAC'H APPROACHES

Depths in Metres

48° 38' N

4° 38' W

Plan 38. L'Aber-Wrac'h approaches

L'Aber-Wrac'h, lifeboat slip bearing 123°.

(elevation 55m, range 12M) at a range of at least 5M and Ile Wrac'h red light (elevation 19m, range 7M) at a range of at least 3M. By day it is possible to enter in lesser visibility, provided the yacht's position can be fairly accurately plotted whilst looking for the outer marks.

The popular anchorage at La Palue is conveniently near the entrance, but not always fully sheltered. The river above Pointe Cameleut is a snug retreat, sheltered by steep wooded banks.

Approaches

GRAND CHENAL

By day

Make a position from which Ile Vierge lighthouse (elevation 77m), which has a radiobeacon *VG* 314 kHz range 70M, bears 090° distant 3M; with Ploudalmézeau tall steeple on the skyline in transit with Lampaul-Ploudalmézeau steeple (nearer, below the skyline) bearing 186°.

Steer to follow a line keeping Ploudalmézeau steeple open to the west of Lampaul steeple allowing for strong cross tides, and leaving the overfalls over the Basses Occidentales du Libenter shoals to port.

Head with La Petite Fourche W cardinal spar buoy fine on the port bow until Le Libenter W cardinal pillar light and whistle buoy with radar reflector is abeam, distant 0·25M, to port. Usually the whistle in

this buoy can be heard for over a mile (not to be relied on). See plan 38.

Then alter towards La Petite Fourche buoy until the leading marks for the Grand Chenal come into line: Ile Wrac'h lighthouse (square white tower with red top on white house, elevation 19m) in line with Lanvaon rectangular tower (pointed top painted white towards the transit, elevation 55m). Plouguerneau belfry farther inland is also on this line bearing 100°. A tall thin columnar water tower can be seen to the north of Lanavaon tower (see photograph). Alter course to follow this line (D).

If visibility is poor, having found the Libenter buoy, identify Trépied port buoy 0·6M bearing 109° from Libenter buoy and steer to leave it 100m to port.

This line leaves the following marks on the sides shown:

Libenter W cardinal pillar light and whistle buoy with radar reflector 0·15M to port.

Trépied port buoy 100m to port.

Grand Pot de Beurre port pyramid 0·1M to port. (This mark is deceptive and looks rather like a large pillar buoy from a distance.)

Petit Pot de Beurre E cardinal beacon tower 80m to port.

Plate Aber-Wrac'h port buoy 150m to port.

However, just before this latter buoy is abeam, alter course to starboard to follow line E: La Palue former lighthouse (white tower with red top), St-

153

The three leading marks for Grande Chenal, repainted 1991. Note water tower to left of line.

Amer de la Pendante (rear marker for Chenal de la Pendante, repainted), just visible on skyline, halfway between front mark (white roundel) on fort Ile Cézon and green tower Breac'h Vert.

Chenal de la Malouine at half tide. From left to right: 1. La Malouine, 2. Karreg Bazil port town, 3. Petit Pot de Beurre (in transit with Petite Ile white beacon left centre), 4. Water tower, 5. Grand Pot de Beurre port tower right.

Antoine former lighthouse (white tower with red top) and the new white light pillar by the lifeboat house, in line bearing 128° (line E). The line leaves the following marks on the sides shown:

Petite Ile de la Croix white pyramid 0·25M to starboard.

Basse de la Croix starboard buoy 180m to starboard.

Bréac'h Ver starboard beacon tower 80m to starboard.

Fort Ile Cézon, a small stone fort with a circular black-and-white mark painted on its northern wall, 0·1M to starboard.

Enez Terc'h port buoy 50m to port.

Roche aux Moines starboard beacon tower 65m to starboard. (Towards high water a small yacht working to windward may choose to pass over the oyster beds to the SW of this rock, the SW corner of which is marked by a white beacon tower. This passage dries 3·2m LAT, i.e. has 1·5m of water at half tide and 3·2m at MHWN.)

Continuing up the main channel, when the Roche aux Moines starboard beacon tower is abeam to starboard, alter course to 110° for about 0·2M leaving the next port buoy about 50m to port.

Then alter to port as though to leave Touris port beacon tower 75m to port. A large round mooring buoy lies to the NNW of the jetty and may be passed on either side. Enter the anchorage or go alongside the pontoon.

If bound up the river steer to leave the small starboard buoy SW of the Perros slip close to starboard. There is a shoal with only 1m over it LAT, situated midstream about 0·175M upstream of Touris beacon tower, but there is nearly always enough water over this.

Keep close to the lines of moorings off the slipway on the north side of the river at Perros and upstream of Pointe Cameleut and thereafter keep near the middle of the river all the way to Paluden, leaving Beg an Toul starboard beacon tower close to starboard. For much of the way deep water is indicated by moorings, but it is easier for a stranger to proceed up the river at half tide, when oyster withies will be seen on each side of the channel.

By night

Approaching from the north or east, bring Ile Vierge light Fl.5s to bear 090° distant about 3·5M with Corn Carhai light Fl(3)12s, bearing 223°. From this position Libenter W cardinal light and whistle buoy, with radar reflector, Q(9)15s, will bear 140° distant 1·1M.

Steer 180° to avoid the overfalls on Basses Occidentales du Libenter and continue to make good this course, allowing for a cross tide, until the leading lights for the Grand Chenal bear 100°: Ile Wrac'h (front) Q.R.7M, in line with Lanvaon (rear) DirQ.12M (intensified 090°-110°).

Then alter to follow this transit (line D) until the green sector of l'Aber-Wrac'h Oc(2)WRG directional light comes into view, then stand by to alter course to follow the white sector on a course of 128° (line E).

Approaching from the west or southwest, navigate to ensure that Grande Basse de Portsall W cardinal light and whistle buoy, VQ(9)10s, is left at least 1M to starboard before coming on to the leading line.

CHENAL DE LA MALOUINE

This channel is narrow and when using it for the first time it is probably advisable to leave rather than to enter by it so that the marks can be positively identified for future use.

By day only

From a position on line B, 1·5M west of Ile Vierge lighthouse, identify La Malouine a large rock (see photograph), and La Pendante a lower rock to the west of it. In the gap between these rocks identify Le Petit Pot de Beurre E cardinal squat beacon tower and the white pyramid on Petite Ile de la Croix.

Bring these into line bearing 176° and steer to follow this line, making allowance for the cross tide (line H.) This channel carries a least depth of 3m, but passes very close to an isolated rock drying 1·7m, 0·17M NNW of La Malouine and to the NE end of the Plateau de la Pendante, which has a least depth of 0·3m and over which the sea commonly breaks at all states of the tide. In heavy weather this broken water is said to extend right across the channel, and a yacht should then use the Grand Chenal. The line leaves the following marks on the sides shown:

La Malouine rock 100m to port.

Carrec Bazil port beacon tower 90m to port.

Réan Bras rock (dries 6·4m LAT) 90m to starboard.

Bar-ar-Bleiz port buoy 100m to port.

When the latter is abeam, quit the leading line and steer midway between Petit Pot de Beurre E cardinal beacon tower and Plate Aber-Wrac'h port buoy.

Then bring La Palue former lighthouse (white tower red top), St-Antoine former lighthouse (white tower red top) and the new white-sectored light pillar by the lifeboat house into line bearing 128°, and follow this line as for *Grand Chenal*, above.

CHENAL DE LA PENDANTE

In 1990 it was only possible to identify the rear marker for this channel by walking up to it, after which it still could only be located from the channel with binoculars. In 1991 it had been repainted and was conspicuous. Dangers lie close on each side of the channel and the line must be precisely held so that, as with La Malouine channel, departure, in good conditions, is preferable to entry.

By day only

From a position on line B, 2·5M west of Ile Vierge lighthouse, identify Fort Ile Cézon, a small stone fort on an island with a black-and-white circular mark painted on the wall of the fort, and Amer de la Pendante black tower, with a white stripe and an orange conical top among trees and to the left of houses on the skyline a short distance to the right of the conspicuous fishery school building. The Amer de la Pendante tower is among the tall, thin, floodlight poles of the rugby field, with three houses to the right. There is a conspicuous water tower about 300m to the west of it which assists in identification. These marks in line bearing 136° mark the Chenal de la Pendante (line J). This channel carries a least depth of 3·6m, but it passes very close to drying rocks on the NE side of Le Libenter and the SW side of the Plateau de la Pendante. It should not be attempted unless the leading marks have been positively identified before approaching, nor in heavy weather, and not in poor visibility. The leading marks must be held exactly. Follow the leading line which leaves La Pendante, an anvil-shaped above-water rock, painted white, 0·1M to port.

When Grand Pot de Beurre port beacon bears 175°, quit the leading line and steer for the Bar-ar-Bleiz port buoy, but when Petit Pot de Beurre E cardinal beacon tower comes into line with Petite Ile de la Croix white pyramid (line H) alter course so as to pass midway between the Petit Pot de Beurre E cardinal beacon tower and Plate Aber-Wrac'h port buoy. From here follow line E and proceed as for the *Grand Chenal* above.

Anchorages

Once prohibited, BA *1432* and SHOM *7094* show a deep-water anchorage in 8m between Fort Ile Cézon and Enez Terc'h. Otherwise:

1. Large yachts usually anchor about 0·2M east of Roche aux Moines in 10m LAT, sand, but this position is rather exposed with the wind from the west or northwest. There is a foul patch only 100m northwest of the anchorage position marked on plan 37.
2. There is better shelter in the fairway to the south and southeast of Touris beacon tower, in 3 to 7·6m, sand. The farther south the better, but the edge of the bank is steep and it is possible to take a sounding in deep water and hit the mud before the next is taken. Much of this anchorage is now taken up by permanent moorings, which are available for visitors with boats over 10m long. Some are rather close together and yachts may touch if one is wind-rode and the other tide-rode.
3. A berth may be available at the yacht pontoon east of the jetty. The outer three berths on each side are available to boats of less than 10m length, the inner berths are restricted to yachts of 8m or less. This is very convenient for all purposes.
4. There is perfect shelter anywhere in the fairway above Pointe Cameleut, in depths of 4·8 to 6·1m LAT, mud, as far as Beg-an-Toul; and in depths of 1·8 to 3·6m LAT, mud, from Beg-an-Toul to Paluden, but space in this reach is limited by local moorings. The position shown on the plan to the east of Pointe Cameleut is a good one. Land on the foreshore (mud at LW) and follow the road over a mile to l'Aber-Wrac'h.
5. Below the small quay on the west bank at Paluden is a long trot of dumbbell moorings and it is usually possible to find a berth. There is a good drying berth alongside the quay, drying 2·4m

Slipway at curve of river above l'Aber-Wrac'h, half tide. Starboard buoy warns of oyster beds.

Looking downstream to moorings at Paluden (1990). These were more crowded in 1991.

LAT, muddy shingle, but this is sometimes required by coasters. There is a charge for anchoring in the vicinity of the quay but not (1991) farther down river. The large pool above the quay dries.

Facilities

La Palue, or Port de l'Aber-Wrac'h

If lying to one of the visitors' buoys, three blasts on the foghorn will bring a harbour launch for free transport ashore. A charge is made for the mooring, boats lying to their own anchors pay half price. Manoeuvring under sail in the port is not allowed. Yachts without engine must hail a harbour attendant. Insurance of yachts is compulsory, although one's word is taken for this, otherwise a premium is charged by the harbour attendant.

Visiting yachts are issued with a temporary membership card for the Yacht Club des Abers which is current for the period covered by the berthing fee.

Water on the pontoons, petrol and diesel on the quay.

The yacht club provides WCs, showers (0830–1200 and 1500–1900, not cheap), telephone, sail washing, battery charging, charts, weather forecast, rest rooms and bar, which has limited opening hours.

Chandler, supplying charts near the pontoon. Small food store open in summer.

Marie-Jo's Restaurant with l'Escale Bar, 200m along the road to the west of the chandler is excellent. She is a character and welcomes yachtsmen, especially from the West Country! *Crêperie* near quay. Takeaway oysters from Belon des Abers. Buses to Brest stop at the café near the root of the mole.

Walk up the hill, a little over a mile to Landéda, viewing the Amer de la Pendante en route. The village sports a bank, bars, a *dépôt de pain*, an *alimentation général* (*sérieuse* according to Marie-Jo) and on the left as you enter the square a *huit à huit* supermarket owned by Charlie Alouch, a keen rugby player and coach who speaks English (no comment from Marie-Jo).

A little over 2M SE of l'Aber-Wrac'h and about a mile uphill from Paluden is Lannilis, a pleasant small town with good shopping facilities and restaurants.

Paluden consists of a few cottages and a good hotel. There are no local shops, but it is possible to obtain milk and other farm produce locally. Simple meal at Café Breton and Relais des Abers, half a mile up the road. On the bank opposite to the quay is a small sailing/rowing club which can supply water when open.

Bus from La Palue/l'Aber-Wrac'h to Lannilis.

36. L'Aber-Benoît

Charts
BA *1432, 3668*
Imray *C35*
SHOM *7094*

Tidal data

Tidal heights (approx)
HW +0025 Brest, +0535 Dover
MTL 4·7m. Index 7B
Heights of tide above chart datum
MHWS 8·1m, MLWS 1·1m, MHWN 6·4m, MLWN 3·0m

Tidal streams
1. Off La Petite Fourche buoy the ENE-going stream begins at −0515 Brest (−0005 Dover) and the west-going stream begins at +0055 Brest (+0605 Dover). Both streams attain 2·8 knots at springs.
2. South of Ile Guénioc the flood stream begins at −0500 Brest (+0010 Dover) and the ebb at +0100 Brest (+0610 Dover), reaching 2·5 to 3 knots. In the river itself the flood begins 15 minutes earlier and both streams reach about 3 knots.

General
Lying only 2M SW of l'Aber-Wrac'h, this little river offers excellent sheltered anchorage in beautiful surroundings. It is known locally as La Rivière de Saint-Pabu.

It can be entered at any state of the tide, but only in daylight and reasonable visibility. In strong westerly or northwesterly winds the northern approach described below is said to be dangerous, owing to broken water.

Approaches
NORTHERN APPROACH
By day only
Approach from any direction, make for La Petite Fourche W cardinal spar buoy. From a position 20m west of this buoy steer to make good 168° (line C) leaving Rusven Est starboard conical buoy 50m to starboard.

Continue on this course until Basse du Chenal port beacon, south of Ile Guénioc, bears about 125° and the highest point of Ile Guénioc is abeam to port, then steer 134° to leave Basse du Chenal port beacon 150m to port, Karreg ar Poul Doun port beacon 200m to port and Men Renead starboard buoy 30m to starboard.

With Men Renead buoy abeam, alter to starboard to leave the conspicuous La Jument rock, marked with a patch of red paint and a port beacon, 40m to port, whence follow the channel on 142°, marked by Ar Gazel and Kervigorn starboard buoys and Le

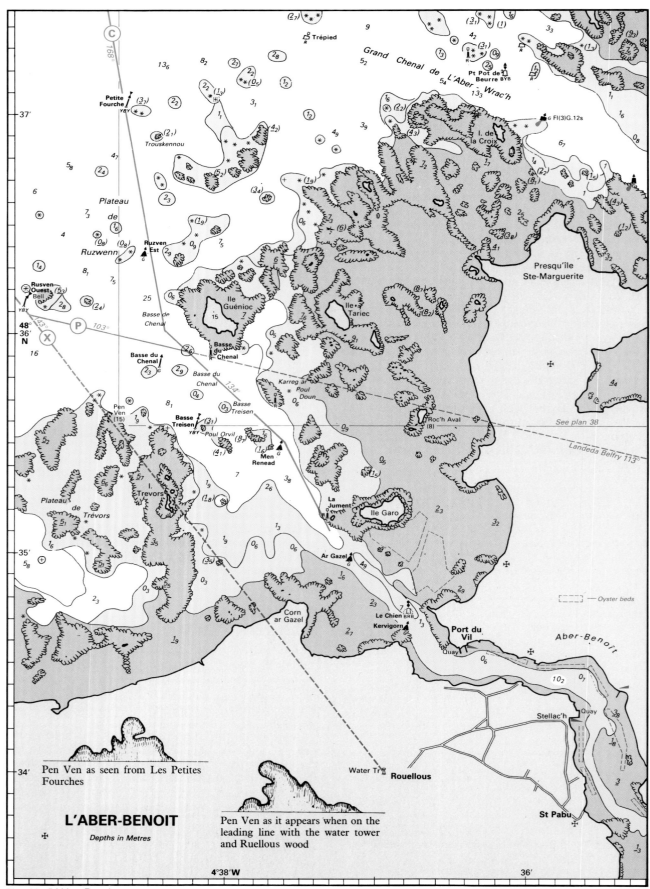

Pen Ven as seen from Les Petites
Fourches

L'ABER-BENOIT

Depths in Metres

Pen Ven as it appears when on the
leading line with the water tower
and Ruellous wood

Plan 39. L'Aber-Benoît

Aber-Benoît, looking east.

Chien isolated danger beacon tower which should be left to port. Depths in the channel and upriver are unpredictable due to dredging and soundings should be taken as a precaution, but 2m or more can be expected at LW as far as Stellac'h (formerly Le Passage).

After passing Kervigorn starboard buoy and leaving the small-craft on moorings in the sandy bay of Kervigorn to starboard, the channel is indicated by yacht and fishing-boat moorings (with due regard to those fitted with legs!)

There are oyster beds on the north bank as far as Stellac'h and they then continue on both sides of the river. The channel turns south at Stellac'h and there is a drying bank extending over halfway out into the river, opposite to and south of the quay.

WESTERN APPROACH

By day only

This is the best approach in bad weather.

From the north, with Rouellou water tower, just below the wood of that name, held open to the right of the prominent Pen Ven rock (see sketch) at about 143° (line X), follow this line to leave Rusven Ouest W cardinal spar buoy 50m to port.

On passing Rusven Ouest buoy, turn onto 103° with Landéda belfry in transit with the left-hand edge of Roc'h Aval (elevation 8m) (line P). Leaving

Basse du Chenal starboard buoy to starboard continue on this transit for 300m and then turn to starboard onto 134° and at this point join the *Northern approach* above.

From the Rélec channel see page 165 (*Eastbound passage, Chenal du Rélec*), when Le Rélec E cardinal buoy is abeam to port, steer 085° for Rusven Ouest W cardinal buoy thus avoiding Le Trépied rocks to the east of Le Rélec.

When Landéda belfry is in transit with the left-hand edge of Roc'h Aval (elevation 8m) bearing 103° (line P), turn onto this bearing and proceed as above.

The preferred channel for entry was for some years to the south of Poul Orvil rocks, but the introduction of port beacons and three starboard buoys has made the channel to the north easier to follow.

Anchorage

Anchor anywhere in the pool clear of moorings, on either side of the Pointe du Stellac'h, or borrow a mooring by arrangement. The depths vary due to dredging and there are some patches of rock. There is also anchorage near the entrance in the sandy bay of Kervigorn if the wind is offshore. Anchor in deep water just north of the local yachts and boats on moorings and land by dinghy on the sands.

La Jument rock with red patch to be left to port; starboard buoy, centre of picture, to starboard.

Facilities

If healthy exercise is required, this is the place to visit. With regard to replenishment of stores, the returns are not great.

There is a good dinghy landing at all states of the tide on each side of the river at the Pointe du Stellac'h, especially on the south side. Land at the quay, upstream just round the point, where there is a tap and a public telephone. From the quay walk half a mile up the hill in a westerly direction to find two small shops, a garage, doctor and chemist, several café bars and a small restaurant. A left turn on the hill above the quay leads half a mile south past Saint Pabu church to a small restaurant, a *crêperie*, a snack bar and a *bar-tabac*. Water can be obtained from a pipe in Kervigorn bay.

37. Portsall inner passage

Charts

BA *1432*
SHOM *7094*

Tidal data

Tidal streams

The directions and rates of the tidal streams vary in different parts of the channels between spring and neap tides and are influenced by the formation of the plateaux and rocks between which they run. They are, for example, particularly rapid north of Ile Verte where, towards low water, the streams are compressed between the island and the shoals north of the channel. In the more open parts of the channels the streams tend to be more moderate.

The following table shows the approximate rates and directions of the streams in the main channels.

	East-going stream				*West-going stream*		
		Spring				*Spring*	
Position	*Direction*	*Rate*	*Begins*		*Direction*	*Rate*	*Begins*
Chenal du Rélec	NE	3·5–4	−0500 Brest (+0010 Dover)		SW	3·5–4	+0130 Brest (+0640 Dover)
Chenal du Raous	ENE	4·5–5	−0500 Brest (+0010 Dover)		WSW	4·5–5	+0130 Brest (+0640 Dover)
Chenal Méridional	ENE	3·5–4	−0500 Brest (+0010 Dover)		W	4–5	+0130 Brest (+0640 Dover)

General

This passage inside Portsall rocks, as well as giving access to Portsall itself, provides a short cut between l'Aber-Wrac'h and l'Aber-Benoît to and from the Four channel, together with an interesting exercise in rock dodging. It can be used only in clear weather and, if sailing, with a leading wind. Preferably it will not be used at spring tides as the stream is very strong, especially in the vicinity of Portsall. At low water the rocks are clear, but some of the back leading marks may be masked for a considerable distance by the front marks, standing high above low water. In places the channel between rocks is so narrow that an error would be dangerous, and great care is necessary when navigating through it for the first time, which is best done east to west. The channels carry 2·1m LAT (3·3m MLWS) but as there are rocks in the vicinity of the Chenal du Rélec it is sensible to regard them as having 0·3m LAT (1·5m MLWS). For reasons which will appear later, it is better to make the passage when the soundings are 3·6m above datum.

The passage passes through three named and one unnamed channel. From east to west: first there is the Chenal du Rélec from La Petite Fourche to Ile Longue; next the Chenal du Raous to the rock Bosven Kreiz, with a continuation (unnamed) channel to Bosven Aval; finally the Chenal Méridional de Portsall which is the passage from Portsall leading south of Le Four lighthouse into the Chenal du Four between the mainland and Ouessant. This inner passage is known to a number of cruising people, but it would be irresponsible not to emphasise that it is dangerous in strong winds or poor visibility. The overfalls in the narrows with a spring tide against a SW gale, west of Ile Verte, are said to be as severe as in the famous Raz de Sein and the Chenal Méridional is described as *extrêmement mauvais* under such conditions.

Le Rélec E cardinal buoy, recently installed, is a great help in locating the northern entrance (westbound passage). Corn Carhai (Corn ar C'haé) lighthouse bearing 250° just visible to right of buoy. Le Rélec rock at a safe distance far right!

Westbound passage

CHENAL DU RELEC
By day only

From the Petite Fourche W cardinal spar buoy, situated on the south side of the entrance to l'Aber-Wrac'h by the Grand Chenal make good 255° for about 0·75M when the leading marks for the Chenal du Rélec should be identified on a bearing of 218°.

The front mark is a tall beacon painted white on its north side (but this may not be obvious if seen against the light), on the north side of the steep Petit Men Louet rock or islet. If this cannot be identified from this position it means that the weather is too thick for a stranger to attempt the passage for the first time.

The beacon stands on the islet at the east end of the Men Louet group of rocks which dry high at low water as shown on the photograph on page 164. It will not be confused with Grand Men Louet beacon standing on the islet 200m west of it, which is squat and painted white only on its south side.

The rear mark, distant 5·5M, is a white beacon with a red top on Pointe de Landunvez just west of the ruins of a semaphore building, and about 0·2M SE of the headland. Do not bring the beacons in line, but keep Landunvez beacon just open to the left of Petit Men Louet beacon and follow this lead. The transit on SHOM *7094* is shown as 218·5°, but few yachts can be steered with such accuracy. According to this chart the line leaves Queyn-an-Treis (only 1·3m LAT) only a few metres to port. As the rock is dangerous at LW springs or in a large swell or rough seas, borrow to starboard temporarily when in its vicinity, to hold Le Rélec E cardinal buoy on a bearing of 220°. When the rock has been passed return to the leading line.

The channel then passes between Le Rélec on the northwest side (which dries 5·3m), marked by the E cardinal buoy and Le Trépied plateau on the southeast side (which dries 2·5m in parts).

PORTSALL INNER PASSAGE

Depths in Metres

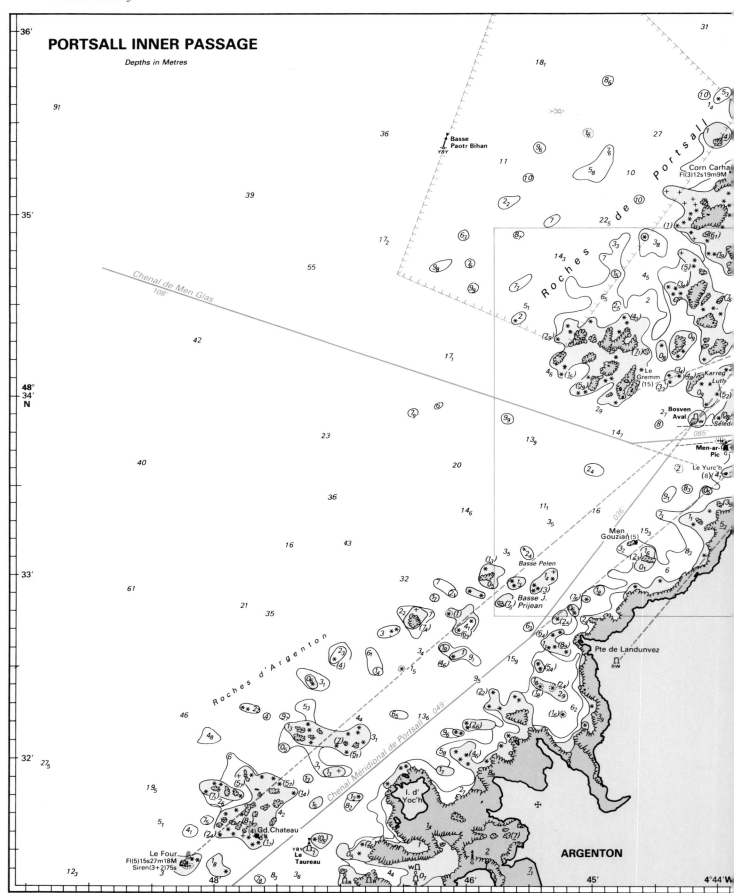

Plan 40. Portsall inner passage

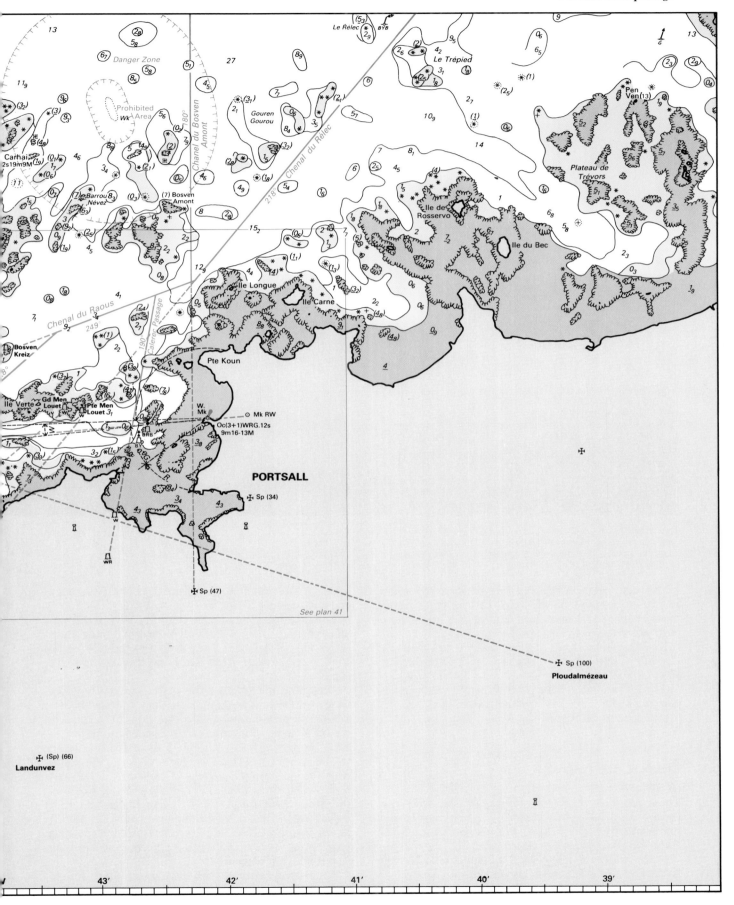

PORTSALL

Chenal du Rélec leading marks, Pointe de Landunvez beacon in transit with Petit Men Louet on 218°. Steer with the Landunvez beacon just open to the left of Petit Men Louet. The visibility here is better than average!

Chenal du Rélec leading marks, left of picture. Grand Men Louet centre of picture and Le Yurc'h, the other eastbound passage 'gunsight' mark, just right of the motorboat. *Capelan* has turned to starboard into the Chenal du Raous.

The next dangers are the line of scattered rocks known as Gouren Gourou which lie very close on the starboard hand. When in their vicinity borrow to port where there is plenty of water.

The line then leads a little over 0·15M off Ile Longue which is a low rocky area, mostly covered at HW.

Course is altered when Ile Longue is abeam to port, to make good 249° on the transit of the marks for the Chenal du Raous.

CHENAL DU RAOUS

By day only

These are Bosven Kreiz (a rock or islet with two apexes and a white beacon), in line with the southernmost high rock (15·8m above datum, 8·2m above MHWS) of Le Gremm group.

At low water the rear rock is hidden behind Bosven Kreiz and the track must be held despite the set of the stream. When at least 0·25M from Bosven Kreiz, make good 228° with Le Four lighthouse just open south of Bosven Aval (a rock or islet with one apex and a white beacon).

The transit on the SHOM chart is shown as 227·8°. This channel is most difficult between Karreg Luth (dries 5·2m LAT) and reefs drying to the NW of Ile Verte. At low water it is clearly defined as the rocks can be seen.

According to the chart the channel is nearly 200m wide, but at low water it looks less and the stream attains its maximum rate, so that a yacht is quickly set off course. Bosven Aval is a steep islet, but at LAT there is a shoal with only 0·4m extending 100m to the east of it. There is also a rock to the south which dries 1·5m. Southwest of Ile Verte is Sélédran rock which dries 0·8m LAT and, to avoid this and the dangers off Bosven Aval, when Bosven Kreiz is in line with Barrou Néves (almost covered at HWS) astern bearing 025°, alter to follow this line making good the reciprocal 205° until Ile Verte is abeam then alter slightly to starboard.

When Men Gouzian rock touches the tip of Pointe de Landunvez bearing 210°, alter to maintain this transit, leaving Sélédran rock close to port.

Once past Bosven Aval and the rock to the south of it navigation becomes easier.

If bound for Portsall bear to port (see Portsall) but if continuing in the inner passage when Men ar Pic starboard beacon tower is abeam to port bring Bosven Kreiz and Bosven Aval into line astern bearing 036° and make good the reciprocal 216°.

Identify Le Yurc'h rock which is left about 0·4M to port, one of the next marks. Continue on this line for about 1·5M until about 0·1M west of Pointe de Landunvez. Great care should be taken to keep exactly on the transit when approaching Landunvez as many vessels have been lost on the drying rocks of Basse Pelen and Basse J Prijean 0·1M northwest of the transit, and there are also dangers to the southeast.

At half tide, Castel Braz (or Le Grand Château), an above-water rock, to be left to starboard on entering the Chenal Meridional de Portsall from the south. Le Four lighthouse bearing 250°.

Chenal Meridional leading marks, Grand Men Louet beacon tower in 'gunsight' of Le Yurc'h (arrowed), on 049°. Men Gouzain rock is just to the left of Le Yurc'h and must be left to starboard on the new course. Landunvez beacon is far right of the picture, and the turn to port for the Bosven Aval, Bosven Kreiz transit of 036° is made when Sabloc, the large rock in the centre of the picture, is abeam to starboard.

CHENAL MERIDIONAL DE PORTSALL
By day only

When the beacon on Grand Men Louet, which is painted white on the SW side and is about 0·1M west of Petit Men Louet beacon (grey on this side), is in line with the cleft on the top of Le Yurc'h bearing 049°, alter to make good the reciprocal 229°.

The cleft is like a gunsight and except perhaps at high water, the beacon is lost immediately the yacht deviates to one side or the other, which is easily done on a stern transit. This line leads about 0·1M north of the prominent Ile d'Yoc'h, about 0·1M south of Grand Château rock (Castel Braz on BA *1432* of 1986) which is 11m above datum and has outliers to the south and east which dry 2·2m, and leaves Le Taureau W cardinal beacon tower 0·1M to port. The line then leads into open water about 0·3M south of Le Four lighthouse.

Eastbound passage

This passage should not be attempted for the first time with visibility of less than 5M since this will be needed for the last pair of leading marks. However some may prefer to make the passage eastbound rather than westbound, as it can be taken on a rising tide and usually with a fair wind. Le Rélec E cardinal buoy, recently introduced, makes a good mark to steer for, as the stern transit beacons fade into the haze.

CHENAL MERIDIONAL DE PORTSALL
By day only

First identify Le Grand Château (Castel Braz) rock which is 11m above datum and lies about 0·4M NE of Le Four lighthouse, and Le Taureau W cardinal beacon tower 0·6M E by N from the lighthouse. The line runs about midway between these, bearing 049°, with Grand Men Louet beacon, painted white on the SW side, in line with the cleft on the top of Le Yurc'h. The cleft is like a gunsight and except perhaps at high water the beacon is lost immediately the yacht deviates to one side or the other. A help is to keep Men Gouzian, which is easily distinguished, just open west of Le Yurc'h.

Looking N. Bosven Aval (front) and Bosven Kreiz, the second pair of marks when making the eastbound passage. See text.

When Bosven Kreiz and Bosven Aval white pyramids come into line, bearing 035°, follow this line exactly until Men ar Pic starboard beacon tower is abeam to starboard, then alter course to make good 030°, keeping the east side of Men Gouzian rock touching the tip of Pointe de Landunvez on a stern transit bearing 210°. Follow this line leaving Sélédran rock (dries 0·8m) close to starboard and Bosven Aval 120m to port.

When Bosven Aval is abaft the beam, alter slightly to starboard to bring Bosven Kreiz in line with Barrou Néves (almost covered at HWS) bearing 025°. Follow this transit until Le Four lighthouse is just open of Bosven Aval astern bearing 228°, when alter to follow this line making good 048°.

Take care to note the cross stream at this point particularly as Karreg Luth (dries 5·2m) is very close to port.

CHENAL DU RAOUS

By day only

When the southernmost rock of Le Gremm is in line with Bosven Kreiz on the port quarter bearing 249°, alter to make good 069° and follow this line until the white beacon with red top on Pointe de Landunvez and the tall beacon painted white on its north side, on the north side of the steep Petit Men Louet rock or islet, are in line astern bearing 218·5°.

CHENAL DU RELEC

By day only

Then make good 038° to follow this line, passing between Le Rélec E cardinal buoy (marking an isolated rock which dries 5·3m) on the north side and Le Trépied plateau (which dries 2·5m in parts) on the south side.

When Le Rélec buoy is abeam to port, if northward bound, steer north to avoid Queyn-an-Treis (only 1·3m LAT) which is only a few metres to starboard of the line; or if bound for l'Aber-Benoît, turn onto 085° for Ruzven Ouest W cardinal buoy, avoiding a rock with 0·6m LAT 0·2M SSW of the buoy. Then, leaving Ruzven Ouest buoy 100m to port, enter the river by line P (see page 161, *Western approach*).

38. Portsall and Kersaint

Charts

BA *3668, 1432*
Imray *C35*
SHOM *7094*

Tidal data

Tidal heights (approx)
HW +0010 Brest, +0520 Dover
MTL 4·8m. Index 7B
Heights of tide above chart datum
MHWS 8·1m, MLWS 1·5m, MHWN 6·5m, MLWN 3·4m

Tidal streams

1. Offshore at Grande Basse de Portsall 3M NW of Portsall, the NE-going stream (reaching 4 knots at springs) begins at −0430 Brest (+0040 Dover), and the WSW-going stream (reaching 4 knots at springs) at +0200 Brest (+0710 Dover).
2. For Portsall inner passage see page 160. The streams in the Chenal de Men Glas have the same characteristics as Chenal du Rélec.
3. In the approach south of Ile Verte and in the outer anchorage, the flood stream begins at −0530 Brest (−0020 Dover) in an easterly direction south of Ile Verte and ENE in the anchorage, both streams reaching 2 knots at springs. The ebb stream runs west in both positions beginning at +0100 Brest (+0610 Dover), also reaching 2 knots.
4. In the entrance NNW of Beg ar Galéti the flood (east) begins at −0500 Brest (+0010 Dover), 1·5 knots at springs; and the ebb (west) at +0130 Brest (+0640 Dover), 1·7 knots at springs.

General

A pretty, drying, fishing harbour with one drying berth alongside the quay and good outside anchorages during offshore winds in settled weather. The outer approaches can be very rough with wind against tide.

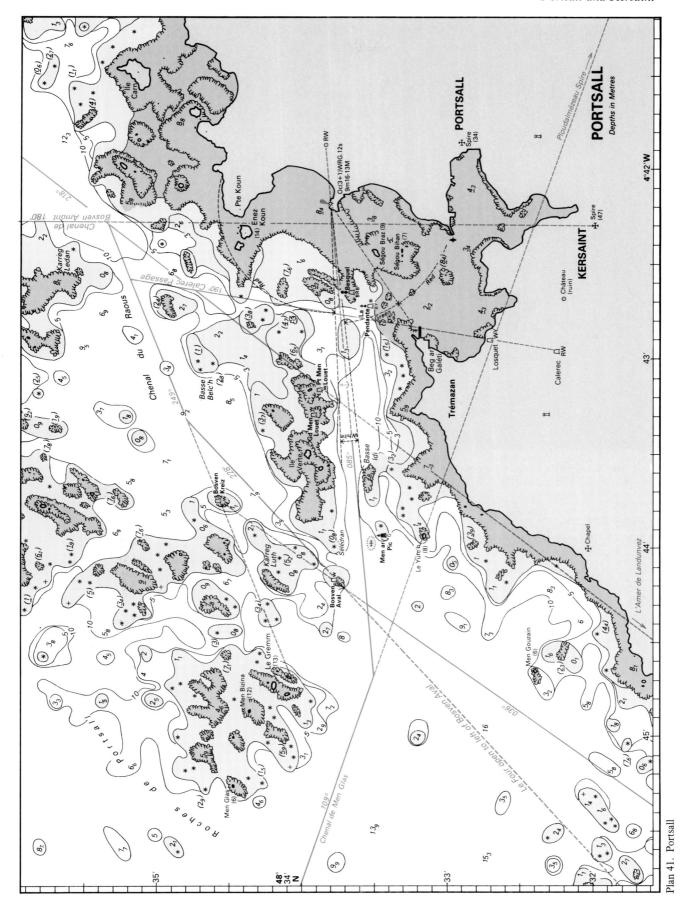

Portsall, looking SE. Petit Men Louet right foreground, lifeboat,
La Pendante beacon tower and middle of pier in transit on 225°.

Approaches

CHENAL DE MEN GLAS

By day

From a position 1·25M SW of the Basse Paupiane W
cardinal spar buoy, identify Ploudalmézeau church
steeple and Le Yurc'h rock (see photograph page 164
which shows the rock viewed from the north) which
lies 0·125M south of Men ar Pic starboard beacon
tower, and bring Le Yurc'h and Ploudalmézeau
steeple into line bearing 109°. Steer on this transit,
allowing for tidal stream, leaving Portsall rocks (Men
Glas, Men Bizina and Le Gremm) just over 0·25M to
port. The channel is wide and there is deep water
southwards in this part of the approach.

When Le Gremm rocks bear about N (or when the
more conspicuous Bosven Aval islet with white
beacon on top bears 070°) identify the next leading
marks. These are two rectangular column beacons on
the land: front is white with a silver radar reflector
along the top, and rear is white with a red top; the
bearing being 085°. They are not easy to distinguish
among the houses in their vicinity, and should not be
confused with a white water tower south of the Beg
ar Galéti which is not a leading mark.

Steer on this transit leaving Men ar Pic starboard
beacon tower 150m to starboard and Ile Verte a
similar distance to port. The danger on this approach

is Basse Idic which lies about 300m east of Men ar
Pic and has rocks on it drying 0·5 and 2·8m LAT.
The leading line leaves these about 80m to starboard.

Identify La Pendante N cardinal beacon tower to
the right of Besquel isolated danger masonry beacon.
When La Pendante beacon tower is in line with
Ségou Braz (9m), which may have a painted white
patch, bearing 094°, follow this line into the
anchorage.

By night

The characteristics of Portsall light are: Oc(3+1)
WRG.12s16-13M, elevation 9m, 058°-G-084°-W-088°
-R-058°. The approach may be made in the 4° white
sector as far as the outer anchorage. Portsall light is
more useful for departure at night than for entry by a
stranger.

CALEREC PASSAGE

By day only

When entering from the NE by Chenal du Rélec and
Chenal du Raous instead of proceeding to the
Bosvens there is a short cut west of Ile Longue which
can be used with sufficient rise of tide, over a rock
which dries 0·6m LAT and others near which dry
1m.

Entering Portsall at HW. Outer leading mark far left, lifeboat at anchorage, La Pendante BY beacon tower right.

About 0·25M west of Ile Longue when on the Bosven Kreiz–Le Gremm transit, note two pyramids: Losquet (white with red top, front) and Calerec (white with red top, rear) bearing 190°.

Alter course and follow this transit precisely for about 0·75M heading just west of La Pendante beacon tower.

Before reaching La Pendante alter course to enter the anchorage as described before. This channel is very narrow and the leading marks must be held precisely in transit. It is considered better locally than the pass from Bosven Kreiz to Bosven Aval, which involves a detour and where the seas are often more rough.

However, should identification of the leading marks be uncertain, it would be better to leave rather than enter by this passage.

CHENAL DU BOSVEN AMONT

This approach passes through the *Zone dangereuse, Plongée sous marine interdite*, outside the *Zone interdite* surrounding the wreck of the *Amoco Cadiz*. Since 1990 it has been possible to use this passage again (see plan 40, *Portsall inner passage*).

From a position 1M west of Le Rélec E cardinal buoy, the leading line is with the bell tower of Kersaint church between Pointe Koun and Enez Koun islet (16m high) on a bearing of 180°. This transit leaves Bosven Amont rock (height 7m) 0·14M to starboard, but with a drying rock halfway between it and the transit.

0·4M past Bosven Amont turn to starboard to join the Chenal du Raous with the southernmost of the Roches du Gremm in transit with the white pyramid on Bosven Kreiz bearing 249°.

The harbour may then be entered by the Calerec passage if so desired.

Anchorages

The recognised anchorage is about 0·1M SW of Petit Men Louet beacon in 11 to 12m, or in a position where La Pendante N cardinal beacon tower bears SSE 100m and Besquel isolated danger masonry beacon bears E distant about 100m, in soundings from 4m LAT to 2·4m a little to the east. This position is used as a temporary anchorage by the lifeboat. Another anchorage nearby with 4m LAT is on the line of the white leading marks at 085°, with Besquel beacon tower bearing 125° distant about 180m. These anchorages are exposed to all westerly and northerly winds and the streams are strong in the more westerly anchorage. Both anchorages are far from the harbour landing, and the easterly positions are in rather confined waters.

At neap tides, or between neaps and springs, a more convenient anchorage is 60m southeast of La Pendante beacon tower. There are fishing-boat moorings in this area and it may be possible to borrow one. Soundings should be taken as there are rocks 70m to the east, 50m south and 60m southwest of La Pendante. Avoid also the rocks on which the beacon tower stands and the little rock close to the east. On an ordinary spring tide there is 2m at low water; sand bottom. Take soundings as more water can be found a little northward and it shoals to the south. Distance to the lifeboat slip and harbour is under 0·5M.

Harbour approaches

By day only

Follow the leading line until Petit Men Louet is abeam to port then alter to 131°, bringing the old water tower, standing on four legs, open of the breakwater (see photographs page 170).

Identify the above-water rock to the SW of Ile Ségou Braz and steer to leave this about 100m to port (see top photograph on page 170), then steer to pass close to the end of the mole.

Entry to drying harbour, HW and LW. Old water tower open of end of jetty on 133°.

Go alongside or anchor (see bottom photograph). The harbour bottom is hard sand and taking the ground or taking off is uncomfortable in any NW swell. In these circumstances it is advisable to visit at HW and move out to the anchorage in good time.

Facilities

Those of a small fishing village and lifeboat station. Small cafés at the port. Supermarket (closed on Mondays) and garage at Barr ar Lann between Portsall and Kersaint. Small shop and Restaurant de Famille at Kersaint, about 1M south of Portsall, where the 12th-century *château* is worth visiting.

39. Argenton

Charts
BA *2694, 3668, 3345*
Imray *C35*
SHOM *7094, 7149, 7122*

Tidal data

Tidal heights (approx)
HW +0010 Brest, +0520 Dover
MTL 4·7m. Index 7B
Heights of tide above chart datum
MHWS 7·6m, MLWS 1·2m, MHWN 6·1m, MLWN 3·0m

Tidal streams

One mile west of Le Four lighthouse the E-going stream (reaching 3·5 knots at springs) begins −0545 Brest (−0035 Dover) and the W-going (4 knots at springs) at +0100 Brest (+0610 Dover). The inshore streams SE of Le Four turn about 10 or 15 minutes earlier.

General

A village with an open anchorage and drying harbour, situated 2M east of Le Four lighthouse. At neap tides, during offshore winds and in the absence of swell, this is an interesting anchorage. The approach channel is deep but passes close to a 0·9m LAT rock SE of Brividic port masonry beacon and passes close to rocks east of Brividic beacon. There is a jetty on the mainland east of Ile Dolvez.

Approach

By day only

Make a position 0·2M south of Le Four lighthouse, and heading to make good 085°, identify a port buoy (marking the destroyed Le Belier port beacon tower) and two port beacon towers to port, with Melgorn Vihan rock (elevation 12m) to starboard.

Approach to pass midway between the red buoy and Melgorn Bihan. Before the latter comes abeam, identify the leading marks on Ile Dolvez. The front

Argenton entrance at LW. Le Four lighthouse bearing 273°.

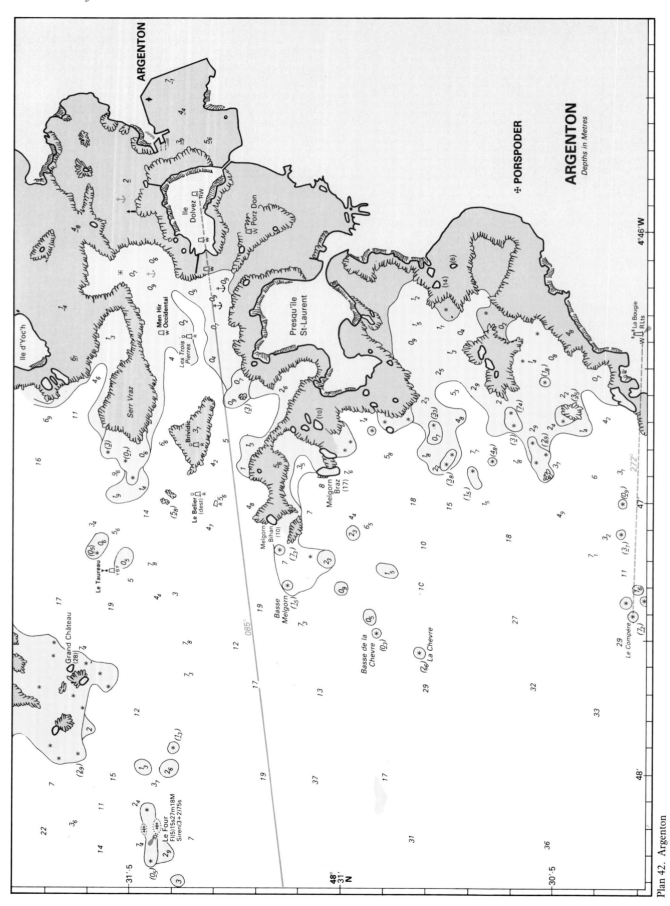

Plan 42. Argenton

Argenton entrance, left to right, Le Belier R buoy, Brividic R beacon tower, white beacon tower, Les Trois Pierres R beacon tower, white leading marks over white fishing boat bearing 084°, water tower, Melgorn Bihan. There is a strong N-going stream.

mark is a small, low, round white beacon tower on the foreshore of Ile Dolvez and the rear is a white pyramid on the island itself. There is also a white wall mark east of the latter, which can be obscured by gorse. Steer in on their transit of 085°.

Approaching on this line Melgorn Bihan rock will be left 200m to starboard when a strong cross tide may be experienced, after which the leading line must be followed exactly, as there are dangers to starboard, including an isolated rock drying 3m LAT and a shoal to its north with a depth of 0·9m LAT.

With adequate rise of tide, Le Belier port buoy will be left to port as also will the fat port beacon tower Brividic. The channel is 4m or more deep as far as Brividic, but note the reef shown on the plan, extending ESE of Brividic beacon tower. The channel here is at its narrowest, only about 100m between the extremity of the reef to port and the isolated rock previously mentioned.

With sufficient rise of tide the rest is easy, once these dangers have been passed. Hold on to the leading line leaving Les Trois Pierres port masonry beacon tower about 100m to port, and so to the anchorage, see below. If proceeding to the jetty, with sufficient tide above MTL, navigate to the north round Ile Dolvez, rounding the starboard beacon and the breakwater which runs out to a rock which never covers.

Anchorage

There is anchorage on the leading line off the Ile Dolvez, about 100m off the outer white beacon in 0·9m LAT (2·1m MLWS or 3·9m MLWN), or the same distance SW of the beacon. A mooring buoy moored between Les Trois Pierres and Ile Dolvez is reserved for the lighthouse tender. There is 0·9m LAT depth midway between Men Hir Occidental white beacon tower and the starboard beacon pole north of Ile Dolvez. The SHOM chart shows about

1m LAT south and east of Les Trois Pierres port masonry beacon and SE of the mooring buoy. This has not been verified and the bottom may be rock.

The anchorage is partially sheltered from the north by Ile d'Yoc'h and rocks, and from E through S to SSW by land. It is exposed to all westerly winds and swell (which is said to be enormous) so even the approach would be dangerous in strong onshore winds. Under suitable conditions the anchorage is pleasant, though far from the jetty and the village. Shallow-draught yachts will find better anchorage in the bay NE of Ile Dolvez where there is a large area of weed-covered sand which dries 2m LAT so would have 0·1m at neaps. It is said locally that there is 1·8m.

The harbour consists of a short west jetty against which a yacht can dry out on the south side on sand bottom – not rock as shown on the charts. (See bottom picture opposite.) The west jetty dries about 3m but is covered at high water springs. Another jetty and slip to the east is used by racing dinghies. There is less water there and it is not recommended for berthing, although it might be possible. The west jetty is stated locally to be safer than Portsall jetty, and is protected from all directions except north by the mainland and Ile Dolvez. A northwest sea or swell could penetrate between Ile d'Yoc'h and the mainland when the rocks are covered. A yacht might be weather-bound alongside the jetty and unable to beat out of the approach channel in the event of an unexpected westerly gale or the swell in advance of one, but under ordinary weather conditions the harbour is snug enough, which is why it has been adapted as a centre for dinghy sailing.

Facilities

Water at jetty. Yacht club with showers and toilets. Small shops in Argenton. Porspoder one mile south with more shops, two banks, post office, garage with camping gas. Bus to Brest.

The three Argenton leading marks to the right of disused lifeboat house.

40. Melon

Charts
BA *3345, 2694*
SHOM *7149, 7122*

Tidal data
See under Argenton, above.

General

A small drying harbour lying between the island and the village of the same name, about a mile north of l'Aber-Ildut. The island is 14m high and bordered by low cliffs. The port offers good shelter except at high water and with a NW wind. Entry provides an interesting exercise in pilotage.

Approaches

The main approach is from the NNW. First identify the conspicuous white radar tower, aptly named by the locals *La Bougie* (the candle), position 48°30'·32N 4°46'·21W on SHOM *7122*, close to and north of three radio masts (see photo and plan 43). Le Compère rock 6·6m above datum according to SHOM charts and therefore covering at high water except at neaps, lies 0·5M offshore on an approximate bearing of 272° from La Bougie, with Le Four lighthouse bearing 334° distant 1·25M. If the rock is clear of the water, pass about 0·1M to the SW of it, then bring it into line (astern) with Le Four lighthouse. Steer to make good 154° keeping on the transit. This line leads to the anchorage over a

least depth of 6·2m, but passes very close to drying rocks on either hand.

The approach from the south, inside the Ile Melon, is intricate, and no adequate directions can be given.

Anchorages

1. In easterly weather, a yacht may anchor in 6·7m sand with Le Compère rock in line with Le Four lighthouse and the north end of Ile Melon, distant 0·2M. In this position the north end of the small Ile Mazou-Bras bears about 050°, but be sure to anchor clear of the rocky shoal to the SW of the anchorage.
2. The port contains a number of small fishing boats on drying moorings but has no quays or facilities, and dries from 2·5m to 5m LAT.

Melon, looking southeast near LW.

'La Bougie' tower in transit with Le Compère rock on 092°.

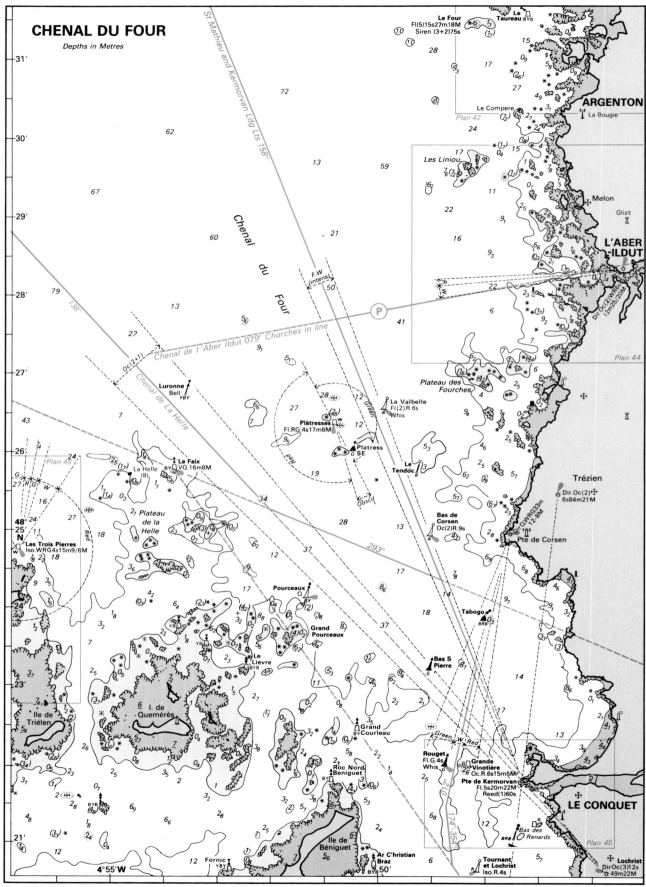

CHENAL DU FOUR

Depths in Metres

St Mathieu and Kermorvan Ldg Lts 158°

72

62

13

59

Chenal du Four

67

60

Chenal du Four

79

138°

13

22

9₁

Chenal de l'Aber Ildut 079° Churches in line

Chenal de La Helle

Oc(2+1)

F.W (intens) 50s

21

41

P

5₄

Luronne Bell YBY

43

7

Le Faix BY☐ VQ.16m8M

Plan 46

G R W

27

24

16

2₅ (1₇)

La Helle (8)

48 25'N

Les Trois Pierres Iso.WRG4s15m9/6M W

11

Plateau de la Helle

34

12

37

Pourceaux Q BY

18

17

Grand Pourceaux

18

37

293°

17

Le Lievre BYB

Grand Courleau BY

35

12

11

I. de Quemérès

6

Ile de Triélen

26'

23'

21'

4°55'W

50'

Roc Nord Beniguet BY

Fornic YBY

Ile de Béniguet

Ar C'hristian Braz BYB

12

Le Four Fl(5)15s27m18M Siren (3+2)75s

Le Taureau BYB

ARGENTON La Bougie

Plan 42

24

Le Compere

Les Liniou

17

Melon

22

16

L'ABER-ILDUT

Dir.Oc(2)WRG6s 12m25/20M

Plan 44

Plateau des Fourches

La Valbelle Fl(2)R.6s Whis

Platress SE G

Le Tendoc R

Bas de Corsen Oc(2)R.9s R

13

Trézien Dir.Oc(2) 6s84m21M

Fl.WRG33m 12.8M

Pte de Corsen

17

14

18

Tabogo BRB

Bas S Pierre BYB

14

17

Rouget Fl.G.4s Whis G

Green W Red

Grande Vinotière Oc.R.6s15m5M

Pte de Kermorvan Fl.5s20m22M Reed(1)60s

174°354°

12

Bas des Renards BRB R

LE CONQUET

Plan 45

Tournant et Lochrist Iso.R.4s R

Lochrist DirOc(3)12s 49m22M

Plan 43. Chenal du Four

41. L'Aber-Ildut (Lanildut)

Charts
BA *3345, 2694*
Imray *C36*
SHOM *7149, 7122*

Tidal data

Tidal heights (approx)

HW +0005 Brest, +0515 Dover
MTL 4·6m. Index 4B
Heights of tide above chart datum
MHWS 7·6m, MLWS 1·2m, MHWN 5·7m, MLWN 3·0m

Tidal streams

1. About 3M west of l'Aber-Ildut the NNE-going stream begins at −0520 Brest (−0010 Dover) and the SSW-going at +0030 Brest (+ 0540 Dover). Both streams reach 2·8 knots at springs. Close inshore the coastal streams probably turn earlier.
2. The ebb tide from l'Aber-Ildut near the entrance sets to the NW on the off-lying rocks, reaching 3 knots at springs.

General

This small natural harbour was once shown on charts as drying right out, but for many years *sabliers* or sand dredgers have been taking sand off the entrance and from the bed of the harbour for building construction and agricultural use. As a result, it provides an attractive and sheltered anchorage in which small craft can lie afloat at LW springs.

A stony spit runs north from the southern headland at the entrance, immediately to seaward of Le Crapaud, the prominent rounded rock close off the light structure and joined to the northern shore by a jetty. This spit reduces the width of the channel by half but, by keeping to port, 4m can be found at MLWS. In 1990 a deep-laden *sablier* was seen to enter without trouble, shortly after soundings had been taken with a leadline.

L'Aber-Ildut, looking east.

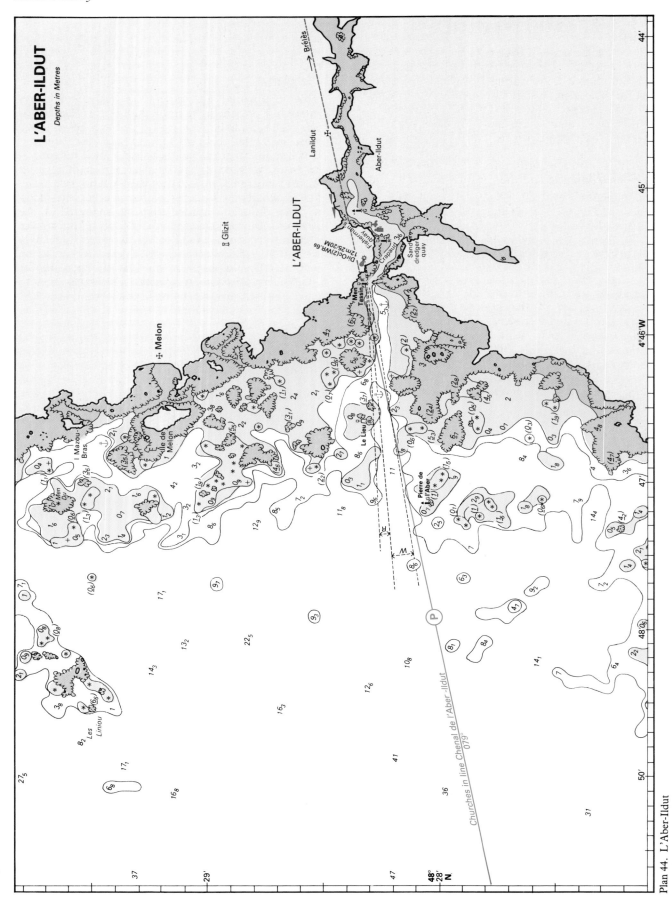

Plan 44. L'Aber-Ildut

Approaches

By day

The recommended approach for a stranger is to keep Brélès church spire (see plan 44) in line with Lanildut church spire bearing 079° (line P). However these marks blend so well with the surrounding trees and houses that they are virtually impossible to identify from a distance, and the most prominent feature in the approach is Le Lieu port beacon tower.

Coming from the north, a fix can be obtained using Le Four lighthouse and the conspicuous white radar tower, aptly named by the locals *La Bougie* (the candle), position 48°30'·32N 4°46'·21W, close to and north of three radio masts. The prominent water tower (Glizit) 0·6M north of the entrance can be identified and Le Lieu port beacon tower located. Steer towards the entrance when Le Lieu bears 080° and, if the two spires can be seen, keep in the deep channel by steering with Brélès, the distant spire, open to the left of the near spire. Should they continue to be invisible steer to leave Le Lieu 100m to port and Pierre de l'Aber starboard beacon (replaced by a buoy 1991) 300m to starboard.

Coming from the south, keep outside the Plateau des Fourches and locate the Glizit water tower in order to identify the entrance and Le Lieu port

tower. With Le Lieu tower abeam to port, it should be possible to identify the unusual l'Aber-Ildut light structure. The front wall of this structure has an aperture, the right-hand half being open and the left-hand part with a red window. The light itself shines through a window to the rear of this aperture. On closer approach steer so as to centre the window through which the light shines in the open part of the aperture bearing 083°. Keep clear of the red sector as there are drying rocks east of Le Lieu beacon tower.

When 0·3M from the light structure, borrow to starboard to keep in the deep channel and identify the port beacon Men Tassin which will be seen to the left of the light structure. This beacon is directly opposite the stony spit which halves the width of the channel. Steer in to leave Men Tassin no more than 30m to port and then turn to starboard on 117°, leaving Le Crapaud rock, which juts out from the north bank, 15m to port. Steer for the quay on the south bank until the second port beacon is abeam, when turn to port into the harbour.

By night

If in doubt as to the general position of the entrance bring Keréon (Oc(2+1)WR.24s in R sector) into line astern with La Jument (Fl(3)R.15s) on 257°(see plan 188). This line crosses the centre of the white sector of l'Aber-Ildut light, DirOc(2)WR.6s25/20M, 081°-

L'Aber-Ildut approach. Le Lieu port beacon tower bearing 084° with the two spires visible to the left of Le Lieu.

L'Aber-Ildut leading light building to left of motorboat. Le Crapaud rock behind sail.

W-085°-R-087°. Keep in this white sector until very close to the entrance, then proceed as above if visibility permits; otherwise bring up in one of the outer anchorages.

Anchorages

1. With Le Lieu beacon tower bearing about 285° distant 0·15M. The least depth here is 7m.
2. With the light structure bearing about 075° distant about 0·2M in about 3·6m, sand. There has been considerable dredging in the vicinity of this anchorage and, with the help of soundings, it is possible to anchor further to the south of the position marked on the plan.
3. The fishing boats are by the quay on the north side of the estuary. The creek to the south dries and is full of motorboat moorings. Further up harbour are a large number of dumbbell moorings for local boats and visitors. There is very little, if any, room left to anchor.

Facilities

Water and diesel can be obtained from the fishermen's quay on the north side by the entrance. The tide runs hard through the fishing-boat moorings and, when coming alongside the quay near low water, it is essential to have someone ashore to take lines, as the wall is high. Apply to the café/bar proprietor near the quay for diesel. Petrol is not available.

L'Aber-Ildut and Lanildut merge together. Water from the pump by the slip is not for drinking. Repairs to wooden vessels can be undertaken and there is a marine engineer but no sailmaker. Post office by the church, patisserie and two grocers. Hotel, restaurants and bars. No bank, buses to Brest.

L'Aber-Ildut. Entrance at low water springs looking out towards Le Lieu port beacon town, over tip of spire.

Surroundings

The shores of the harbour are of sand and rock, with landing slips at the villages. The great disused quarry on the right bank of the river once supplied stone for the construction of many of the ocean harbours of France and for several works in England, including the Thames Embankment. A trip up the estuary by dinghy can be interesting.

42. Le Conquet

Charts

BA *3345, 2694*
SHOM *7122, 7149*

Tidal data

Tidal heights (approx)
HW −0005 Brest, +0505 Dover
MTL 4·6m. Index 4B
Heights of tide above chart datum
MHWS 7·2m, MLWS 1·4m, MHWN 5·6m, MLWN 2·9m

Tidal streams

1. In the northern approach to the Chenal du Four about west of l'Aber-Ildut the NNE-going stream begins at −0520 Brest (−0010 Dover) and the SSW-going stream at +0030 Brest (+0540 Dover). Both streams attain 2·5 knots at springs.
2. Off St-Pierre starboard buoy some 2M NW of Pointe de Kermorvan the N-going stream begins at −0600 Brest (−0050 Dover) and the S-going stream at +0100 Brest (+0610 Dover). Both streams attain 2·5 knots at springs, but note the sharp increase in rates to the south which are referred to in (3).
3. In the southern end of the Chenal du Four, between Grand Vinotière port beacon tower and Basse du Chenal, west of Pointe de St-Mathieu, the N-going stream begins at −0550 Brest (−0040 Dover) attaining 5·6 knots at springs, and the S-going at +0015 Brest (+0525 Dover) attaining 5 knots at springs.
4. At the anchorage there are eddies on the flood stream, sometimes setting towards the entrance, but on the ebb the stream is very weak.

General

Le Conquet is on a lee shore in most westerly winds, but receives a measure of protection from Ile de Beniguet. The outer harbour is sheltered from north through east to SSW although there is limited space to anchor. The inner harbour dries and is ideal for yachts that can take the ground.

Le Conquet, looking east.

Le Conquet entrance. La Louve port beacon tower left centre, outer breakwater head right.

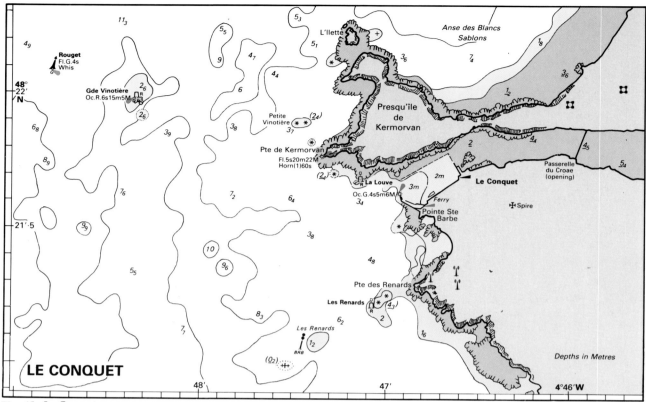

Plan 45. Le Conquet

Approaches

By day

From the north, this is by the Chenal du Four which is entered between La Valbelle port pillar light buoy and Les Plâtresses white beacon tower, on the transit of Kermorvan lighthouse (front) square white tower, and St-Mathieu lighthouse (rear) square white tower, bearing 158°. Steer to make good this course.

When l'Ilette is abeam steer 180° so as to pass 0·2M west of Pointe de Kermorvan and to avoid La Petite Vinotière and other drying rocks to the north of the point.

When Pointe de Kermorvan lighthouse is abeam alter course to port leaving La Louve port beacon tower to port. Les Renards port beacon tower is left 0·5M to starboard. The only feature of navigation in this easy approach is allowance for the cross-tidal streams which may attain 5·5 knots.

On a spring flood a yacht is set rapidly towards Pointe de Kermorvan and the stream only relaxes when it gets under the tidal lee of Pointe St-Barbe at the entrance. Avoid the rock which dries 2·6m LAT, situated about 0·15M east of La Louve, north of the outer breakwater.

Approach from the south presents no problem as long as a berth of 0·15M is given to Les Renards isolated danger buoy which may be passed on either side.

By night

From the north, identify Kermorvan light Fl.5s, and St-Mathieu light Fl.15s, with DirF light intensified 157·5°-159·5° (there are F.R lights on a radio mast 1·7M ENE of St-Mathieu).

Make a position from which Les Plâtresses light (Fl.RG.4s on this bearing) bears 190° distant 1M when the leading lights will be in line bearing 158·5°. Steer to make good this transit and if visibility permits proceed as *By day* above. Otherwise when Pointe de Corsen light (DirQ.WRG) changes from green to white bearing 012° alter course to make good 192° and keep in the white sector and pass between La Grande Vinotière beacon tower (Oc.R.6s) and Rouget starboard pillar buoy Fl.G.4s.

When well past these steer for the Oc.G.4s light on the outer breakwater, making due allowance for the cross tide.

From the south, taking care to avoid the unlit starboard buoy La Fourmi, 0·8M W by S of Vieux-Moines tower (Fl.R.4s), steer to leave Tournant et Lochrist port buoy (Iso.R.4s) to starboard, passing out to the west of the directional Trezien light (DirOc(2)6s).

With the buoy abeam to starboard, steer to hold Pointe de Kermorvan light on not less than 025° with due allowance for tidal set, until the breakwater light (Oc.G.4s) bears 060°, whence steer to enter the harbour.

Anchorage and harbour

In 1990 the outer harbour between the Môle Ste-Barbe and the Môle St-Christophe was dredged to 2m south of La Basse du Filet rock and a quay was constructed, with a slip, along the south side. This area is well protected but is largely occupied by fishing boats on moorings secured to ground chains and it is essential to buoy the anchor and to allow room for the manoeuvres of the ferry which arrives with considerable *élan*.

The inner harbour dries and contains a number of small fishing boat and yacht moorings. It has a mole, alongside the eastern side of which vessels can lie, with fair protection from offshore winds. The mole dries about 2·4m and berths alongside are often occupied by commercial vessels.

In southerly weather an alternative anchorage is in the Anse des Blancs Sablons, which can be approached direct from the leading line, and is useful whilst waiting a fair tide or clearance of fog. Gradually shelving shore and good sands for bathing. Sometimes a swell finds its way in. There are many fishermen's floats in the SW corner. Short walk over the Kermorvan peninsula to Le Conquet.

Facilities

Many shops and restaurants. Hôtel de Bretagne is well spoken of. Water from tap by wall in inner harbour. Petrol, etc. available half a mile along main road.

43. Ile de Molène

Charts

BA *2694*
SHOM *7123P, 7122P, 7149P*
Imray *C36*

Tidal data

Tidal heights (approx)
HW +0010 Brest, +0520 Dover
MTL 4·4m. Index 5B
Heights of tide above chart datum
MHWS 7·6m, MLWS 1·2m, MHWN 5·7m, MLWN 3·0m

Tidal streams

1. In the Chenal de la Helle at the northern entrance the ENE-going stream begins at −0520 Brest (−0010 Dover) reaching about 3 knots at springs, and the SW-going at −0045 Brest (+0425 Dover), reaching about 4 knots at springs. At the SE end where the channel joins the Chenal du Four the streams are only 2·5 knots.
2. In the middle of the Passage du Fromveur the ENE-going stream, reaching 9 knots at springs, begins at −0515 Brest (−0005 Dover), and the WSW stream, reaching 8 knots, at +0045 Brest (+0555 Dover).
   Near Kéreon lighthouse streams attain the same rates but they start earlier and the directions differ. The NNE-going stream begins at +0550 Brest (−0125 Dover) and the SSW-going stream at −0030 Brest (+0440 Dover).
3. Between Ile de Molène and Plateau de la Helle the N-going stream begins at −0615 Brest (−0105 Dover) and the S-going at −0015 Brest (+0455 Dover). Both streams reach 2·8 knots at springs.
4. In the channel NW of Ile de Molène the streams turn at the same times as in 3 above but the directions and rates differ: at the west end of the channel NNE and SSW reaching 3·8 knots; at the east end ENE and WSW attaining 6 knots.
5. In the Chenal des Las the N-going stream begins at −0600 Brest (−0050 Dover) and the S-going at −0215 Brest (+0255 Dover). Both streams reach 2·8 knots at springs.

General

Molène is a small island situated halfway between Le Conquet on the mainland and Ouessant. Viewed on a small-scale chart the approach looks difficult, being beset by rocks and fierce tidal streams. However, under the right conditions, preferably at neaps, it is easily approachable from north; easier, for example, than Ouessant or Ile de Sein. There is an anchorage, usually sheltered from east through south to WSW. The tiny island has a character of its own, less rigorous than Ouessant or Ile de Sein. In late spring the editor was surprised at the sight of four cuckoos flying and calling in company!

Approaches

NORTHERN APPROACH

By day

First make a position about 0·5M to the north of Le Faix N cardinal lighthouse situated on the north side of Plateau de la Helle. From here steer to make good about 270°, leaving a distinctive solitary rock, La Helle, about 0·5M to port (never covers, 11m). See plan 43.

When just over 0·5M west of this rock identify the first leading marks which are the North Mill (a stumpy stone tower, with the top painted day-glow red, on the north of Ile de Molène), in line with Les Trois Pierres (white light tower, situated about 0·75M NE of Ile de Molène). At 2M distant, the mill appears lower than Les Trois Pierres and therefore, to be seen, can be opened to either side, but preferably to the west. The transit is 215° which should be followed.

When within 0·5M of this light tower, turn to starboard to leave it 0·3M to port and identify Bazou Réal BYB beacon tower, marking Men Réal rocks and the Roche Goulin W cardinal spar buoy 0·2M SSW of Les Trois Pierres lighthouse. On the island will be seen a church spire with, to the right a coastguard tower and to the left a white framework telephone-link mast.

Keeping the church spire midway between Bazou Réal beacon tower and the W cardinal spar buoy on about 199°, pass between the tower and buoy and continue on into the anchorage, leaving a line of rocks, which never cover, to port and the outer (northern) breakwater to starboard.

ILE DE MOLENE

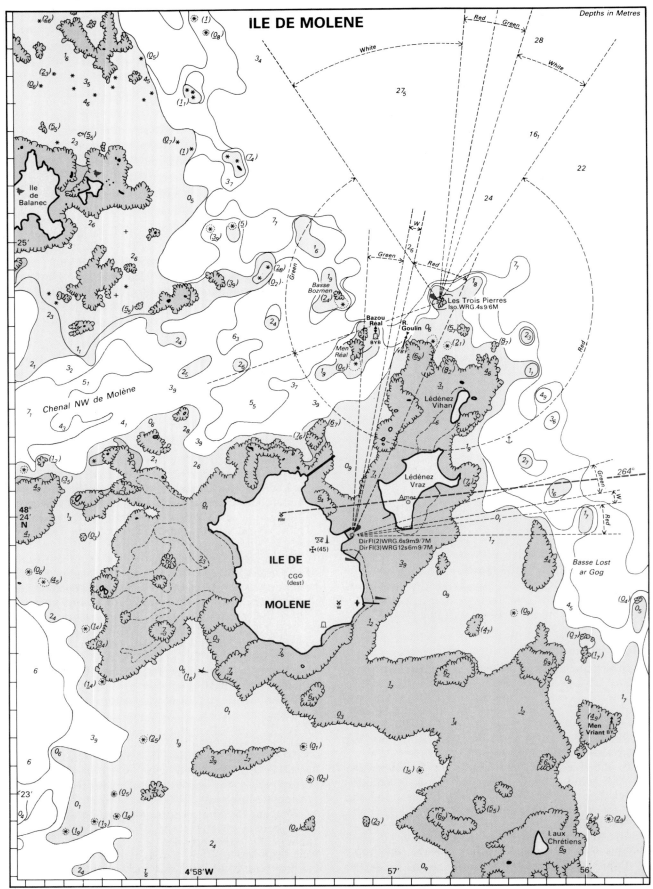

Plan 46. Ile de Molène

Ile de Molène looking west.

Note that at springs the streams will be strong (up to 6 knots) across the approach off Les Trois Pierres.

By night

Les Trois Pierres lighthouse to the NE of Molène has the following characteristics: Iso.WRG.4s9–6M 070°-G-147°-W-185°-R-191°-G-197°-W-213°-R-070°. Approach in either white sector, preferably on the northern edge of the narrow NE white sector at 197°.

When 0·3M off Les Trois Pierres alter course to starboard to enter the narrow white sector of Molène WRG light from 190° to 192°, which from this direction is Fl(3)12s.

Steer in this sector until 0·1M after passing between Bazou Réal tower and Roche Goulin W cardinal spar buoy (both unlit) when bear to starboard and continue in the green sector.

SOUTHERN AND EASTERN APPROACH CHENAL DES LAZ

By day only

In hazy conditions it is not easy to identify the Molène leading marks for this approach. For a first visit it is preferable to use the northern approach for entry and, if desired, leave by the eastern approach. BA *2694* or SHOM *7122* are recommended for this approach.

Use as a stern transit the leading marks for the Chenal de la Helle which are Kermorvan lighthouse (front, square white tower, elevation 20m) and Lochrist (rear, octagonal white tower, red top, elevation 49m) by making good 318°.

When about 0·5M NE of Chaussée des Porceaux N cardinal pillar buoy, bring the white beacon on Lédénez Vraz to bear 264° and steer to make this good as a course, allowing for cross stream.

As soon as the North Mill (a stumpy stone tower, with the top painted day-glow red, on NW of Ile de Molène) is identified, bring the two in line and steer to follow this transit strictly bearing 264°.

When the west end of Ile de Quéménès bears 170° and not before, alter course to 315°, heading 0·4M northeast of Les Trois Pierres lighthouse and bring Le Grand Crom N cardinal beacon tower and Le Lièvre E cardinal beacon tower open to the east of Men Arouet S cardinal beacon tower, on a stern bearing of approximately 125°.

Steer to make good 315° to follow this line until approaching Les Trois Pierres lighthouse, which leave 0·3M to port as there are shoals east and ENE of the lighthouse. Before turning to round the lighthouse, join the northern approach to Ile de Molène *By day* as above. Be alert for tidal sets, which can be up to 3 knots N and S, to the east of, and up to 6 knots E and W, to the northwest of Les Trois Pierres.

Anchorage and harbour

In the pool about 0·1M northeast of the northern jetty there is about 1·9m at LAT. Depths decrease to the south but with soundings it will usually be possible to find a berth to the south of this and at neap tides to anchor between the northern jetty and the old pier. The shelter in the outer position depends on tidal conditions and at springs is pretty well open from WSW through north to east. The holding ground of sand and rock is said to be poor and the anchor should be buoyed.

Northern entry, church spire bearing 198°.

Much of the harbour has a rocky bottom but there are positions where a yacht could dry out alongside, if local advice is obtained. Vessels that can take the ground can anchor with care or borrow a mooring by arrangement among the fishing boats to the southeast of the old pier. This anchorage is open to the east and south at high water.

The French and British charts show there to be an anchorage ENE of the northern tip of Lédénez Vraz in 9m sand and mud, but this would appear to be exposed to the west at high water and unprotected from all easterly sectors.

Facilities

Post office, a good *Huit à Huit* supermarket, other small shops, a co-operative where some chandlery can be obtained, a small hotel/restaurant, a hotel/bar and a café/bar. Water is scarce and there is no fuel.

Molène is an oval-shaped island, about ¾M from north to south and ½M from east to west. The houses above the harbour are dense, so that viewed from a distance it looks like a town. The principal buildings are the semaphore tower and the church. The clock tower on the latter was a gift from England in recognition of the services of the men of Molène when the *Drummond Castle* was wrecked on Les Pierres Vertes. The bodies of 29 of the passengers are buried in the cemetery. A local industry is gathering kelp from nearby islets and rocks. It is just a remote windswept island with magnificent views over the islets and rocks standing in the fierce tidal streams towards Ouessant.

Neaps anchorage. *Capelan* centre right.

44. Ouessant (Ushant)

Charts

BA *2694*
Imray *C36*
SHOM *5287 (P), 7123 (P)*

Tidal data

Tidal heights (approx)

HW −0005 Brest (+0505 Dover)
MTL 4·5m. Index 5B
Heights of tide above chart datum
MHWS 7·6m, MLWS 1·2m, MHWN 5·7m, MLWN 3·0m

Tidal streams

1. For streams between Ouessant and the mainland and in the Passage du Fromveur, where they can reach 9 knots at springs, see page 000.
2. At Baz Veur (0·75M NNW of Nividic lighthouse at the west end of the island) the NNE-going stream begins at −0550 Brest (−0040 Dover) and the SSW-going stream at +0045 Brest (+0555 Dover). Both streams reach 5·6 knots at springs.
3. The streams S and SW of the entrance of Baie de Lampaul vary in direction, time and rate within a relatively small area of sea.

Off La Jument lighthouse and Ar Vridic 0·5M NW of the lighthouse, at springs the NW-going stream begins at +0435 Brest (−0240 Dover) and the S-going at −0045 Brest (+0425 Dover), both streams reaching 4·7 knots at springs.

About 3M west of the entrance to Baie de Lampaul the streams differ again and are sometimes quite clearly defined by overfalls in one tidal area and smooth water in the other. Here the NW-going stream begins at +0535 Brest (−0025 Dover) and the S-going at +0030 Brest (+0540 Dover), both streams reaching 3 knots.

General

Ouessant (Ushant or, in Breton, Enez Eussa), although one of the most important milestones on the world's sea traffic lanes, is not often visited by yachts. This is partly due to its lack of good anchorages, and partly to a general feeling that the extreme NW corner of Brittany is no place for loitering, whether outward or homeward bound. It also has more days when visibility is less than 1km than any other north French port, with a maximum in July.

Baie du Stiff. Breakwater bearing 260°.

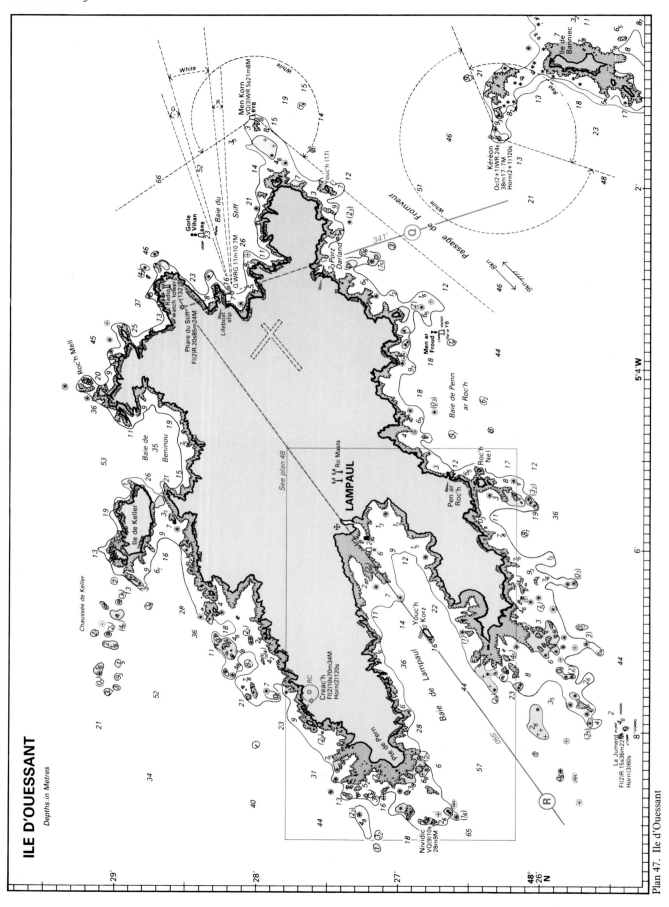

ILE D'OUESSANT

Depths in Metres

Ile de Banniec

Kéréon
Oc(2+1)WR 24s
38m17·7M
Horn(2+1)120s

Men Korn
VQ(3)WR 5s21m8M
BYB

Youc'h (17)

Gorle Vihan
BYB

Baie du Stiff

Q.WRG 11m10·7M

Radio watch tower (132)
Phare du Stiff
Fl(2)R.20s85m24M

Lifeboat slip

Porz
Darland

Passage de Fromveur

341°

8kn
9kn

Men ar
Froud

Roc'h Mell

Baie de
Beninou

Baie de Penn
ar Roc'h

See plan 48

Ile de Keller

Chaussée de Keller

Ro Masts

LAMPAUL

Pen ar
Roc'h

Roc'h
Nel

Creac'h
Fl(2)10s70m34M
Horn(2)120s
RC

Baie de Lampaul

Youc'h
Korz

Pte de Pern

Nividic
VQ(9)10s
28m9M

La Jument
Fl(3)R 15s36m22M
Horn(3)60s

R

48°
26'
N

29'

28'

27'

6'

5'4'W

2'

Plan 47. Ile d'Ouessant

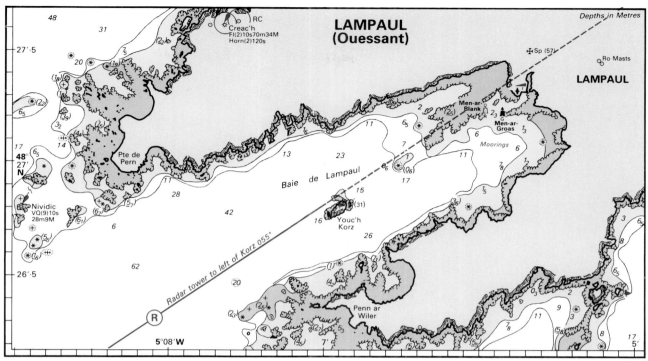

Plan 48. Lampaul (Ouessant)

Approaches

Provided account is taken of the strong tides, particularly in the Passage du Fromveur, of the overfalls which these can create especially with adverse winds, and of the possibility of a deterioration in visibility, approach to the island in daylight from the mainland is straightforward whether direct from the east or from the south via the Chenal de la Helle.

Baie de Lampaul

In spite of being open to the SW this bay is the chief anchorage at Ouessant.

Approach

A line (R) formed by the conspicuous Le Stiff radar watch tower (elevation 132m) open to the left of Youc'h Korz (a rock about 34m high) and bearing 055°, clears all the outer dangers comfortably. Pass either side of Youc'h Korz, which has drying rocks extending about 100m on its northern side, then leave the leading line and keep well over to the east to avoid the shoals which fill the northern corner of the bay.

If proceeding to the harbour alter course when the port beacon tower Men-ar-Blank bears north, and steer between this beacon tower and the starboard beacon tower Men-ar-Groas.

Anchorage and harbour

In the approach, if space can be found, anchor near the mooring buoys in 5·7 to 9·1m, sand and mud, good holding ground or, further from the landing place, secure to one of a number of white or orange-red visitors' buoys in the bay southeast of Men-ar-Groas green beacon tower in 7 to 4m.

The port of Lampaul (or Porz-Pol) consists of what may be termed the outer harbour with 1·8 to 2·1m LAT near the entrance and a quay for the mail steamer, and the inner harbour which dries out and is almost closed by two short jetties, leaving a gap about 7·9m wide through which small vessels may pass when the tide serves.

There may be room to anchor in the outer harbour, in the channel, roughly on the line from the port beacon tower to the quay. There are two white mooring buoys used by the lifeboat and the ferries on this line, and soundings should be taken if deviating to the north or south of them, as the basin is only a little over 100m wide with drying rocks on each side and contains some fishing-boat moorings.

There is 2·3m LAT between the beacon towers with rock bottom 2m north of the starboard beacon tower and about 0·6m to 0·9m LAT off the steamer jetty. The water shoals rapidly beyond the lifeboat slip. If one adds 1·2m at MLWS, or 3m at MLWN, it will be seen that there is usually plenty of water for a yacht in the anchorage. This is protected from north and east by land and from the south there is a fetch of less than 0·5M. From the west the anchorage receives some protection from rocks which dry out north of the port beacon tower, but at high water it might be dangerous with strong winds blowing into the bay.

The best dinghy landing is at the lifeboat slip, which dries out at low water, at which time land at a ladder to the west of it.

Baie du Stiff, looking NW, showing visitors' orange-red mooring buoys.

Lampaul lifeboat slip. Visitors' moorings out of picture to right.

Facilities

Facilities for visiting yachts are being improved. Water may be obtained from an hotel and fuel from garage a quarter of a mile from harbour. The engineer will deal with marine engines. No chandler or sailmaker in 1990. Post office, banks, several food shops. Taxi, car and *vélo* hire, small hotels and good restaurants.

Ferries to Le Conquet and Brest, air connections to Brest.

Baie du Stiff (Porz Liboudou)

This bay is sheltered from S through W to NW, but heavy weather from any quarter sends in a huge swell which makes the anchorage untenable. The holding ground is only moderate.

Approach

Straightforward but avoid Gorle-Vihan rocks in the middle of the bay, marked by an isolated danger beacon tower.. The small bay 0·2M south of Le Stiff lighthouse receives the submarine cable from l'Aber-Ildut, and is a prohibited anchorage.

Anchorage

There are heavy white mooring buoys for the ferries and supply vessel. South of the white buoys a number of moorings (with orange-red buoys) have been laid for visiting yachts, in 5m or more. These leave little room to anchor but appeared on examination to be adequate for a night's stay. Room to anchor might be found but avoid a rocky patch in the south corner of the bay. Do not anchor between the white buoys and the jetties where the ferries need room to manoeuvre. It is possible to land by dinghy at all states of tide at the lifeboat slip which is behind the inner jetty.

Facilities

Café/bar above the lifeboat station, open in the summer, where *vélos* may be hired. All facilities at Lampaul two miles away.

Ferries to Le Conquet and Brest. Air connections to Brest.

Porz Darland

This consists of a small drying inlet partly protected by a jetty on its SW side. The end of the jetty dries 1·5m.

Approach

Approach with Le Stiff lighthouse (twin connected white towers, elevation 85m) in line with the right edge of the beach, east of the jetty, bearing 341° (line Q). On close approach, turn towards the jetty head, leaving the white mooring buoy close to port and avoiding a rock (4·8m, never covers) off the north shore.

Lampaul on a calm evening.

Anchorage

There is a temporary anchorage in 3·6m LAT, sand, with the end of the jetty bearing about NW distant 0·1M. There is also a mooring buoy near this position which may be used if vacant but in northerly winds it is used by the mailboat.

There is a landing slip on the north side of the jetty.

Baie de Penn ar Roc'h

This bay offers very little shelter, but is used by the mail steamer during strong westerly winds.

Approach

Approach is straightforward and the dangers can be seen on plan 48.

Anchorage

There is a temporary anchorage in about 12m LAT, sand, with Roc'h Nel bearing about 200°, distant 0·15M. There is a landing slip which can be used at all states of the tide.

Appendix

I. NAUTICAL TERMS

ENGLISH – FRENCH

English	French
aboard	à bord
afloat	à flot
aft	arrière
aground	à terre
anchor	ancre (f)
to anchor	mouiller
anchorage	mouillage (m)
ash (wood)	frêne (m)
awash	à fleur de l'eau
baler	écope (f)
ballast	lest (m)
bank (of river)	digue (f), rive (f)
bar (of river)	mascaret (m)
barge	chaland (m)
basin	bassin (m)
battery (electric)	batterie (f)
baulk (of wood)	tin (m)
bay	baie (f)
beach	plage (f), grève (f)
beacon	balise (f)
beacon tower	tourelle (f)
beam (width)	largeur (f)
bearing (direction)	relèvement (m)
to beat to windward	louvoyer
to belay	frapper une amarre
belfry	clocher (m)
bell	cloche (f
below	en bas
bend (of a channel)	coude (m)
to beware of	se méfier de
black	noir
block (pulley)	poulie (f)
to blow	souffler
boat	bateau (m), canot (m), embarcation (f)
boat-building shed	chantier (m)
boathook	gaffe (f)
bollard	bitte d'amarrage (f)
boom	bôme (m)
bore (tidal)	mascaret (f)
bottom (sea bed)	fond (m)
bows	avant (m)
bowsprit	beaupré (m)
breaker (surf)	brisant (m)
breakwater	brise-lames (m)
breeze	brise (f)
bridge (of river)	pont (m)
broken down	en panne
buoy (navigational)	bouée (f)
buoy (mooring)	corps mort
burgee	guidon (m)

English	French
cabin	cabine (f)
calm	calme
can buoy	tonne (f)
canal	canal (m)
canvas	toile (f)
cape	cap (m)
to capsize	chavirer
to cast off	larguer
to caulk	calfater
chain	châine (f)
channel	manche (f), chenal (m), canal (m), passage (m)
chart	carte (marine) (f)
to clean	nettoyer
to clear (an obstacle)	franchir
cliff	falaise (f)
close-hauled, to come	ranger le vent
clump of trees	bouquet de bois (m)
coast	côte (f)
coaster	caboteur (m)
coasting, coasting trade	cabotage (m)
cockpit	baignoire (f)
compass	boussole (f), compas (m)
copper	cuivre (m)
corrected time	temps compensé (m)
course	route (f)
cove	anse (f)
crane	grue (f)
creek	crique (f), anse (f)
crew	équipage (m)
cruise	croisière (f)
Custom house, Customs	douane (f)
Customs officer	douanier (m)
current	courant (m)
cutter (rig)	côtre (m)
daymark	amer (m)
deck	pont (m)
depth	profondeur (f)
diesel oil	gasoil (m)
dinghy	canot (m), annexe (f)
to disembark	débarquer
diver	plongeur (m)
dockyard	chantier (m)
downstream	aval
to drag (anchor)	chasser
draught	tirant d'eau (m)
to dredge	creuser
dredge	gabarre (f), dragueur (m)

English	French
to dry out	échouer
dyke	digue (f)
east	est (m)
eastern, easterly	oriental
ebb tide	marée descendante, jusant (m)
eddy	remous (m)
elapsed time	temps réel
to embark	embarquer
engine	machine (f)
English Channel	la Manche
fathom (French)	brasse (f) (5ft 4in)
fender	défense (f)
ferry	bac (m)
fish	poisson (m)
fish hook	hameçon (m)
fish pond	vivier (m)
fisherman	pêcheur (m)
fishing boat	bateau pêcheur (m)
fire	feu (m)
flag	pavillon (m)
flood tide	marée montante, flot (m)
fog	brouillard (m), brume (f)
forward	avant
fresh water	eau douce
gaff	corne (f)
gale	coup de vent (m)
galley	cuisine (f)
galvanised	zingué
gangway	passerelle (f)
graving dock	forme de radoub (f)
grease	graisee (f)
grid	gril de carénage (m)
grounding	echouage
gunwale	plat-bord (m)
to gybe	empanner, gambeyer
half tide	mi-marée (f)
halyard	drisse (f)
harbour	darse (f), havre (m)
harbourmaster	capitaine du port (m)
hard astarboard!	tribord tout!
hard (adj.)	dur
to haul	haler
to heave the lead	jeter la sonde
to heave-to	mettre en panne
high water	haute marée, haute mer, pleine marée

193

to hoist	*hisser*	nautical mile	*mille marin*	sail loft,	*voilerie (f)*
holding ground	*tenue (f)*	neap tide	*marée morte,*	sail-making	
horse power	*chevaux (pl)*		*mort eau*	sailmaker	*voilier (m)*
hose (pipe)	*manche (f)*	net	*filet (m)*	sand	*sable (m)*
to hug (pass		north	*nord (m)*	sandbank	*banc de sable (m)*
close to)	*rallier, ranger*			sandy	*sableux*
hull	*coque (f)*	oak	*chêne (m)*	schooner	*goëlette (f)*
hydrant	*prise d'eau (f)*	oar	*aviron (m),*	screw (propeller)	*hélice (f)*
			rame (f)	to scrub	*nettoyer à labrosse*
insurance	*assurance (f)*	offing	*large (m)*	sea (ocean)	*mer (f)*
iron	*fer (m)*	oilskin	*cirés (m) (pl)*	sea (wave)	*coup de mer (m)*
island	*île (f)*	open sea	*pleine mer,*	seaweed	*goémon (m)*
			large (m)	to seize	*amarrer*
jetty	*jetée (f)*	owner	*propiétaire (m)*	shackle	*maillon (m)*
jib	*foc (m)*	oyster bed	*parc à huitres (m)*	sheet	*écoute (f)*
				shells	*coques*
keel	*quille (f)*	painter (rope)	*bosse (f)*	sheltered	*abrité*
kelp	*goémon (m)*	paraffin	*pétrole (m)*	shingle	*cailloux (m) (pl)*
ketch	*ketch (f)*	to pass to the	*laisser dans l'est la*	ship	*navire (m)*
knot	*noeud (m)*	westward of the	*balise*	shoal	*haut-fond (m)*
		beacon		shrouds	*haubans (m) (pl)*
ladder	*échelle (f)*	passenger	*passager (m)*	side light	*feu de*
landfall	*atterrage (m)*	passengers	*embarcation (f)*		*navigation (m)*
landing slip	*cale (f)*	passport	*passeport (m)*	sill (of lock)	*radier (m)*
to lash	*amarrer*	pebbles	*cailloux (m) (pl)*	slack (stream)	*étale*
launching	*mise à l'eau*	peninsula	*presqu'île (f)*	sluice	*pertuis (m),*
lead (sounding)	*sonde (f)*	petrol	*essence (f)*		*vanne (f)*
lead (metal)	*plomb (m)*	pier	*jetée (f)*	soft	*mou (m), molle (f)*
to leak	*faire eau*	pierhead	*musoir (m)*	to sound (depth)	*sonder*
to leave (to	*laisser (par*	pilot	*pilote (m)*	south	*sud (m)*
port, etc.)	*babord, etc.)*	pine (wood)	*pin (m)*	speed	*vitesse (f)*
legs (of a boat)	*béquilles (f)*	pool	*fosse (f)*	spinnaker	*spinnaker (m)*
length	*longueur (f)*	poop	*dunette (f)*	splice	*épissure (f)*
to let go	*larguer*	port (harbour)	*port (m)*	spring tide	*grande marée,*
lifeboat	*canot de*	port (side)	*bâbord (m)*		*vive eau*
	sauvetage (m)	pump	*pompe (f)*	standing rigging	*gréement*
lifebuoy	*bouée de*	to pump	*pomper*		*dormant (m)*
	sauvetage (f)			starboard	*tribord (m)*
lifejacket	*ceinture de*	quay	*quai (m)*	stay	*étai (m)*
	sauvetage (f)	quicksand	*sables mouvants*	staysail	*voile d'étai (f)*
lighter	*chaland (m),*			steel	*acier (m)*
	gabarre (f)	race	*course (f)*	steeple	*clocher (m)*
lighthouse	*phare (m), feu (m)*	radio	*T.S.F. (f)*	to steer for	*gouverner sur,*
lightship	*bateau feu (m)*	rain	*pluie (f)*		*mettre le cap sur*
lock (of canal,	*écluse (f)*	ready about!	*paré à virer!*	steps	*escalier (m)*
etc.)		to recaulk	*calfater*	stern	*arrière (m)*
low water	*basse marée,*	red	*rouge*	stove	*étuve (f)*
	basse mer	reef (of rock)	*écueil (m)*	straits	*pertuis (m)*
low water mark	*étiage (m)*	reef (of sail)	*ris (m)*	stream	*ruisseau (m)*
lubricating oil	*huile de*	to reef	*riser*	surf	*ressac (m)*
	graissage (f)	to reeve	*passer*	surge, swell	*houle (f)*
lugger	*lougre (m)*	to refit, to repair	*remettre à neuf*	to swim	*nager*
		riding light	*feu de*	swinging room	*évitage (m)*
mahogany	*acajou (m)*		*mouillage (m)*		
mainsail	*grande voile*	rig	*gréement (m)*	tackle	*palan (m)*
to make fast to	*amarrer sur*	river	*rivière (f)*	teak	*teck (m)*
mast	*mât (m)*	roads	*rade (f), anse (f)*	tidal	*de marée*
masthead height	*tirant d'air*	rock	*rocher (m), roche*	tide	*marée (f)*
methylated spirits	*alcool à brûler (m)*		*(f), écueil (m)*	tide gauge	*échelle de marée (f)*
mile	*mille (m)*	rope	*cordage (m),*	tide mill	*moulin a l'eau (m)*
mizzen	*tapecul,*		*corde (f)*	tide race	*raz (m)*
	artimon (m)	rough (of sea)	*dur*	tiller	*barre (f)*
mole	*digue (f)*	to row	*nager*	timber yard	*chantier (m)*
to moor to	*amarrer sur*	rowlock	*dame de nage (f)*	ton	*tonne (f)*
mooring dolphin	*Duc D'Albe*	Royal Navy	*marine de l'état (f)*	topping lift	*balancine (f)*
mooring ring	*organeau (m)*	rudder	*gouvernail (m)*	topsail	*hunier (m)*
moorings	*corps morts*	runnel	*ruisseau (m)*	to tow	*remorquer*
mouth (of river)	*bouche (f)*			towage	*touage (m)*
mud	*vase (f)*	sail	*voile (f)*	towpath	*chemin de*
muddy	*vaseux*				*halage (m)*

trawl	*chalut (m)*
trawler	*chalutier (m)*
trysail	*voile de cape (f)*
tug (boat)	*remorqueur (m)*
upstream	*amont*
wall beacon	*amer (m)*
warp	*aussière (f)*
warping	*touage (m)*
water (fresh)	*eau douce*
water point	*prise d'eau*
wave	*vague (f)*
way, to get under	*appareiller*
weather (met)	*temps (m)*
weather forecast	*la metéo (f)*
to weigh anchor	*appareiller, lever l'ancre*
well (water)	*puits (m)*
west	*ouest (m)*
western, westerly	*occidental*
wet dock	*darse (f), bassin à flot (m), bassin (m)*
wheel (steering)	*roue (f)*
white	*blanc*
wind	*vent (m)*
wire	*fil (m)*
wireless	*T.S.F. (f)*
wreck	*naufrage (m)*
yacht	*yacht (m)*
yawl	*yawl (m)*

FRENCH – ENGLISH

French	*English*
abrité	sheltered
acajou	mahogany
acier	steel
alcool à brûler	methylated spirits
amarrer (sur)	to moor, make fast (to), to tie, to seize
amer	daymark, wall beacon
amont	upstream
ancre	anchor
annexe	dinghy
anse	creek, cove
appareiller	to weigh anchor, get under way
arrière	aft, stern
artimon	mizzen
assécher	to dry out
assurance	insurance
atterrage	landfall
aussière	warp
aval	downstream
avant	forward, bows
aviron	oar
bâbord	port (side)
bac	ferry
baie	bay
baignoine	cockpit
balancine	topping lift
balise	beacon
banc de sable	sandbank
barre	tiller

basse marée, basse mer	low water
bassin	basin, dock
bassin à flot	wet dock
bateau	boat
bateau feu	lightship
bateau pêcheur	fishing boat
batterie	battery (electric)
beaupré	bowsprit
béquilles	legs (of a boat)
bitte d'amarrage	bollard
blanc	white
bôme	boom
à bord	aboard
bosse	painter
bouche	mouth (of river)
bouée	navigational buoy
bouée de sauvetage	lifebuoy
bouquet de bois	clump of trees
boussole	compass
brasse	French fathom (5ft 4in)
brisant	breaker (surf)
brise	breeze
brise-lames	breakwater
brouillard	fog
brume	mist
cabine	cabin
cabotage	coasting, coasting trade
caboteur	coaster
cailloux	pebbles, shingle
cale	landing slip
calfater	to caulk
calme	calm
canal	channel, canal
canot	boat, dinghy
canot de sauvetage	lifeboat
cap	cape
capitaine du port	harbourmaster
carte (marine)	chart
ceinture de sauvetage	lifejacket
chaîne	chain
chaland	lighter, barge
chalut	trawl
chalutier	trawler
chantier	timber yard, boatbuilding shed, dockyard
chasser	to drag (anchor)
chavirer	to capsize
chemin de halage	towpath
chenal	channel
chêne	oak
chevaux	horse power
cirés	oilskins
cloche	bell
clocher	belfry, steeple
compas	compass
coque	hull
coques	shells
cordage, corde	rope
corne	gaff
corps morts	moorings
côte	coast
côtre	cutter (rig)
coude	bend (of a channel)

coup de mer	sea (wave)
coup de vent	gale
courant	current
course	race
creuser	to dredge
crique	creek
croisière	cruise
cuisine	galley
cuivre	copper
dame de nage	rowlock
darse	wet dock, harbour
débarquer	to disembark
défense	fender
digue	bank, dyke, mole
douane	customs house, customs
douanier	customs officer
dragueur	dredger
drisse	halyard
duc d'albe	mooring dolphin
dur	hard (adj.), rough (of sea)
eau douce	fresh water
échelle	ladder
échelle de marée	tide gauge
échouage	grounding
écluse	lock (of canal, etc.)
écope	baler
écoute	sheet
écueil	reef, rock
embarcation	small boat, passengers
embarquer	to embark
empanner	to gybe
en bas	below
épissure	splice
équipage	crew
escalier	steps
essence	petrol
est	east
étai	stay
étale	slack (stream)
étiage	low water mark
étuve	stove
évitage	swinging room
falaise	cliff
faire eau	to leak
fer	iron
feu	lighthouse, fire
feu de mouillage	riding light
feu de navigation	sidelight
fil	wire
filet	net
à fleur de l'eau	awash
flot	flood (tide)
à flot	afloat
foc	jib
fond	sea bed
forme de radoub	graving dock
fosse	pool
franchir	to clear (an obstacle)
frapper une amarre	belay
frêne	ash (wood)

gabarre	lighter, small dredger
gaffe	boathook
gambeyer	to gybe
gasoil	diesel oil
gôelette	schooner
goémon	seaweed, kelp
gouvernail	rudder, helm
gouverner sur	to steer for
graisse	grease
grande marée	spring tide
grande voile	mainsail
gréement	rig
grève	beach
gril de carénage	grid
grue	crane
guidon	burgee
haler	to haul
hameçon	fish hook
haubans	shrouds
haussière	(see *aussière*)
haut-fond	shoal
haute marée, haute mer	high water
havre	harbour
hélice	screw (propeller)
hisser	to hoist
houle	surge, swell
huile de graissage	lubricating oil
hunier	topsail
île	island
jetée	jetty, pier
jeter la sonde	to heave the lead
jusant	ebb
ketch	ketch
laisser dans l'est	to pass to the westward of the beacon
laisser par bâbord	to leave to port
large	offing, open sea
largeur	beam (width)
larguer	to cast off, let go
lest	ballast
lever l'ancre	to weigh anchor
longueur	length
lougre	lugger
louvoyer	to beat to windward
machine	engine
maillon	shackle
manche	hose (pipe), channel, English Channel
marée	tide
de marée	tidal
marée descendante	ebb tide
marée montante	flood tide
marée morte	neap tide
marine de l'état	Royal Navy
mascaret	bore
mât	mast
se méfier de	to beware of
mer	sea (ocean)

metéo	weather forecast
mettre en panne	to heave-to
mettre le cap sur	to steer for
mi-marée	half tide
mille	mile
mille marin	nautical mile
mise à l'eau	launching
molle (f), mou (m)	soft
montée d'eau	height of tide
morte eau	neap tide
moulin à l'eau	water mill, tide mill
mouillage	anchorage
mouiller	to anchor
musoir	pierhead
nager	to swim, to row
naufrage	wreck
navire	ship
nettoyer	to clean, to scrub
noeud	knot
noir	black
nord	north
noroît	northwestern
occidental	western, westerly
organeau	mooring ring
orienta	eastern, easterly
ouest	west
palan	tackle
en panne	broken down, hove-to
parc à huitres	oyster beds
paré à virer!	ready about!
passage	channel
passager	passenger
passeport	passport
passe	to reeve
passerelle	gangway
pavillon	flag
pêcheur	fisherman
pertuis	straits, sluice
pétrole	paraffin
phare	lighthouse
pilote	pilot
pin	pine (wood)
plage	beach
plat-bord	gunwale
pleine marée, pleine mer	high water
plomb	lead (metal)
plongeur	diver
pluie	rain
poisson	fish
pompe	pump
pomper	to pump
pont	deck, bridge
poulie	block
presqu île	peninsula
prise d'eau	water point, hydrant
profondeur	depth
propriétaire	owner
puits	well (water)
quai	quay
quille	keel

rade	roads
radier	sill (of lock)
rame	oar
rallier, ranger	to hug (pass close to)
ranger le vent	to come close hauled
raz	tide race
relèuement	bearing (direction)
remettre à neuf	to refit, repair
remorquer	to tow
remorqueur	tug (boat)
remous	eddy, dead water
ressac	surf
ris	reef (of sail)
riser	to reef
rive	bank
rivière	river
rocher, roche	rock
roue	wheel (steering)
rouge	red
route	course
ruisseau	runnel, stream
sable	sand
sables mouvants	quicksand
sableux	sandy
sas	lock
sonde	lead (sounding)
sonder	to sound (depth)
souffler	to blow
spinnaker	spinnaker
sud	south
suroît	southwestern
tapecul	mizzen
tech	teak
temps	weather (met)
temps compensé	corrected time
temps réel	elapsed time
tenue	holding ground
à terre	aground
tin	baulk of wood
tirant d'eau	draught
tirant d'air	masthead height
toile	canvas
tonne	ton, can buoy
touage	towage, warping
tourelle	beacon tower
tribord	starboard
tribord tout!	hard astarboard!
T.S.F.	radio
vague	wave
vase	mud
vaseux	muddy
vent	wind
vitesse	speed
vive eau	spring tide
vivier	pond or enclosure for live fish
voile	sail
voile de cape	trysail
voile d'étai	staysail
voilerie	sail loft, sailmaking
voilier	sailmaker
youvou	dinghy
zingué	galvanised

THE BRETON LANGUAGE

It is of interest, and sometimes actually of value to the navigator, to know the meanings of some of the commoner Breton words which appear in place names. Those who have cruised on the Celtic fringes of Britain will recognise some of them; the Irish *inish* corresponds to the Breton *inis*, and those who have cruised in Western Scottish waters will know the meanings of *glas* and *du*. I have no pretensions to a knowledge of Breton, but set down here the results of a few investigations.

The pronunciation is, or should be, more like English than French, with the final consonants sounded. The letters *c'h* represent the final sound of Scottish *loch* or Irish *lough* (not English *lock*); there is indeed a word *loc'h*, meaning a lake or pool; *ch* is pronounced as in *shall*. The French books and charts do not always distinguish between these, and there may be some errors in this book in consequence. In France, as in England, mobility and the radio/TV are killing regional differences and *Raz* is now usually pronounced *Rah*; *Penmarc'h*, pronounced *Penmargh* a generation ago, is now often *Painmar* and *Bénodet* has gone from *Benodette* to *Bainoday* and collected an accent in the process. The most misleading exaple of this process is *porz*, which means an anchorage, possibly quite exposed and/or lacking all shore facilities, not a port. This gets frenchified into *port*, and the French word *port* does mean a port, and not an anchorage which is *anse* or *rade*.

A Breton glossary is hard to use, because initial letters are often mutated into others, following complicated rules, depending on the preceding word. I have tried to meet this by suggesting, after the relevant letters, other(s) from which the initial might have come. Thus suppose that one wants to find the meaning of *I. ar Gazek* (which is quite likely since *The Mare* seems to be the commonest name given to an islet). There is no word *gazek* in the glossary, but after G it says 'try K'; *kazek* means a mare; it mutates into *gazek* after *ar*. Mutations of final letters also occur, but these do not usually cause difficulty in finding a word.

Breton	English
al, an ar	the
arvor	seaside
aven	river

B (try **P**)

bann, benn	hilltop
baz	shoal
beg	point, cape
beniget	cut, slip
benven	above-water rock
bian, bihan	small
bir	needle, point
bras, braz	large
bre, brenn	small hill
breiz	Brittany
bri, brienn	cliff

C (try **K**)

D (try **T**)

daou	two
don, doun	deep
du	black
enez	island
er	a, an, the

G (try **K**)

garv	rough
gavr	goat
glas	green
gromil, gromilli	roaring
gwenn	white, pure
hi	long
hoc'h, houc'h	pig
inis	island
karn	cairn
karreg	rock
kastel	castle
kazek	mare
ker	house, hamlet
kern	summit
koad	wood
kornog	shoal
koz	old
kreiz	middle
kriben	crest
lan, lann	monastery
marc'h	horse
melen	yellow
men	rock
mor	sea
nevez	new
penn	head, point
plou, plo	parish
porz, porzig	anchorage
poul	pool, anchorage
raz	strait, tide race
roc'h	rock
ros	wooded knoll
ruz	red
ster	river, inlet
teven, tevenneg	cliff, dune
toull	hole, deep place
trez, treaz	sand, beach

V (try **B, M**)

W (try **Gw**)

yoc'h	group of rocks

II. CHARTS AND PUBLICATIONS

British Admiralty charts

Chart	Title	Scale
1432	Le Four to Ile Vierge	25,000
	L'Aber-Wrac'h	15,000
2643	Ile d'Ouessant to Pointe de Penmarc'h	200,000
2644	Ile d'Ouessant to Ile de Batz	150,000
2668	Ile Vierge to Plateau des Roches Douvres	150,000
2669	Channel islands and adjacent coast of France	150,000
2694	Le Four to Goulet de Brest including Ile de Ouessant	50,000
2700	Port St Malo and approaches	15,000
3345	Chenal du Four	25,000
3656	Plateau des Minquiers and adjacent coast of France	50,000
3659	Cap Fréhel to Iles Chausey	50,000
3668	Le Four to Anse de Kernic	50,000
	Port de Pontusval	20,000
3669	Anse de Kernic to Les Sept Iles	50,000
3670	Les Sept Iles to L'Ost-Pic	50,000
3672	Harbours on the northwest coast of France:	
	Riviere de Treguier: Granville	15,000
	Erquy: Perros-Guiréc: Port Blanc	20,000
	Saint Quay-Portrieux	25,000
3673	Lézardrieux and Paimpol with approaches	20,000
	Rivière de Trieux	10,000
3674	L'Ost Pic to Cap Fréhel	50,000
	Le Légué	

French SHOM charts

P = available folded on waterproof material

Chart	Title	Scale
824P	De Cancale à Bricqueville, baie du Mont Saint-Michel, îles Chausey	45,200
831	Des Héaux de Bréhat à Paimpol, plateaux des Roches Douvres et de Barnouic	45,000
832P	De l'île de Bréhat aux roches de Saint-Quay, partie de la baie de Saint-Brieuc	45,200
833P	De Portrieux au cap Fréhel, baie de Saint-Brieuc	45,500
	Cartouche: Port de Légué	10,000
844P	Du cap Fréhel à Cancale, abords de Saint-Malo	45,200
967P	De l'Ile Grande aux Héaux, les Sept Iles, rivière de Tréguier	45,100
972	Passes de la rivière de Tréguier	14,400
973	Rivière de Tréguier	14,400
974	Les entrées de Perros et du Port-Blanc	14,400
4233	La Rance de Saint-Servan au Chatelier	15,000
	Cartouche: Partie amont, du Chêne Vert au Chatelier	15,000
4599	Plateau des Minquiers, entrée de la Déroute	45,000
5644	De la pointe de Rothéneuf à la pointe de La Houle, rade de Cancale	15,000
5646	Du cap Fréhel à la pointe du Décollé	20,000
5724	D'Erquy au cap Fréhel	20,000
5725	De la pointe du Roselier à la pointe de Plouha	20,000
6930P	Des roches de Portsall au plateau des Roches Douvres	150,000
7094P	Du phare du Four à l'île Vierge – Port de l'Aber-Wrac'h	25,000
	Cartouche: A – Aber Wrac'h	15,000

Chart	Title	Scale
7095P	Baie de Morlaix – De l'île de Batz à la point de Primel	20,000
	Cartouche: A– Ports de Roscoff	10,000
	B – Rivière de Morlaix	15,000
7122	De la Pointe de Saint-Mathieu au Phare du Four	25,000
7123	Ile Molène, Ile d'Ouessant	20,000
7124P	Baie de Lannion – De la pointe de Primel à l'île Grande	20,000
	Cartouche: A – Le Léguer (Rivière de Lannion)	20,000
	B – Port de Lannion	7,500
7127	Port en anse de Paimpol	14,400
7130	Abords de St-Malo – De l'île des Hébihens à la pointe de la Varde	15,000
7149P	De Portsall à la pointe de Saint Mathieu, chenal du Four et environs de l'île d'Ouessant	45,500
7150P	De Portsall à l'Anse de Kernic	50,000
7151P	De l'Anse de Kernic à l'île Grande	50,000

P = Plastic sheets

Imray charts

Charts	Title	Scale
C10	Western English Channel Passage Radiobeacons, Lights, Tides	400,000
C33b	Channel Islands (South)	121,000
	St Peter Port, Omonville, Goury, Portbail, Dielette, Carteret, Gorey, Alderney, Beaucette Marina, Creux Harbour, St Sampson	
C34	Cap d'Erquy to Ile de Batz	110,000
	R de Tréguier, Primel, R de Lannion, Port de Légué, Port Clos, Port de la Corderie, Loguivy, Anse de Perros, R de Portrieux and Anse de Paimpol, Port Blanc, Lézardieux, Tréguier, Paimpol	
C35	Baie de Morlaix to L'Aber-Ildut	76,000
	Ile de Batz, Approaches to L'Aber-Wrach and L'Aber-Benoit, Argenton, Pontusval, Mogueriec, Porsal, L'Aber-Ildut	
C36	Ile d'Ouessant to Raz de Sein	77,000
	Le Conquet, Brest, Morgat, Camaret, Dournenez, Lampaul, Marina du Moulin Blanc	

NORTH BRITTANY

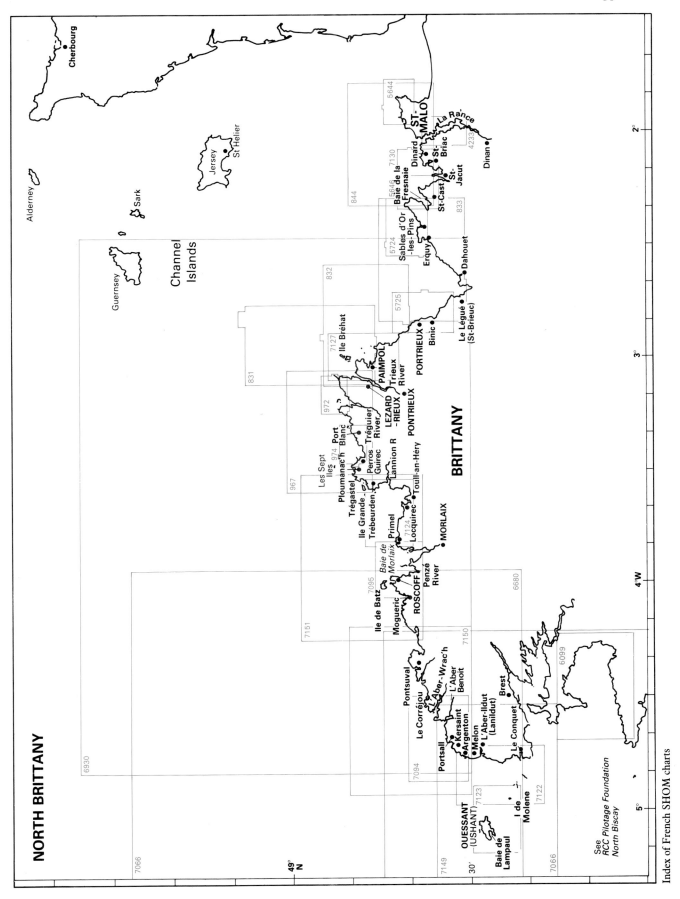

Cherbourg

Alderney

Jersey
St Helier

Sark

Guernsey

Channel
Islands

6930

7066

49°
N

30'

7066

7149

7123

7122

I de
Molene

OUESSANT
(USHANT)

Baie de
Lampaul

7094

6099

6680

Le Conquet

Brest

L'Aber-Ildut
(Lanildut)

Melon
Argenton
Kersaint
Portsall

L'Aber
Benoit

Aber-Wrac'h

Le Corréjou

Pontsuval

7150

7151

7095

ROSCOFF
Mogueric

Ile de Batz

Baie de
Morlaix

Penzé
River

MORLAIX

7124

Primel
Locquirec

Ile Grande
Trébeurden

Trégastel
Ploumanac'h

Les Sept
Iles

967

974

Perros
Guirec

Port
Blanc

Tréguier
River

Lannion R

Touli-an-Héry

831

972

7127

Ile Bréhat

832

LEZARD
-RIEUX

PONTRIEUX

PAIMPOL
Trieux
River

PORTRIEUX

Binic

Le Légué
(St-Brieuc)

5725

Portrieux

Le Légué

Dahouet

5724

Erquy

Sables d'Or
-les-Pins

844

5646

Baie de la
Fresnaie

St-Cast

St-
Jacut

833

7130

Dinard

St-
Briac

4233

Dinan

La Rance

ST-
MALO

5644

BRITTANY

4°W

5°

3°

2°

See
*RCC Pilotage Foundation
North Biscay*

Index of French SHOM charts

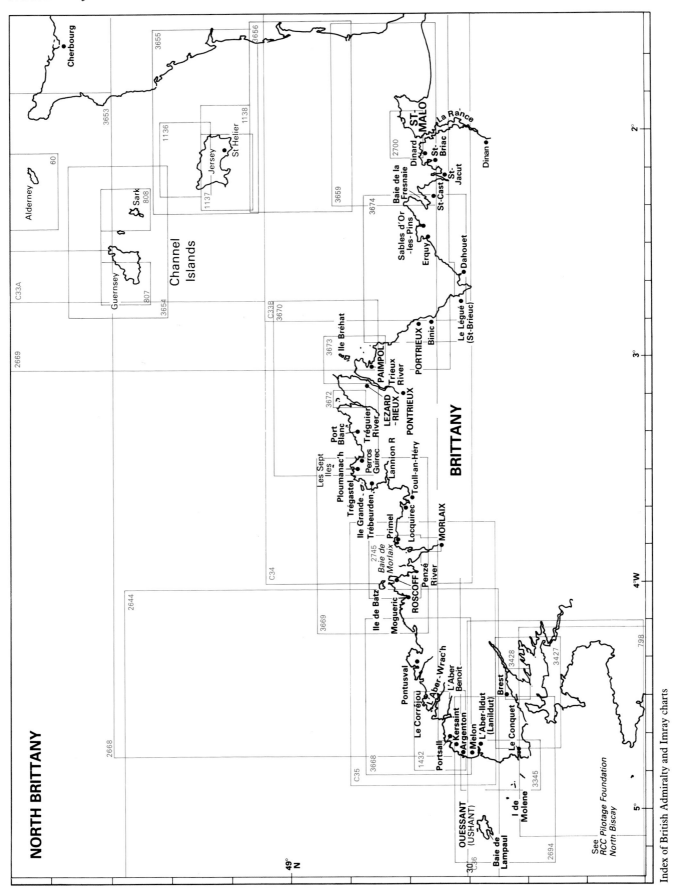

NORTH BRITTANY

Index of British Admiralty and Imray charts

See
RCC Pilotage Foundation
North Biscay

Navigational publications

British Admiralty publications

Channel Pilot, NP27.
List of Lights, Volume A, NP74.
ALRS, Coast Radio Stations, Volume 1, NP281(1).
ALRS, Radio Navigational Aids, Volume 2, NP282.
ALRS, Radio Weather Services and Navigational Warnings, Volume 3, NP283.
ALRS, Port Operations, Volume 6, NP286(1).
Tide Tables, Volume 1, European Waters, NP201.
Tidal Stream Atlas for the English and Bristol Channels, NP250.
Tidal Stream Atlas for the Channel Islands and Adjacent Coasts, NP264.
Admiralty Tide Tables for Yachtsmen, NP192. New (1992) and very useful.

Other British publications

The Cruising Association Handbook.
Tidal Streams North Coast of France between Cape Barfleur and Pointe de Penmarch. Imray, Laurie, Norie & Wilson Ltd.
Reed's Nautical Almanac
Macmillan & Silk Cut Nautical Almanac

French SHOM publications

Instructions Nautiques, No. C 11A, Côtes Nord et Ouest de France.
Annuaire des Marées and supplement *Tables des Hauteurs d'Eau pour les Côtes Françaises de la Manche et de L'Atlantique.*

Other French publications

Almanach de Marin Breton (Roux, Le Fret, Finistère, France).
Pilote Côtier Fenwick de Saint-Malo à Brest, Alain Rondeau (Praxys Diffusion 68 rue des Bruyères 9 3260 Les Lilas).
Votre Livre de Bord – Manche et Atlantique. Bloc Marin. Distributed by Imray, Laurie, Norie & Wilson Ltd.

III. CONVERSION TABLES

metres–feet

m	ft/m	ft
0·3	1	3·3
0·6	2	6·6
0·9	3	9·8
1·2	4	13·1
1·5	5	16·4
1·8	6	19·7
2·1	7	23·0
2·4	8	26·2
2·7	9	29·5
3·0	10	32·8
6·1	20	65·6
9·1	30	98·4
12·2	40	131·2
15·2	50	164·0
30·5	100	328·1

centimetres–inches

cm	in/cm	in
2·5	1	0·4
5·1	2	0·8
7·6	3	1·2
10·2	4	1·6
12·7	5	2·0
15·2	6	2·4
17·8	7	2·8
20·3	8	3·1
22·9	9	3·5
25·4	10	3·9
50·8	20	7·9
76·2	30	11·8
101·6	40	15·7
127·0	50	19·7
254·0	100	39·4

metres–fathoms–feet

m	fathoms	ft
0·9	0·5	3
1·8	1	6
3·7	2	12
5·5	3	18
7·3	4	24
9·1	5	30
11·0	6	36
12·8	7	42
14·6	8	48
16·5	9	54
18·3	10	60
36·6	20	120
54·9	30	180
73·2	40	240
91·4	50	300

kilometres–statute miles

km	M/km	M
1·6	1	0·6
3·2	2	1·2
4·8	3	1·9
6·4	4	2·5
8·0	5	3·1
9·7	6	3·7
11·3	7	4·3
12·9	8	5·0
14·5	9	5·6
16·1	10	6·2
32·2	20	12·4
48·3	30	18·6
64·4	40	24·9
80·5	50	31·1
120·7	75	46·6
160·9	100	62·1
402·3	250	155·3
804·7	500	310·7
1609·3	1000	621·4

kilograms–pounds

kg	lb/kg	lb
0·5	1	2·2
0·9	2	4·4
1·4	3	6·6
1·8	4	8·8
2·3	5	11·0
2·7	6	13·2
3·2	7	15·4
3·6	8	17·6
4·1	9	19·8
4·5	10	22·0
9·1	20	44·1
13·6	30	66·1
18·1	40	88·2
22·7	50	110·2
34·0	75	165·3
45·4	100	220·5
113·4	250	551·2
226·8	500	1102·3
453·6	1000	2204·6

litres–gallons

l	gal/l	gal
4·5	1	0·2
9·1	2	0·4
13·6	3	0·7
18·2	4	0·9
22·7	5	1·1
27·3	6	1·3
31·8	7	1·5
36·4	8	1·8
40·9	9	2·0
45·5	10	2·2
90·9	20	4·4
136·4	30	6·6
181·8	40	8·8
227·3	50	11·0
341·0	75	16·5
454·6	100	22·0
1136·5	250	55·0
2273·0	500	110·0
4546·1	1000	220·0

Index

Bold type indicates the page number for the relevant plan.